THE ULTIMATE EU CAREER
DEVELOPMENT BOOK

Also from John Harper Publishing

The Ultimate EU Test Book – Administrator edition
The Ultimate EU Test Book – Assistant edition
The Ultimate EU Test Book – Assessment Centre edition

For full details of these and other books on how the EU works

www.johnharperpublishing.co.uk

For the online tool that accompanies this book

https://www.johnharperpublishing.co.uk/the-ultimate-eu-career-development-toolkit/

THE ULTIMATE EU CAREER DEVELOPMENT BOOK

Jan De Sutter

JOHN HARPER
PUBLISHING

The Ultimate EU Career Development Book
ISBN 978-0-9934549-3-6

Published by John Harper Publishing
27 Palace Gates Road
London N22 7BW, United Kingdom.
www.johnharperpublishing.co.uk

Sales and distribution: Turpin Distribution Services Ltd.

Typeset mainly in 9 & 10/11pt Palatino
Printed and Bound in the EU at the Gutenberg Press, Malta.

TABLE OF CONTENTS

CHAPTERS

ANNEXES

ABOUT THE AUTHOR

After a career in IT, defence systems and people management, Jan De Sutter joined the European Economic and Social Committee in 2000, where he was Head of Unit of the budget and finance department. While at the EESC Jan served on EPSO Selection Boards and was president of a Selection Board for IT specialists. Since 2013 Jan has worked as an independent entrepreneur and coach, focusing on personalised coaching and preparation for the EPSO Assessment Centre and other aspects of career development in the EU administration. He is happy to share his knowledge and experience in this book – and in person through individual face-to-face coaching or classroom training. Jan's full biography can be found on LinkedIn at https://be.linkedin.com/in/jandesutter

FOREWORD AND ACKNOWLEDGEMENTS

I had been playing with the idea of writing a book on the topic of personal development for quite some time, and it was more of a coincidence than careful planning that made it happen.

When I left active service in the EU and started my own coaching and training business I met András Baneth, creator of 'The Ultimate EU Test Book' series. Gradually, the idea emerged of us working together on a new volume in that series, covering exclusively the topic of the Assessment Centre. This book finally hit the bookstores in the summer of 2015, and it turned out to be a great and immediate success with candidates in EPSO competitions.

Then in discussions with our publisher, John Harper, I put forward the idea of writing a book with a wider scope than merely the EPSO competitions – a book that would be relevant to those already working in the EU administration. The underlying idea was that developing your working skills and competencies is not just something you should do while preparing for a competition, but a life-long endeavour, extending far beyond the period of a competition. It is the key to a successful and fulfilling career. Both András and John were immediately enthusiastic about the idea, and I want to thank them both for their support and encouragement.

As the project developed another dimension opened up as it became obvious that one aspect of what I was attempting – self-assessment in the EU competencies – while feasible in the pages of a book, could be more elegantly and creatively accomplished by providing a supporting online tool. This concept was then expanded to allow full 360-degree feedback online with input from friends and colleagues. Used together the book and the online tool create a very flexible resource for both self-assessment and personal development: the online tool is extensively referenced in the book, and I would encourage readers to take advantage of its benefits.

Of course, a book with this ambition cannot be put together by just one man. I consulted many of my former colleagues, most of them now high-ranking EU officials, with a vast experience in the EU realm. I would like to mention Donal Carey (Head of Unit at DGT) in particular, but some other important contributors of ideas and expertise preferred to stay anonymous: they will know who they are, and I thank them all.

Career development is a sensitive topic. Individual interests and the interests of the employer are sometimes conflicting, and this is the point where the trade unions come in. Since I wanted to give a balanced overview I decided to consult some of the main EU staff trade unions. I want to thank in particular Alan Hick (EESC) and Félix Geradon (European Council) for their contributions.

Good communication is about conveying the right message to the right audience. That is why I asked a number of future and current EU officials to proofread the book, and tell me whether or not it could add value to their own career development. I will only mention Marco Bernardini (European Commission), Frederik Duym (European Council), and Dirk Homann (future Data Protection Officer). Their comments were valuable for putting everything into the right perspective.

Last but not least, I want to thank Helen Williams. Helen is an experienced occupational and coaching psychologist and member of the team at Sten10, a leading business psychology consultancy that specialises in designing people assessments. Helen's particular passion is for the delivery of one to one coaching adopting a solution-focused, cognitive-behavioural approach. Helen did a very thorough proofreading of this book, sharpened my theoretical and scientific insights, and helped make this book a practical and hands-on tool for its intended audience.

It is customary – but no less true – to add that the final responsibility on all issues of fact, interpretation and balance is mine alone. When it comes to the challenges of personal development tackled in this book, there is rarely a definitive 'right' or 'wrong' approach: each individual is different and each situation has its nuances. I will warmly welcome any feedback that reflects on such nuances.

Jan De Sutter

Brussels
February 2016
jan.de.sutter@scarlet.be

All cartoons in this book courtesy of Ted Goff cartoons, http://www.newslettercartoons.com

1. Upgrading your core competencies

'Wanderer, your footsteps are the path, and nothing else; wanderer, there is no path, the path is made by walking.' – Antonio Machado[1]

The EU institutions form a unique mix of politics, diplomacy and administration with an impact on the lives of 500 million Europeans. This is what makes working for the EU something special.

According to Trendence[2], in 2015 the EU institutions were Belgium's third most attractive employer amongst business students, and at the European level they still occupy an honourable fifteenth place in a list of renowned multinational companies. Not surprisingly, more than 50.000 candidates present themselves at the European Personnel Selection Office (EPSO) competitions every year, but only around 1200 are recruited. This means that people who work for the EU are amongst Europe's finest – and they are proud of it.

However, it is not enough to have a high potential to become a high-achiever. Potential has to be converted into *performance*. Performance has to be fostered and managed, both by the employee and his employer. That is what this book is about.

Performance development is a broad term that includes performance management and employee development. It describes both assessing and managing the work that needs to be done and providing opportunities for professional growth and development. There are significant benefits to employees, and organisations, that invest time and thought into performance development practices. When done consistently and well, these practices result in better performance at the individual and organisational levels, higher satisfaction and self-actualisation[3], and safeguarding of strong performers.

Many organisations have a *performance appraisal* process as part of their human resources policy, and so do the EU institutions. A performance appraisal is a systematic and periodic process that assesses an employee's job performance and productivity in relation to pre-established criteria and organisational objectives, as well as the identification of potential for future improvement, etc. Performance appraisals play an important role in putting talent to the best possible use and rewarding staff for good work.

The European Commission, too, is working on an organisation-wide talent management policy. This initiative took off under Commissioner Maroš Šefčovič and has been continued by the Juncker Commission under Vice President for Budget and Human Resources Kristalina Georgieva. In his 'Mission Letter'[4] to Georgieva, Commission President Juncker states:

> 'During our mandate, I would like you to focus on the following, in your role as Vice-President: […] Coordinating the personnel and administrative policy of the Commission, maintaining high standards in recruitment, improving staff mobility and their skills and ensuring a secure working environment. In the context of the

---

1   Antonio Machado (1875–1939), was a Spanish poet and one of the leading figures of the Spanish literary movement known as the Generation of '98.

2   Trendence is Europe's leading research institute specialising in employer branding, personnel marketing and recruiting.

3   'The full realisation of one's potential, and of one's true self' (Abraham Maslow).

4   https://ec.europa.eu/commission/sites/cwt/files/commissioner_mission_letters/georgieva_en.pdf

"Ooops. I didn't mean to tell you
how great your work has been.
I meant that you're doing just
okay and to try harder.

ongoing staff reduction and pressures on our administrative budget, it will be key to develop a corporate talent management policy, further rationalising our ways of working and matching the allocation of human resources with our priorities. By the end of our mandate, I would like us to achieve 40% of female senior and middle management in the Commission. I will also ask you to pay particular attention to gender equality in the recruitment process and throughout the career path.'

The level of the sponsorship of this undertaking can only underline its importance. The Commission seeks to enable staff to achieve their full potential and be rewarded appropriately while ensuring that the right people are in the right jobs at the right time, in the interests of the organisation. Even though the Commission employs only part of the total EU staff, the impact of this initiative on the other institutions cannot be overstated: one can expect initiatives from the other institutions and agencies to align their policies with those of the Commission over the coming years.

However, in this book I intend to focus on the employee's side of performance development: personal development. *Personal development* is the process of understanding and developing oneself in order to achieve one's fullest potential. Personal development is a vital part in a person's growth, maturity, professional success and personal fulfillment.

Unfortunately, not everyone is aware of the importance of personal development. Often, people tend to give more importance to academic and professional achievement rather than personal growth. Such lack of self-understanding and of a principle-centered way of living blocks one's ability to live an enjoyable and successful life.

I will introduce and lay out a methodology for individuals to take care of and foster their personal performance development. Since this book is intended for EU staff, I will concentrate on the competencies that matter most for the EU administrations, as described in EPSO's competency framework.

This book is written from a coach's point of view. The essence of coaching is raising awareness and responsibility, two vital ingredients of performance. *Awareness* increases input, interest, learning and recall. Offering choice that leads to self-esteem, confidence and self-motivation generates *responsibility*. Both awareness and responsibility are states of mind, and the mind is key. Knowledge and experience are important for performance but neither is half as important as state of mind, and that is the area in which coaching works. Coaching lifts the focus of attention to future possibilities, so leaving behind past mistakes and fixed ideas that can hold you back.

Offering choice not only values the individual, but also capitalises on the unique qualities and contributions of each individual. No two people are the same in mind or body; we all think differently and act differently. So often in the past these differences were actively discouraged for the sake of control, standardisation, ease of administration – and because management thought they knew best. Standardisation was the key to most growth and success in the previous century, giving us mass-production and economies of scale. However, it also had side effects including over-control, cultures of blame and criticism and low individual buy-in, disaffection and stress in the workplace because of the loss of choice and responsibility. Ironically enough, this created poor performance in the post-industrial age …

Organisations have only begun to unleash the potential of their people and allow them to see the world – and the workplace – through more holistic eyes. That is the blueprint for high performance in the future.

Why performance development is important

In 2014, EPSO announced 60 reserve lists filled via open competitions, with in total 1200 laureates. The latest figures show that the vast majority (80%) of laureates are recruited. Also in 2014, EPSO's budget amounted to €27,2M of which some €3,4M was invested in the activities of the European School of Administration.

Making allowance for the other activities of EPSO, and for the costs for the non-permanent members (which are on another budget), these figures mean that the 'total cost per hire' is around €25K. This may seem high, but one should consider that, in the private sector, executive recruiters (head-hunters) charge 20% or more of the total yearly salary (social security, taxes and bonuses included) of the people they select on behalf of their clients. Of course, EU officials are not really 'executives', but the long-term risk of hiring a 'bad' official is much higher since officials are appointed for life and there is not the high turnover of staff seen in many areas of the private sector.

Working for the EU is a two-way street: a very big investment by the institutions in recruiting long-term staff – so a necessary corollary of that has to be staff commitment to developing their competencies. It is a 'serious relationship'.

General competencies

A competency is a set of observable behaviours that provide a structured guide enabling the identification, evaluation and development of the behaviours in individual employees. Competencies are job-related: for every job a different set of competencies is needed. Hence, during the selection process an employer will try to assess if a candidate has the necessary competencies for the job. Once the employee has been hired he or she will be – formally or informally – evaluated, which will have an impact on their further development and career with that employer. As such, employees are responsible for the development of their own competencies, but the employer may provide facilities (coaching, mentoring, training, time) to help.

General competencies are competencies – or behaviour – that are expected from all employees regardless of their position or function in the organisation. General competencies are not to be confused with intelligence or professional competency; they are – in fact – part of another dimension of what we are as human beings (Figure 1.1).

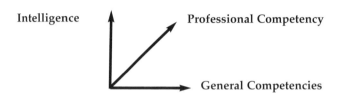

Figure 1.1

The definition of *intelligence* is somewhat controversial amongst psychologists, but by far the most widely used in practical settings is the psychometric approach, trying to capture the complex concept into a single score known as the Intelligence Quotient, or IQ. The IQ is influenced by environmental and genetic factors, the relative importance of which has been the subject of much research and debate. A person's IQ is derived from the results of standardised tests and is supposed to be stable over time.

For recruitment and job selection purposes more specific ability tests in verbal, numerical and abstract reasoning are preferred. However, it is possible to influence the outcome of these tests by intensive practice over an extended period of time. Does this mean that a person who scores better on these tests is necessarily smarter or more intelligent than others? Of course not; this person is simply better at performing these tests.

The IQ score bell curve

With standardised IQ tests, the tests are designed so that their scores have a 'bell curve' distribution in the general population with an average of 100. This curve has a peak in the middle where most people score and elongated ends where only a few people score. In statistics this is called a 'normal distribution.'

An IQ of 115 or more can be considered to be a high IQ score or level; it is one standard deviation above the average. Only 15% of the population have an IQ level of 115 or above.

Around 2% of the population has an IQ greater than 130, which is 'gifted' intelligence. This is an IQ of two standard deviations from the average IQ.

At the age of 21, Nikola Tesla[5] earned his first PhD. He ultimately held four PhD degrees (Philosophy, Physics, Electrical Engineering, and Mechanical engineering). His exact IQ score is not known, because there were no tests at the time he lived, but it is estimated to be around 200, which is exceptionally high.

5   Nikola Tesla (1856–1943) was a Serbian-American inventor best known for his contributions to the design of the modern alternating current (AC) electricity supply system. The name of Tesla is now used by a well-known American company that designs, manufacturs, and sells electric cars.

"Well, you certainly have a lot of
experience in tech support."

Professional competencies are skills, knowledge and attributes that are valued by the
other professionals that are connected to your profession; professional competencies
may also be referred to as 'technical competencies'. You could say: 'It takes one to
know one.' Only other engineers can properly assess the professional competencies of
an engineer, or lawyers those of a lawyer. Professional competencies are usually
assessed on the basis of a person's (formal) education and their (proven) experience in
the professional field through an in-depth interview conducted by another – preferably more experienced – professional in that field.

Having the mental capacity (IQ) and the professional knowledge and know-how is
still no guarantee that you will be a proficient employee; you still have to act properly.
Here is where your general competencies come in. General competencies are all about
behaviour, and behaviour can be changed – but it takes awareness and responsibility.

Competencies, anchors and indicators

General competencies are further divided into *'behavioural anchors'*. Behavioural
anchors are specific, easy-to-apply *examples* of behaviours that demonstrate the competency.

With every anchor, there are a number of positive and negative *indicators*, or specific associated behaviours. Indicators – or behaviours – can be associated with multiple anchors, as is depicted in Figure 1.2. A behavioural anchor is something that can
be used, for example, to define the level someone has reached on a particular competency from 1 to 10. In this sense it is very similar to an indicator, but indicators tend to
be simple 'positive' and 'negative' poles, whereas the anchors define all points in
between.

For instance, 'team working' would be a behavioural anchor for the 'working with
others' competency, which is further translated into positive indicators such as 'listens
to others' or 'waits for another to finish speaking before voicing their own contribu-

tion'. This behaviour is also considered as part of the 'communicating' and even 'leadership' competencies.

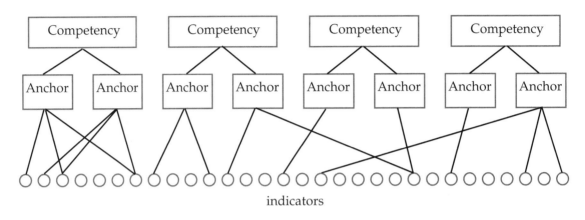

indicators

Figure 1.2

This means that competencies are interrelated. Certain behaviours (indicators) are the hallmark of a given competency but have a clear relation with some other competencies as well.

The concept of anchors and indicators will also be used in this book, in particular to shape the self-assessment questionnaires in the annexes. These anchors are not exactly the same as the ones used by EPSO; in fact they are more comprehensive, because it would be impossible to apply all these in EPSO's selection procedures. The competencies, however, are exactly the ones as used by EPSO.

The competency framework

The competency framework used by the European Personnel Selection Office is the result of a comprehensive job analysis undertaken in 2009 for all entry grades of EU officials across the institutions. All officials recruited at the entry grades between 2004 and 2007 were interviewed and, in parallel, line managers and senior stakeholders were also questioned. The outcome of the job analysis was the development of the competency framework. The emphasis was on identifying those competencies common to all European institutions and therefore suitable for use in open competitions. As a result, the EU institutions are looking for employees who demonstrate the general competencies listed in Table 1.1:

A more detailed description of these competencies, and how to improve them, will be given in chapters 3 to 10.

In 2014, EPSO organised a stakeholder's survey, the results of which were unequivocal: all existing competencies are important and there is no need to add additional ones. The current competency framework – including the related behavioural anchors – will therefore be maintained.

Analysis and Problem Solving	Identify the critical facts in complex issues and develop creative and practical solutions
Communicating	Communicate clearly and precisely both orally and in writing
Delivering Quality and Results	Take personal responsibility and initiative for delivering work to a high standard of quality within set procedures
Learning and Development	Develop and improve personal skills and knowledge of the organisation and its environment
Prioritising and Organising	Prioritise the most important tasks, work flexibly and organise own workload efficiently
Resilience	Remain effective under a heavy workload, handle organisational frustrations positively and adapt to a changing work environment
Working with Others	Work co-operatively with others in teams and across organisational boundaries and respect differences between people
Leadership	Manage, develop and motivate people to achieve results

Table 1.1

The competency passport

People who have gone through an Assessment Centre in a European Personnel Selection Office competition will receive a *competency passport*, which consists of an overview of their general competencies – in a graphical format as in Figure 1.3, along with a textual description of the strong points and the opportunities for improvement. This competency passport is inserted into your personnel file.

Figure 1.3

In this book, you will get the opportunity to construct your own competency pass-port (Annex 9), based on a self-assessment with the worksheets in Annexes 1-8. This overview will allow you to identify your possible development areas and set up a plan for your own personal development (Annex 10). You can also do this via our online assessment toolkit, as described more fully later in this chapter.

Key events in your EU career

Since this book is about developing your EU career it is only natural to highlight the key events in an EU official's professional trajectory. In Figure 1.4 these key events are shown as arrows (horizontal, vertical or oblique) – these are transitions from one state (temporary or permanent, AD or AST, on probation or established, lower grade or higher grade) to another.

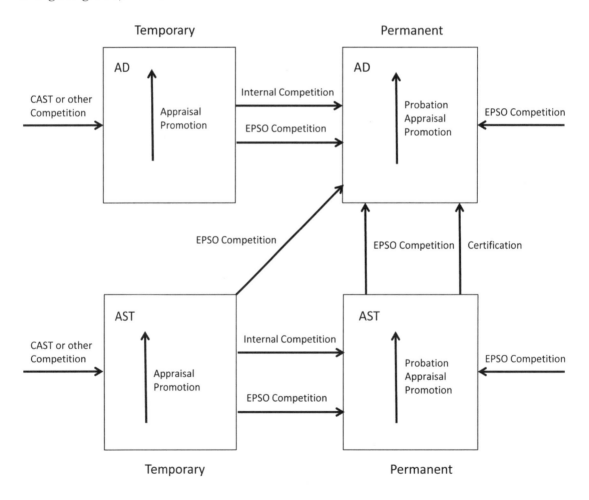

Figure 1.4

The point I want to make here is that for any of these events your core competencies will be scrutinised, and the outcome of this assessment will determine whether or not the transition will take place. I hope that you will understand now why developing your core competencies is so important.

In the following paragraphs I will cover in somewhat more detail some of these events.

Appraisal

Article 43 of the Staff Regulations[6] stipulates:

'The ability, efficiency and conduct in the service of each official shall be the subject of an annual report as provided for by the appointing authority of each institution in accordance with Article 110. That report shall state whether or not the performance level of the official has been satisfactory. The appointing authority of each institution shall lay down provisions conferring the right to lodge an appeal within the reporting procedure, which has to be exercised before the lodging of a complaint as referred to in Article 90(2).

As of grade AST 5, the report may also contain an opinion as to whether the official, on the basis of his performance, has the potential to carry out an administrator's function.

The report shall be communicated to the official. He shall be entitled to make any comments thereon which he considers relevant.'

Article 44 (first paragraph) continues:

'An official who has been at one step in his grade for two years shall automatically advance to the next step in that grade, unless his performance has been evaluated as unsatisfactory pursuant to the last annual report referred to in Article 43. An official shall advance to the next step in his grade after no later than four years, unless the procedure laid down in Article 51(1) is applied.'

In the 'Special Report N° 10/2012'[7] the European Court of Auditors made the observation that the appraisal and promotion system in place until 2011 did not sufficiently distinguish between good performers who develop their skills and poor performers who do not. The new system introduced in 2012 aimed to make a clearer distinction and not to promote those whose performance is below average.

The Commission has three main systems for providing information on the existing skills of its staff:

– *Recruitment assessments:* as part of the recruitment processes all new Commission staff are assessed by the European Personnel Selection Office against eight core competencies. The results of the assessment are recorded on a competency passport.

6   http://eur-lex.europa.eu/legal-content/EN/TXT/?uri=CELEX:32013R1023
7   http://www.eca.europa.eu/en/Pages/NewsItem.aspx?nid=1944

STRUCTURE OF SKILLS ASSESSED BY ANNUAL APPRAISAL IN USE UNTIL 2011 AND EPSO COMPETENCY PASSPORT FOR NEW RECRUITS		
Annual appraisal until 2011		**EPSO Competency Passport**
Efficiency	Organising and planning work	Prioritising and organising
	Performing work and ensuring quality	Delivering quality and results
Ability	**Technical skills**	
	Oral and written communication	Communicating
	Communication in meetings	
	Negotiation skills	
	Analysing problems and applying solutions	Analysis and problem solving
	Awareness of the working environment	
	People management	
Conduct	Teamwork	Working with others
	Service culture	
	Commitment to the job	
	Personal development in the context of work	Learning and development
	Leadership	Leadership
		Resilience

Table 1.2

- *Annual appraisals*: throughout their career the conduct, ability and efficiency of staff in carrying out their job is assessed in the annual appraisal[8]. A new appraisal system has been used from January 2012 onwards.
- *Electronic curriculum vitae (e-CV)*: staff can also record knowledge, skills and experience acquired from current and previous jobs on their e-CV. This provides information on their potential to work in other roles.

These systems, however, do not combine to produce a reliable, consolidated picture of the skills of Commission staff.

The EPSO competency passport is available for staff recruited since 2010. It examines skills in a different structure to that of the annual appraisal in use until 2011 (see Table 1.2). As a result it is not updated or followed up during the appraisal process. The Commission uses the same framework of eight competencies as EPSO in the new appraisal process introduced from 2012, allowing easier alignment between the two tools.

In the Commission, the general provisions for implementing Article 43 and the first paragraph of Article 44 are laid down in the Commission Decision C(2013)8985[9] of 16/12/2013.

---

8   Annex I, Article 43 of Regulation (EC, Euratom) No 723/2004.
9   http://ec.europa.eu/transparency/regdoc/rep/3/2013/EN/3-2013-8985-EN-F1-1.Pdf

Common appraisal standards

In the Commission, the common appraisal standards are based on the description of a performance level that can be expected of any jobholder. These standards are Commission-wide, but may be supplemented by standards specific to each DG, provided that they are approved by DG HR and Security. Where necessary, distinctions are made between the tasks of administrators (AD) and assistants (AST), and jobholders with management functions (MANAGEMENT). For historical reasons they are still classified under the headings of efficiency, ability, and aspects of conduct, as set out in Article 43 of the Staff Regulations, but they now effectively reflect the competency framework as described earlier. Tables 1.3 to 1.5 illustrate this mapping.

Until recently, the Commission also had a 360-degree feedback mechanism as part of the appraisal system for senior managers, but pending approval of a new policy for appraisal of senior staff, this measure has been suspended.

Because all the EU institutions have to respect the Staff Regulation, It is clear that the other institutions have similar appraisal standards, but these may map somewhat differently to the competency framework. Nevertheless, the underlying principles are essentially the same.

You need to take the annual appraisal exercise seriously, because not only will it influence your career progress, there are also potentially serious consequences in case of incompetence. Article 51, first paragraph:

> 'The appointing authority of each institution shall define procedures to identify, deal with and remedy cases of incompetence in a timely and appropriate fashion.
>
> When adopting internal provisions, the appointing authority of each institution shall respect the following requirements:
>
> (a)   an official who, on the basis of three consecutive unsatisfactory annual reports as referred to in Article 43, still shows no progress in his professional competence shall be downgraded by one grade. If the following two annual reports still show unsatisfactory performance, the official shall be dismissed;
>
> (b)   any proposal to downgrade or dismiss an official shall set out the reasons on which it is based and shall be communicated to the official concerned. The proposal from the appointing authority shall be referred to the Joint Advisory Committee provided for in Article 9(6).'

Table 1.3: Efficiency	
Organising/Planning work	
GENERAL	Jobholder draws up a work plan taking into account elements like the order of priority of assigned tasks, and the workload imposed by the tasks.
	Jobholder effectively splits her/his time between the various tasks to be performed, in line with their order of priority.
	Jobholder reacts quickly to unexpected new tasks.
MANAGEMENT	Jobholder distributes tasks in a balanced and transparent manner, and gives clear instructions on the way they are to be handled and the success criteria (oral and written).
	Jobholder gives a strategic vision of the objectives and priorities of the unit and translates it into measurable and attainable objectives for the team members.
Performing work/Ensuring quality	
GENERAL	Jobholder ensures that she/he understands the tasks she/he is asked to perform by listening and by asking questions.
	Jobholder effectively manages a range of projects/dossiers simultaneously
	Jobholder carries out tasks without unnecessary or unjustified delays.
	Jobholder ensures that the DG's/Directorate's/Unit's quality standards are met and policies and procedures followed in the performance of his/her tasks.
MANAGEMENT	Jobholders sets up and runs a supervision system to support her/his team in fulfilling its tasks effectively and achieving objectives.

Table 1.4: Abilities	
Oral & written communication	
GENERAL	Jobholder expresses her/himself clearly, accurately and concisely, showing sensitivity to the multicultural working environment, in a Community language other than her/his native language, depending on the needs of the service.
	The documents the jobholder writes are clear, concise, and structured, requiring only minor corrections.
AD	Jobholder uses the appropriate communication style for different target audiences.
Technical skills	
GENERAL	Jobholder has the requisite basic technical skills to fulfil her/his tasks (e.g. knowledge of computer tools, specific Commission tools, specific financial tools or procedures).
Communication in meetings	
GENERAL	Jobholder generally makes valuable contributions in meetings, pinpointing key issues and proposing constructive solutions.
AD	Jobholder ensures sound organisation and efficient time management of meetings under their responsibility.

cont...

Table 1.4: Abilities – continued	
Negotiation skills	
AD	Jobholder shows good diplomacy skills in negotiations and strives to maintain good relations with the other side. Jobholder generally knows how to deploy an appropriate line of argument to ensure a positive outcome. She/he is aware of negotiating strategies and techniques and has the requisite skills.
Analysing problems and applying solutions	
GENERAL	Jobholder analyses problems accurately, trying to find sources of the problem, taking a methodical and logical approach to her/his work. Jobholder is able to identify viable solutions.
AD	Jobholder weighs up the various possible solutions and shows sound reasoning in identifying the most suitable one. Consults management where appropriate.
AST	Where requested to do so by the management, jobholder weighs up the various possible solutions she/he has identified, using sound and appropriate reasoning.
Awareness of the working environment	
GENERAL	Jobholder is aware of the internal control standards and systematically applies relevant ones when performing her/his tasks. Jobholder is aware of the rules and practices with regard to ethics and integrity and observes them. Jobholder takes into account the multicultural environment and is tolerant of different cultures and opinions.
MANAGEMENT	Jobholder defends the interests of the institution by observing the rules and procedures in force and acts with particular caution when dealing with financial issues.
People management	
GENERAL	Jobholder is able to delegate tasks when appropriate and/or requested. In such cases, she/he ensures that the nature, scope and timeframe of delegated functions/powers/tasks are clear to all concerned.
MANAGEMENT	Jobholder delegates tasks by adapting the style and scope of delegation to the team member's specific background (e.g. education, experience, personality). She/he assesses skills correctly and makes effective use of staff. Jobholder gives and encourages regular feedback to/from her/his team and reacts positively to constructive criticism. Jobholder is able to motivate and inspire team members and fosters their professional and personal development (including training and mobility prospects). Jobholder is able to identify and willingly address problems of low or underperformance in her/his team by taking the necessary action. Jobholder is able to handle conflicts effectively and in an even-handed way.

Table 1.5: Aspects of conduct

Teamwork

GENERAL	Jobholder contributes to the achievement of shared goals.
	Jobholder is willing to accept feedback and learn from mistakes she/he has made.
	Jobholder spontaneously recognises the achievements of other team members.
	Jobholder maintains constructive relations with colleagues, to help them complete their tasks, trying to be sensitive to their needs and giving advice where needed.
	Jobholder keeps her/his superiors and colleagues informed about her/his tasks and shares information which might be of general interest to the team/unit/DG.
MANAGEMENT	Jobholder stimulates teamwork, in particular, by clearly defining roles and tasks, rewarding joint efforts and crating team spirit.

Service culture

GENERAL	Jobholder ensures that she/he knows the needs of stakeholders and seeks the best solution for their needs.
	Jobholder checks whether stakeholders are satisfied with the service provided.
	Jobholder conducts her/himself properly, adapting her/his conduct to suit different persons or situations. She/he is patient, showing due courtesy and respect.
	Jobholder ensures that whatever she/he does gives a positive and professional image of her/his institution.

Commitment to the work

GENERAL	Jobholder takes responsibility for her/his tasks and approaches them proactively. She/he works independently, but, where necessary, does not hesitate to seek advice from colleagues and/or superiors.
	Jobholder is happy to accept changes in her/his responsibilities and tasks.
	Jobholder is committed to meeting her/his targets and those of the unit.

Professional development in the context of work

GENERAL	Jobholder agrees to develop – through training or coaching – new knowledge and skills needed to take on new responsibilities or to adapt to changes in working methods.
	Jobholder takes into account existing best practices and makes use of expertise within her/his DG/Directorate/Unit. Seeks to improve procedures by making constructive suggestions.

Leadership

MANAGEMENT	Jobholder acts with integrity and respect in her/his dealings with all team members and is sensitive to their cultural and social background.
	Jobholder is mindful of the needs for confidentiality when dealing with sensitive tasks or with personnel matters.

Promotion

In virtually all organisations, promotions (or vertical mobility) are a hot topic. A promotion is a way for an employer to express appreciation for the good work, and the loyalty, of the promoted employee. The problem with promotions, especially in bigger organisations, is that it is very difficult – if not impossible – to find a system that is considered to be 'fair' by everybody. If the promotion system is 'automatic' – based on seniority – the risk exists that underperformers are also promoted, and this will make the high-performers unhappy. If, on the other hand, promotion is only based on (perceived) merit, some high-performers may be left behind because they go unnoticed by the management, and underperformers who manage to hide their failures or are their managers' favourites, can get a promotion.

Another tricky thing connected to promotions is the well-known Peter Principle[10]: 'everybody is promoted to his level of incompetence.' A nasty corollary of this principle is that in the highest ranks of an organisation you will only find 'incompetent', so unproductive people. However, even though there is some truth to the Peter Principle, it does ignore the possibility that people can change (or 'grow') throughout their career, by developing their competencies. So, if promotion is based on potential (and not on seniority or merit) the risk of people ending up at the final stage (of incompetence) is significantly diminished.

In the EU institutions, the promotion system is based on a mixture of seniority and merit, and to a certain extent on potential; it is governed by the Staff Regulations (Article 45, first paragraph):

> 'Promotion shall be by decision of the appointing authority in the light of Article 6(2). Unless the procedure laid down in Articles 4 and 29(1) is applied, officials may only be promoted if they occupy a post which corresponds to one of the types of posts set out in Annex I, Section A, for the next higher grade. Promotion shall be effected by appointment of the official to the next higher grade in the function group to which he belongs. Promotion shall be exclusively by selection from among officials who have completed a minimum of two years in their grade after consideration of the comparative merits of the officials eligible for promotion. When considering comparative merits, the appointing authority shall in particular take account of the reports on the officials, the use of languages in the execution of their duties other than the language for which they have produced evidence of thorough knowledge in accordance with point (f) of Article 28 and the level of responsibilities exercised by them.'

Even though the concepts of merit and potential are prominently there, seniority is also taken into consideration. The Staff Regulations provide for the mathematical calculation of the number of promotion possibilities each year. The Appointing Authority (AA) may deviate from this, but the five-year average must comply with these calculations. The European Union Civil Service Tribunal recently ruled against the European Commission[11] for failing to comply with the guaranteed promotion rates, so you can safely bet on it that – in the future – the AAs will repect this rule.

Say, for example, that for a given grade, the average promotion rate is 33%. This

---

10   'The Peter Principle' (1968) by Laurence J. Peter.
11   Judgment in Case F-72/11.

effectively means that – on average – people who are currently in that grade are to be promoted after three years. This does not prevent the AA from promoting an individual after only two years (which is the minimum) or only after five, or six years, or never. In 2005, staff had to wait on average 5.6 years for a promotion. Based on all grades and categories, the average wait is now 3.4 years. That was the promise made in the 2004 reform; although starting salary levels were reduced, faster promotions would ensure at least equivalent 'career earnings'. That promise has been kept.

It should be clear by now that the annual appraisal reports (which are based on your competencies, and thus your potential) play a major role in the promotion procedure. In some institutions (like the Commission) however, there is no formal score given in the appraisal report; the report only gives a qualitative description of the performance over the last year: no points are awarded. It has to be said that the EU trade unions are not very happy with this situation, because it leaves an enormous discretionary power in the hands of the Appointing Authority. Formally speaking, the AA can promote whomever they want, provided that the person is 'promotable' (i.e., after 2 years in the same grade) and that the budget of the institution allows it through the '*tableau des effectifs*'. Likewise, a person can be put on hold forever, if he or she is unlucky enough to be on the 'black list' of the AA. (Officially, these lists do not exist, at least not on paper, but the memory of an administration can be very long…) No wonder that the trade unions are watching the yearly promotion procedures with a very critical eye.

Certification

The 2004 Staff Regulation Reform also provided for the possibility of AST officials to be appointed as AD, as stipulated in Article 45a:

1. 'By way of derogation from Article 5 (3) (b) and (c), an official in function group AST may, from grade 5, be appointed to a post in function group AD, on condition that:

(a) he has been selected in accordance with the procedure laid down in paragraph 2 of this Article to take part in a compulsory training programme as set out in point (b) of this paragraph,

(b) he has completed a training programme defined by the Appointing Authority comprising a set of compulsory training modules, and

(c) he is on the list drawn up by the Appointing Authority of candidates who have passed an oral and written examination demonstrating that he has successfully taken part in the training programme mentioned under point (b) of this paragraph. The contents of this examination shall be determined in accordance with Article 7(2)(c) of Annex III.

2. The Appointing Authority shall draw up a draft list of AST officials selected to take part in the aforesaid training programme on the basis of the annual reports referred to in Article 43 and their level of education and training and taking account of the needs of the services. This draft shall be submitted to a joint committee for its opinion. (…) '

Once again, a good appraisal report – and the continuous development of your competencies – is paramount.

The GROW model

As already mentioned, this book has been written from a coach's point of view. Coaches use models, and the model I am going to use is the GROW model, so before explaining in more detail about the methodology I intend to follow, it will be useful to say a bit more about the underlying concept.

The GROW model is a simple, yet powerful method for goal setting and problem solving. It was developed in the United Kingdom, mainly by Sir John Whitmore[12] and is used extensively in corporate coaching. The principle behind the GROW process is rooted in the Inner Game theory[13] developed by Timothy Gallwey[14]. Both methods start from the observation that many individuals are struggling to achieve their goals because they are not learning from experience, and are not aware of the available knowledge that could help them:

> 'In every human endeavour there are two arenas of engagement: the outer and the inner. The outer game is played on an external arena to overcome external obstacles to reach an external goal. The inner game takes place within the mind of the player and is played against such obstacles as fear, self-doubt, lapses in focus, and limiting concepts or assumptions. The inner game is played to overcome the self-imposed obstacles that prevent an individual or team from accessing their full potential.'

Reference should also be made to the work of Graham Alexander[15] in the early development of the GROW framework.

The power of the GROW model lies in the fact that it leads to a clear result in four simple steps. Because it is the coachee himself who formulates the problem – and generates the ideas – the solution sticks better and leads to lasting results.

The GROW model is a four-step sequence of questions; the acronym stands for:

GOAL	–	What do you want?
REALITY	–	What is happening now?
OPTIONS	–	What could you do?
WAY FORWARD	–	What will you do?

(Note: some authors refer to 'Obstacles' for the 'O', and to 'Will' for the 'W', but the underlying ideas of the model remain unchanged.)

A useful metaphor for the GROW model is that of planning a journey. You start with the map: where do you want to go (Goal) and where are you now (Reality)? Then you look at the possible routes (Options). Finally, you pick one route and plan the journey, taking into account all the conditions and obstacles (Way forward).

---

12 Sir John Whitmore is Chairman of Performance Consultants International, the foremost provider of coaching, and leadership development and performance improvement in the workplace globally.

13 www.theinnergame.com

14 Timothy Gallwey (1938) is a respected American tennis player and coach, who has written a series of books in which he has set forth a new methodology for coaching known as 'The Inner Game'.

15 In 'Excellence in coaching: the industry guide' (2010, 2nd ed.) edited by Jonathan Passmore, p. 83–93.

The GROW model provides a framework for having an effective conversation for achieving any goal or addressing any kind of problem or challenge. GROW is a model, not the truth! It is of little value without the context of awareness and responsibility. *Awareness* increases input, interest, learning and recall. *Responsibility* is generated by offering choice, which leads to self-esteem, confidence and self-motivation.

GROW is flexible in terms of sequence of the steps. The dialogue usually starts with Goal questions and then explores the present with Reality questions. After this, you can move freely between the four elements, as needed. The goal may change along the way. New insights and awareness may require a return to the Reality section, followed by more Options and actions (Will) related to them.

Another coaching model

A somewhat different coaching model is to be found in the Solution Focused Coaching (SFC) approach to problem solving[16]. The SFC approach emphasises listening to the problem, issue or challenge, and when ready considering possible solutions; drawing on core strengths, past experience and successes; understanding exceptions; tapping potential; positive imagery and visioning; action planning with simple, achievable first steps. It is my pleasure to say that one of the contributors to this approach – Helen Williams – also provided input to the book you are now reading, and I wish to thank her for the valuable contributions.

Setting goals

When setting a goal, in the G part of GROW, there are certain parameters, which will make the goal stronger and more achievable.

You may already be familiar with **SMART** goals. SMART is a mnemonic for the 5 steps of specific, measurable, attainable, relevant, and time-framed goals. It is a simple tool mostly used by businesses and organisations to go beyond the realm of fuzzy goal setting into an actionable plan for results, but it can also be used for individual goal setting:

Specific: Goals should be simply written and define clearly what you are going to do. This is your vision for the future.

Measurable: Goals should be measurable so that you have tangible evidence that you have accomplished the goal. Usually, the entire goal statement is a measure on its own, but there are frequently several short-term or smaller measurements built into the goal.

Attainable: Goals should be attainable: they should stretch you sufficiently that you feel challenged, but be defined well enough so that you can actually achieve them.

---

16 'Solution Focused Coaching in Practice: Essential Coaching Skills and Knowledge' (2012) by Bill O'Connell, Stephen Palmer and Helen Williams.

You can meet almost any goal when you plan your steps wisely and establish a timeframe that allows you to carry out those steps. As you carry out the steps, you can achieve goals that may have seemed impossible when you started. On the other hand, if a goal is impossible to achieve, you may not even try to accomplish it. Attainable goals motivate – but impossible goals demotivate.

Relevant: In the context of your performance development, your goals should be linked to a competency and a specific anchor, within the list of your current priorities.

Time-framed: Goals should be linked to a timeframe that creates a practical sense of urgency, or results in tension between the current reality and the vision of the goal. Without such tension, the goal is unlikely to produce a relevant outcome.

When setting yourself goals you should distinguish between final goals and performance goals. A *final goal* may be something like 'I want to run a marathon'; a *performance goal* helps you to achieve your final goals, for example 'I will go jogging for half an hour every morning'.

Sir John Whitmore defined 14 criteria your goals ideally meet (see Figure 1.5).

S	Specific	The Right Goal	C	Challenging
M	Measurable	P	Positive	L	Legal
A	Achievable	U	Understood	E	Environmentally sound
R	Realistic	R	Relevant	A	Agreed
T	Time-based	E	Ethical	R	Recorded

Figure 1.5

Different levels of goals

It is important to recognise that there are different levels of goals, and that we have to attend to each level in our journey.

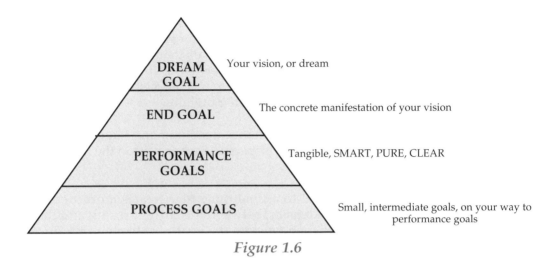

Figure 1.6

A brief guide to SMART goal setting

- Develop several goals. A list of five to seven items gives you several things to work on over a period of time.
- State goals as declarations of intent, not items on a wish list. Use clear, specific language. Start your goal statement with 'To' followed by a verb.
- Attach a date to each goal. State what you intend to accomplish and by when. A good list should include some short-term and some long-term goals. You may want a few goals for the year, and some for two or three month intervals.
- Be specific. Sometimes a more general goal can become the long-term aim, and you can identify some more specific goals to take you there.
- Share your goals with someone who cares if you reach them. Sharing your intentions with your parents, your best friend, or your supervisor will help ensure success.
- Write down your goals and put them where you will see them. The more often you read your list, the more results you will get.
- Review and revise your list. Experiment with different ways of stating your goals. Goal setting improves with practice. Example: *'To run the '20 km of Brussels' in May 20XX and complete the race in under 1,5 hours to beat my personal best time.'*

Methodology

To take the words of the American author David Markson[17]: 'This is not a novel'. A novel is a long narrative, usually in the form of a sequential story. I am not going to tell you a story – or describe a sequence of events. I will walk you through a large number of seemingly unrelated ideas, concepts, and models, which hopefully will lead you to the answers to the same questions we all confront: How do I make the right decisions? How can I motivate my team or myself? How can I change things? How can I work more efficiently? And on a more personal level: What do I really want?

Merriam-Webster defines a *methodology* as 'a set of methods, rules, or ideas that are important in a science or art: a particular procedure or set of procedures'. A methodology does not set out to provide solutions – it is, therefore, not the same as a method.

---

17   'This is not a Novel' (2011) by David Markson.

Instead, a methodology offers the theoretical underpinning to understand which method, set of methods, or so-called 'best practices' can be applied to a specific case, for example, to obtain a specific result.

In this book, I recommend that you follow the GROW model to improve your performance at work. Since this book has been written for EU staff, I will concentrate on the development of your 'general competencies' as introduced earlier in this chapter.

I will dig deeper into the explanation of every competency, in order for you to understand better what is actually expected, and raise your awareness. Without imposing anything I will describe some general models, ideas, and best practices, and make reference to books, websites, or other resources where you can deepen your understanding (Goal) and explore the alternatives (Options).

Developing your general competencies starts with awareness, and ends with responsibility.

If you are not aware that you have a problem with a given competency you will never be inclined to develop it. To build this awareness, the first thing you are recommended to do is **try to complete the questionnaires in the annexes to this book (or use the online toolkit that comes with this book** – described in the next sections of this chapter).

You may find it difficult to do this on your own, because the human mind has a tendency for 'blind spots' when it comes to its own behaviour. You may need external feedback provided by a professional coach or trainer, or someone who knows you very well and is willing to discuss with you in an open and honest manner (and the online toolkit also allows you to get external feedback from others on an anonymous basis). Of course, your EPSO competency passport (if you have one) and the feedback from your superiors come in handy as well.

How to use the self-assessment worksheets

In Annexes 1 to 8 you will find a set of comprehensive questionnaires, covering every competency and allowing you to make a self-assessment. For each competency, there are 10 anchors, and for every anchor there is a list of indicators, ordered from 'Unsatisfactory' to 'Exceptional'. For example, the first anchor for analysis and problem solving in Annex 1 looks like Figure 1.7.

	Unsatisfactory	Improvement Needed	Meets Expectations	Exceeds Expectations	Exceptional	
Anchor	1- Extremely Weak 2- Very Weak	3- Weak 4- Fair	5- Satisfactory 6- Good	7-Strong 8- Very Strong	9- Excellent 10- Outstanding	**Score**
1	Has difficulty distinguising between critical and non-critical issues. Loses focus when resolving larger issues. Misunderstands or misinterprets key elements of information.	Needs help analyzing and prioritizing problems. Tends to focus on simple operational issues.	Solves urgent, high impact problems first.	Analyzes and prioritizes critical problems first. Stays focused on critical problems until they are successfully resolved.	Analyzes and prioritizes critical problems accurately and quickly. Maintains a sense of urgency in solving even complex problems.	

Figure 1.7

The idea is now to identify the indicator that best describes your current behaviour, and determine the score you have for that anchor, by looking at the second header row of the table. Say, for example that you tend to focus on simple operational issues, your score for that anchor would then be 3 (Weak) or 4 (Fair). It's up to you to decide which qualifier is – in your opinion – the best description in your case. Once decided on the score, you write it down in the last column of the row corresponding with this anchor.

It could happen that you think that multiple indicators, in different columns apply. Don't worry, just take the average of the corresponding scores, and use this as your score for the given anchor.

This exercise will have to be repeated for every anchor (10 per competency), and you can then calculate your score for that competency by adding all the scores for the anchors. The result should be a number between 10 and 100 (I consider that it is impossible to have a zero score for any anchor, because that would imply that you are brain-dead).

The resulting scores of the questionnaires can then be plotted on your personal competency passport (Annex 9), giving you a complete idea of where you are (Reality). It is pretty unusual for a person to be equally good – or bad – on all competencies: the resulting spider graph will probably not resemble a circle, but have a more irregular shape. Also, I have never seen a graph with only high scores (over 80). This is because there are certain 'conflicts of interest' in our behaviour. Say, for example that you are a very detail-oriented, analytical person. Your score for analysis and problem solving will then probably be very high. On the other hand, you may have issues in terms of resilience because you are constantly overwhelmed by the details and the richness of your ideas.

Now what is 'good' and what isn't?

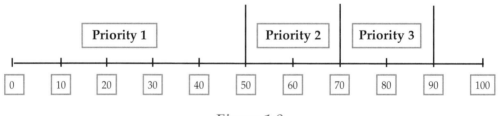

Figure 1.8

If your total score for a given competency is below 50, you really have an important (and urgent) issue. This is definitely a 'priority 1' competency to work on. If your score is between 50 and 70 there is scope for improvement, but it is maybe not so urgent. I would make this your 'priority 2'. If your score is between 70 and 90, then basically all is fine, since you meet and exceed the expectations. So, improving on this competency may not be considered as very important. Be alert to the possibility, however, that since you are already good (aware and responsible) it will probably be easy for you to improve with some fine-tuning of your behaviour through some 'quick wins'. This is your 'priority 3'. Finally, if your score is higher than 90, well, there's not much you can – or should – do; you are exceptionally good at this, so don't bother.

Once you have identified the areas where there is room for improvement – and not before – you can start to think about your options. These may be simple things like reading some books on the topic or getting some formal training in your domain of activity. But sometimes more drastic options have to be considered; if you are really not good at what you do for a living, and training doesn't help, maybe it's time to go for another challenge, and change jobs.

Now that you have listed – and carefully considered – your options, it's time to decide and commit to what you WILL do. Step out of your comfort zone. Start with the 'low hanging fruit' to build confidence. Set yourself SMART operational goals and use an 'agile' and iterative approach. Ask for help. Be patient.

Based on your priorities, the understanding of your goals, your reality, and the available options you can then design your own personal development plan (Will – or Way Forward, see Annex 10).

It is possible to improve every single competency, but there is no point in trying to improve everything at once; this won't work. Once you have a rough idea about your strengths and development areas, make a plan and first try to improve in those areas where your performance is worst. The best approach is to identify your weakest points first, improve and consolidate your development, and then start the process all over again.

Proceed in small, achievable steps. Identify 'quick wins' (process goals) that will make you gain confidence once achieved, before tackling your performance goals. Personal development takes time, a lot of time, and it is too easy to get discouraged when the distant goals are not reached at the first attempt.

And remember: YOU are responsible for your own development, not your manager, your colleagues, your coach, or your mentor. And neither is the HR department.

This book's online toolkit

This book comes with an online self-assessment and 360-degree feedback toolkit. The toolkit is based on the GROW model, much like the book. The output is an actionable development plan, taking into account your priorities in a personalised way.

The foundation of the toolkit is a set of questionnaires, very much like the Annexes of this book, but the online format makes it easy to use, and some extra features have also been added to make it even more useful. Not only can you make a self-assessment by completing these questionnaires, but you can also ask others – friends, colleagues, coaches, and supervisors – to do so if you wish. In this way you can build a Johari window, and gain a better understanding of your own 'blind spots'. This will effectively increase your self-awareness, and allow for better self-development.

The intermediate result of the self-assessment, and the 360-degree assessment, is presented in the form of a competency passport (see screenshot in Figure 1.9) and a Johari window. This concludes the 'Reality' step in the GROW cycle.

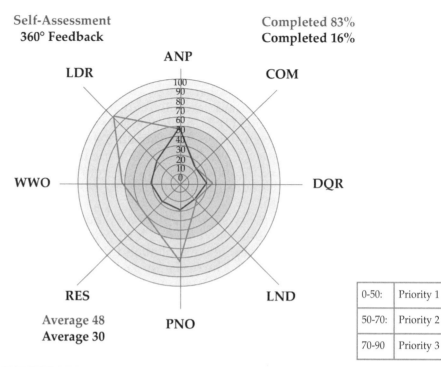

Self-Assessment   Completed 83%
360° Feedback   Completed 16%

0-50:	Priority 1
50-70:	Priority 2
70-90	Priority 3

Average 48
Average 30

Competency	Self-Assessment	360° Feedback
ANP - Analysis and Problem Solving	47	47
COM - Communicating	25	25
DQR - Delivering Quality and Results	34	30
LND - Learning and Development	26	24
PNO - Prioritising and Organising	76	28
RES - Resilience	44	29
WWO - Working with Others	52	29
LDR - Leadership	87	33

10	Extremely Weak
20	Very Weak
30	Weak
40	Fair
50	Satisfactory
60	Good
70	Strong
80	Very Strong
90	Excellent
100	Outstanding

Figure 1.9

Then comes the time for setting your goals. Ideally, your goals are linked to the Priority 1 items, your lowest scores on the competency passport. The tool also encourages you to set SMART goals, at different levels of development (process, performance, end, dream).

The next step is to think about your options. Options are the things you could do to improve this or that competency, without thinking too much about the feasibility (I suggest you use the 'brainstorming' technique for this part).

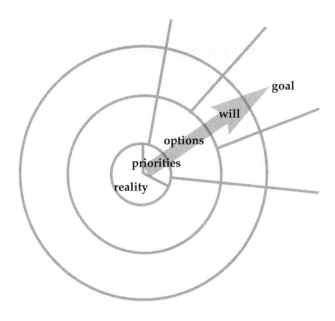

Figure 1.10

Finally, comes the 'Way Forward' – or 'Will' – part of the GROW cycle. Here you make a (realistic) selection of the options, attach timing to them, and commit to the actions you will effectively undertake to achieve your goals.

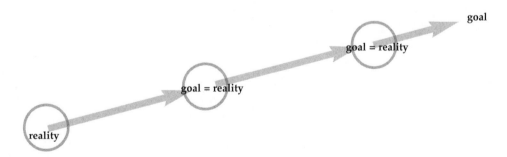

Figure 1.11

The idea is to use this tool (and the book) in an iterative way, building your development in small cycles, as is illustrated in Fig. 1.10. Think in terms of the 'horizontal growth' and the 'vertical transformation' as will be described in the introduction to Chapter 6.

The online toolkit can be found at:

https://www.johnharperpublishing.co.uk/the-ultimate-eu-career-development-toolkit/

Once registered as a user you can use it as long as you want, for free. You can use the toolkit totally anonymously and also get anonymous feedback from others.

Key points to remember

- Having a high-potential is not enough to become a high-achiever.
- Personal development is the process of understanding and developing oneself in order to achieve one's fullest potential.
- Personal development is becoming increasingly important in the EU institutions.
- General competencies are about expected behaviour at work.
- Awareness and responsibility are two vital ingredients of personal development.

Your notes

2. Know yourself to understand others

'If you know others and know yourself, you will not be imperilled in a hundred battles; if you do not know others but know yourself, you win one and lose one; if you do not know others and do not know yourself, you will be imperilled in every single battle' – Sun Tzu[1]

In 1651, Thomas Hobbes[2] used the term *nosce te ipsum*, as the Latin translation of an ancient Greek aphorism inscribed on the temple of Apollo at Delphi, which he translated as 'know thyself' in his famous work, *The Leviathan*. He was contradicting popular thinking at the time that you can learn more by studying others than you can from reading books. He states that one learns more by studying oneself: particularly the feelings that influence our thoughts and motivate our actions. We all have basic skills to lead, coach, or communicate; but most of us have a number of psychological blocks when it comes to applying those skills well and consistently. Knowing yourself, and thereby understanding others, will help you overcome your own blocks and unlock your full potential.

"Everyone says you're really good at office politics. Or were they stabbing you in the back with a compliment like that?"

Theories of human nature

People behave according to certain principles of human nature, the common qualities of all human beings. Therefore, to understand our own behaviour and the behaviour of others it is important to have some knowledge about human nature.

---

1   Sun Tzu (6th century BCE) was a Chinese general, military strategist, and author of 'The Art of War'.
2   Thomas Hobbes, an English philosopher of the 17th century, best known for political philosophy and theory of the social contract.

Maslow's hierarchy of needs

Human needs are an important part of human nature. Ethics, ideas and behaviour differ from country to country and from culture to culture, but all humans have similar needs. Abraham Maslow[3] used the terms 'physiological', 'safety', 'belongingness' and 'love', 'esteem', 'self-actualisation', and 'self-transcendence' to describe the pattern that human motivations generally move through. Maslow's theory suggests that the most basic level of needs must be met before the individual will strongly desire the secondary or higher level needs. The basic four layers of the pyramid contain what Maslow called 'deficiency needs'; esteem, friendship and love, security, and physical needs. If these 'deficiency needs' are not met the individual will feel anxious and stressed. At the top of Maslow's pyramid is self-actualisation. Self-actualisers finally feel themselves – safe and not anxious, accepted, loved, loving, and alive, certainly living a fulfilling life.

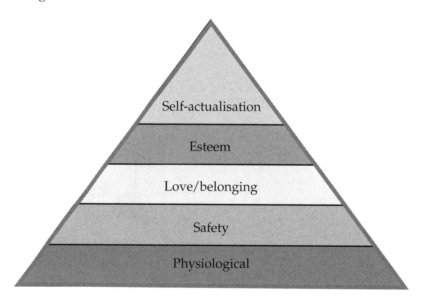

Figure 2.1

Recent research seems to confirm the existence of universal human needs, although the hierarchy proposed by Maslow is questioned. In fact, there is little evidence for the ranking of needs that Maslow described, or for the existence of a fixed hierarchy at all. According to Geert Hofstede[4], the needs and drives of people raised in individualistic societies tend to be more self-centred than those in collectivist societies. In individualistic societies people focus on improvement of the self, with self-actualisation being the apex of self-improvement. In collectivist societies, the needs of acceptance and community will outweigh the needs for freedom and individuality.

3   Abraham Maslow (1908–1970) was a psychology professor at Brandeis University, Brooklyn College, the New School for Social Research and Columbia University.

4   Geert Hofstede (1928) is a Dutch social psychologist and Professor Emeritus of Organisational Anthropology and International Management at Maastricht University in the Netherlands.

Herzberg's hygiene and motivational factors

Frederick Herzberg[5] developed a list of factors, which are based on Maslow's hierarchy of needs but more closely related to work:

'Hygiene Factors' or 'Dissatisfiers':

- Working Conditions
- Corporate Policies
- Salary and Benefits
- Supervision
- Status
- Security
- Fellow Workers
- Work-life Balance

Motivators or Satisfiers:

- Recognition
- Achievement
- Advancement
- Growth
- Responsibility
- Job Challenge

According to Herzberg, Hygiene Factors must be present (without them there is dissatisfaction) before motivators stimulate an employee. He used the term *job enrichment* to describe the process of redesigning work to build motivators.

Theory X and Theory Y

Douglas McGregor[6] developed another view of humanity with his Theory X and Theory Y. These are two opposing perceptions about human behaviour at work.

Theory X is the view that traditional management has taken towards the workforce:

- People have an inherent dislike of work and will avoid it whenever possible.
- People must be coerced, controlled, directed, or threatened with punishment to get them to achieve the organisational objectives.

---

5   Frederick Herzberg (1923–2000) was an American psychologist who became one of the most influential names in business management.

6   'The Human Side of Enterprise' (1960) by Douglas McGregor

- People prefer to be directed, do not want responsibility, and have little or no ambition.

Theory Y is different because:

- Work is as natural as play and rest.

- People will exercise self-direction if they are committed to the objectives.

- Commitment to objectives is a function of the rewards associated with their achievement.

- Creativity, ingenuity, and imagination are widely distributed among the population and people are capable of using these abilities to solve an organisational problem.

- People have potential.

Please observe that Maslow, Herzberg, and McGregor's theories all tie together. Indeed, Herzberg's theory is the application of Maslow to the workplace and McGregor's Theory X is based on workers trapped at lower levels, while Theory Y is applicable to workers at higher levels.

Expectancy theory

In more recent years, probably the most popular motivational theory has been the Expectancy Theory. Although there are several theories found with the same title, they all have their roots in Victor Vroom's work on motivation[7]. Vroom defines motivation as: 'A process governing choices ... among alternative forms of voluntary behaviour.

Imagine an individual, occupying a role in an organisation and faced with a set of alternative voluntary behaviours, all with outcomes attached. The traditional view is that the choice made reflects the strength of the individual's desire for, or avoidance of, a specific outcome at a certain time. Vroom's theory suggests that behaviour results from conscious choices among alternatives whose purpose is to maximise pleasure and minimise pain. The key elements to this theory are called Expectancy (E), Instrumentality (I), and Valence (V):

- *Expectancy* refers to the strength of a person's belief about whether a particular job performance is achievable.

- *Instrumentality* is a probability belief linking one outcome (a high level of performance, for example) to another outcome (a reward).

- The term *Valence* refers to the level of satisfaction people expect to get from the outcome.

The resulting Motivation (M) is given by:

$$M = E * I * V$$

---

7   Victor H. Vroom is a business school professor at the Yale School of Management.

Personality

'*Chassez le naturel, il revient au gallop*'[8] – French proverb

The Oxford dictionaries define 'personality' as 'The combination of characteristics or qualities that form an individual's distinctive character' while the American Psychological Association (APA) says: 'Personality refers to individual differences in characteristic patterns of thinking, feeling and behaving.'

Mussels from Brussels

This is a picture I took from my son's plate after he had enjoyed a yummy dish of Belgian mussels. What does this say about his personality?

Figure 2.2

There are many theories on personality[9], and most are in some way based on – or related to – the work of Carl Jung[10]. There are both type and trait theories; trait personality questionnaires are useful in selection and recruitment as they can be more readily mapped to job requirements, whilst the type models are useful in personal and team development, as the type categories are helpful in understanding oneself and others.

Probably the best-known type theory is the **Myers-Briggs Personality Type Indicator (MBTI)** created by Isabel Briggs Myers and her mother, Katharine Cook Briggs.

Without going into too much detail, suffice it to say that the MBTI is based on the idea that each personality type is composed of four pairs of preferences – or dichotomies – as depicted in Table 2.1, e.g. Feeling.(F) vs. Thinking (T).

8   The closest translation would be: 'A leopard cannot change its spots'.

9   Big Five, Enneagram, Kersey…

10   Carl Gustav Jung (1875–1961) was a Swiss psychiatrist and psychotherapist who founded analytical psychology.

	Subjective	Objective
Deductive	iNtuition vs Sensing	Perception vs Judging
Inductive	Feeling vs Thinking	Introversion vs Extraversion

Table 2.1

As a result, people are classified into one out of 16 'type indicators', such as ISTJ (Introversion, Sensing, Thinking, Judging – see Table 2.2). Based on these type indicators a number of common characteristics can be described like:

> 'ISTJ – Quiet, serious, earn success by thoroughness and dependability. Practical, matter-of-fact, realistic and responsible. Decide logically what should be done and work towards it steadily, regardless of distractions. Take pleasure in making everything orderly and organised – their work, their home, their life. Value tradition ands and loyalty.' (From 'Introduction to TYPE' – sixth edition)

Please note that the terms used for each dichotomy have specific technical meanings relating to the MBTI. For example, extraversion means 'outward-turning' and introversion means 'inward-turning'. These specific definitions vary somewhat from the popular usage of the words. Also, the MBTI instrument measures aptitude; it simply indicates for one preference over another; someone reporting a high score for extraversion over introversion cannot be correctly described as more extraverted: they simply have a clearer *preference*.

ISTJ "Doing What Should be Done"	ISFJ "A High Sense of Duty"	INFJ "An Inspiration to Others"	INTJ "Everything Has Room For Improvement"
ISTP "Ready to Try Anything Once"	ISFP "Sees Much But Shares Little"	INFP "Noble Service to Aid Society"	INTP "A Love of Problem Solving"
ESTP "The Ultimate Realists"	ESFP "You Only Go Around Once in Life"	ENFP "Giving Life an Extra Squeeze"	ENTP "One Exciting Challenge After Another"
ESTJ "Life's Administrators"	ESFJ "Hosts and Hostesses of the World"	ENFJ "Smooth Talking Persuaders"	ENTJ "Natural Leaders"

Table 2.2

A description of each of the sixteen MBTI personality types can be found in Annex 11 of this book.

It is sometimes argued that the MBTI test is unreliable because 50% of people who take the test a second time get a different result. What this really means is that most people who take the test will score near the middle on at least one dichotomy. So on the second taking, that dichotomy could tip one way or the other over the threshold. The real problem with MBTI is not the stability issue, but that many people take the test too literally, especially when they go around classifying people and assuming that they now understand the person because they have found a category. This error is the same as assuming that all people are the same.

Many people who take the MBTI ask whether or not their psychological type can change. According to type theory, basic type preferences for perception or judgement are innate and do not change. However, it is also known that people, as a result of interacting with their environment and through life experiences, also develop behaviours, habits, and strategies that are *not* consistent with their type description.

So why is this important? For one, you may have natural preferences (of innate tendencies) that are not fully used or have been suppressed by your education or environment. Or, you may have facets of your personality that you would like to modify so that you don't fall into the same unhelpful patterns time and again. The elegance of MBTI is that it is a dynamic system that *acknowledges and encourages* an individual to change as a part of healthy type development (even as one's basic type theoretically does not change). There is evidence that either the environment or deliberate intention can indeed bring about these changes. This is very good news indeed!

"You're not going to be upset by
every little thing I point out to you
about your personality, are you?"

Personality tests tend to be referred to as 'questionnaires', as there are no objective 'right' or 'wrong' answers. It is more about understanding what is helpful or less helpful to achieve personal goals and aspirations. I do recommend that you take a personality questionnaire yourself. Ideally, you would have this done by a real specialist, accredited for example in the MBTI, but a good start can be to take a free online test[11]. You will be amazed at how much you will learn about yourself.

I will come back on the more practical application of personality type in the chapters on Working with Others and Leadership.

Who am I?

I am an engineer, brought up and shaped in the Cold War military environment. I started my career in the Belgian Air Force as a technical officer, responsible for an outfit of technicians dealing with the maintenance of military aircraft (Mirage V, the 'Belgian' version of the French Mirage III). When I took the MBTI for the first time the verdict was that I was an ISTJ. I invite you to read again the description of this type above (which is by the way the most frequent amongst men). In hindsight, this really corresponded to who I was, and it was a near-perfect match with the kind of person I was expected to be at that time.

In 1993, shortly after the end of the Cold War, I left the military to join a public sector organisation involved in the socio-medical field. After being an IT project manager I moved into the role of Chief Information Officer. In this role I had responsibility for all aspects relating to the IT environment supporting my employer and had to take a much more holistic view. Then, in 2000, I joined the EU administration, still in a managerial position related to IT. Around 2005 I had the opportunity to become Head of Unit for Budget and Finance and had to take management training for that. During this training I took my second MBTI test and, guess what, I had become an INTJ. INTJ's are described as 'Architects', imaginative and strategic thinkers with a plan for everything. Notice how my previous 'Sensing' preference had turned into a more 'Intuitive' one. In fact, the engineer had turned into a manager. In 2013 I started my own business, as a coach and trainer for people who want to become EU officials. From a manager working for an employer, I had become an entrepreneur. Out of curiosity and in the context of this book, I took another MBTI test. Surprisingly, it turned out that I am an ESTJ now. ESTJ's are 'Executives', excellent administrators, skilled at managing things or people. In short, I went back to the 'Sensing' mode and switched my 'Introversion' preference to 'Extraversion', at least in my behaviour. Please note that the 'Thinking' and 'Judging' aspects of my personality have remained unchanged throughout my entire career. How to make sense of this?

I believe that the consecutive personality types (ISTJ – INTJ – ESTJ) were – and are – pretty close to who I really was or am at these different stages of my life. I was influenced by my environment and adapted my behaviour according to what (I believed) was expected of me. In the role of an engineer I had to behave in the 'Sensing' way, while as a manager and leader I needed to rely more on my intuition. On the other hand, as an employee, I could follow my natural 'Introversion' tendency, while as an entrepreneur I have to behave in the 'Extraversion' mode. I must admit, it took me a number of years before I fully realised this necessity…

MBTI personality types are not evenly distributed throughout the population, nor are they amongst men and women. An interesting treemap in this respect can be found at http://cfcl.com/vlb/Projects/D3/MBTI/MBTI_3.html.

One last thing: there are no 'good' or 'bad' personality types. After all, life would be boring if we were all the same.

---

11   http://www.16personalities.com/personality-types, http://www.truity.com/test/type-finder-research-edition

Culture

11th juror (rising): *'I beg pardon, in discussing…*

10th juror (interrupting and mimicking): *'I beg pardon. What are you so goddam polite about?'*

11th juror (looking straight at the 10th juror): *'For the same reason you're not. It's the way I was brought up'*

(Reginald Rose, 'Twelve Angry Men')

'Twelve Angry Men' is an American theatre play where twelve members of a jury have to decide on the guilt or innocence of a boy accused of murder. The quote cited is part of the confrontation between the tenth juror, a garage owner born and raised in New York, and the eleventh juror, a European-born, Austrian watchmaker.

Every person carries within him or herself patterns of thinking, feeling, and potential acting that were learned throughout that person's lifetime. Much of this was acquired in early childhood, because at that time a person is most susceptible to learning and assimilating. As soon as certain patterns of thinking, feeling, and acting are established, people have to unlearn these patterns before being able to learn something different, and unlearning is more difficult than learning for the first time.

In his bestseller 'Cultures and Organisations'[12] Geert Hofstede uses the analogy of the way computers are programmed. He calls such patterns of thinking, feeling, and acting *mental programs,* or, as per the book's subtitle, *software of the mind.* Allow me to refine this metaphor. Our 'mental programming' can be compared with the Operating System (OS) of our mind (you know, Microsoft Windows, Mac OSX, or Linux). Much like the operating system of a computer determines its basic behaviour, culture determines ours. The normal programs that are run on top of the OS are only 'learned' behaviour, and are much more easy to upgrade or replace. Also, normal programs are only charged in memory when we use them, while the operating system is there all the time.

When applying this to the EU working environment, it is not difficult to understand how the mental program of, for example, a Finnish official who grew up in the cold and dark countryside would be vastly different to the mental programming of a Spanish official who came from the light-filled, warm and vibrant city of Barcelona.

Language and mother tongue constitute an important part of our mental programming. In fact, we actually 'think' in our mother tongue, and you can say that you only have a good command of a foreign language when your mind is capable of skipping the mental translation of your thoughts to the words you speak (or write). There are estimated to be about 150 regional and minority languages in the European Union. These languages may be specific to a region such as Catalan, Basque, Breton, Welsh, Sardinian, or they may be languages spoken by a minority in one state but which are official languages in another EU country, such as Hungarian in Slovakia, or German in southern Denmark. The European languages are vastly different; there are even words

---

12 'Cultures and Organisations – Software of the Mind' (2010) by Geert Hofstede, Gert Jan Hofstede and Michael Minkov.

or concepts that cannot be translated properly: for example Finnish has only gender-neutral pronouns and completely lacks grammatical gender. There has also been some recent research into behavioural differences between speakers of verb-based languages as distinct from noun-based ones. The Sapir–Whorf hypothesis says that linguistic category and usage influence thought and certain kinds of behaviour, but it is seriously questioned in linguistic circles as little empirical evidence has been found.

These facts alone make the EU institutions amongst the most diverse organisations worldwide and not directly comparable to any other multinational or national public

East versus West

There is a much more self-evident behavioural/cultural difference in the EU than issues of language and mother tongue; that is the difference between those staff members brought up under communist rule and those brought up in the Western part of Europe. I find ex-communist officials often require a more planned, collective form of working than do others, who are more able to react to events 'on the fly'. The 'Five-Year Plan' mentality still looms large in some. As it happens, more and more of that particular generation is now making it into senior management across the EU institutions and many don't like the 'directive' approach to management that is appearing as a result.

administration. It is therefore not surprising to see that one of the anchors for the 'Working with Others' competency in EPSO's Assessment Centre deals explicitly with your attitude towards cultural differences: are you aware of, and tolerant of people from other cultures, or – on the contrary – do you ignore cultural differences and judge people based on your own (cultural) standards?

'Everybody has prejudices, but only by facing them, can we fight them.' – Margareta Wadstein, Swedish Ombudsman for Ethnic Discrimination

The advantages of cultural diversity

I once heard a very good example of how the situation in the EU institutions differs from that in a conventional national bureaucracy, from an Englishman who had previously worked in the British public administration. When the British officials were discussing a problem and preparing a decision, he said, there were about ten people in the room who were all in agreement after half an hour. Everybody had the same social origins, spoke the same language, had been to the same university, had the same teachers, in other words they had exactly the same cultural background.

In the EU it is quite the opposite. Participants come from a different country, have different mother tongues and very different backgrounds. They often come from a different social class and went to different universities. The discussions usually last longer, but much more experience is fed into them and they have more input and are more creative. This diversity usually yields a better – more balanced – result.

There is, however, a significant side remark to be made at this point. You only have to travel around Brussels to see there are many people with brown or black skins; and you only have to walk around the EU quarter to see there are virtually none at all. The EU in its recruitment policies gives no recognition to this obvious fact. In contrast the modern British civil service has active policies to recruit from under-represented minorities.

I think this issue will become one of increasing sensitivity and the gloss that the EU institutions tend to put on themselves as beacons of diversity may wear a bit thin...

Xenophobia is the irrational fear of that which is perceived to be different or strange. Xenophobia can manifest itself in many ways such as fear of losing identity, suspicion of the other's behaviour, aggression, and desire to eliminate the other's presence. There is an interesting series of booklets you may already have come across in the bookstores around the EU institutions: 'A Xenophobe's Guide to XYZ'[13], an internationally successful series that highlights the unique character and behaviour of nations. Candid, mocking and funny – almost guaranteed to cure xenophobia.

The essential Belgian

Four hundred years ago Pieter Brueghel the Elder, the greatest of this great family of painters, captured the spirit of his fellow countrymen busily beavering about their villages, skating eagerly on a frozen pond, or celebrating a country wedding, rosy-cheeked with wine and beer, bursting out of their trousers with all that good food, and falling over their comfortable wives in a jolly rustic dance. The hardware has changed, but the spirit remains largely the same.

The Belgians know how to enjoy themselves, but good fun depends upon sound business. Get out there, do an honest day's work for a fair wage, put some away for the future, then spend what's left on having a good time. This, essentially, is what Belgianness amounts to.

(From 'Xenophobe's Guide to the Belgians', p. 17)

Gender and age

Equality between women and men is one of the European Union's founding values. It goes back to 1957 when the principle of equal pay for equal work became part of the Treaty of Rome.

'Men Are from Mars, Women Are from Venus' is a book written by the American author and relationship counsellor John Gray. The book argues that most common relationship problems between men and women are a result of fundamental psychological differences between the genders. However, it is my experience that, at least in the EU institutions, these gender differences don't play a major role in the workplace. I have the impression that men and women of roughly the same age and in comparable positions behave more or less in the same way. Their cultural background matters more than the gender difference. I think that the explanation is rather simple: all EU officials have been selected and recruited through the same gender-neutral process, focusing on what really matters in terms of behaviour at work. Moreover they are governed by the same Staff Regulations, and gender equality is an important part of it. The EU institutions are not quite there yet, especially in the higher – more political – echelons, but they are working very hard to achieve total gender equality over time. Now, I may be biased because I'm a man, but that's the way I see it.

13   www.xenophobes.com

There is no upper age limit when it comes to applying for EU careers and jobs. The minimum age is not specified either, though to meet the formal criteria candidates are certain to be at least 18 years old. EU officials who were in service before 1 January 2014 must normally retire at 65 and EU officials recruited after 1 January 2014 must normally retire at 66; but it is possible in certain circumstances to work up until the age of 67 or exceptionally, until the age of 70. In practical terms this all means that there are soon to be up to four different sociological 'generations' (not the same as family generations) of EU officials crashing into each other at work.

In shorthand terms, Baby Boomers, born between 1946 and 1964, are often pictured as competitive and loyal to their employer. Gen Xers, born between 1965 and 1977, are held to be more likely to be sceptical and independent-minded. Gen Ys – also known as Millennials – were born in 1978 or later, and typically like teamwork, feedback and technology. Finally, there is Gen Z. Born after 1995, they grew up in a highly sophisticated media and computer environment and will supposedly be more internet savvy and expert than their Gen Y predecessors. No other generation in the history of mankind has had the technical ability to connect the majority of people on the planet to each other and in the process to provide the potential opportunity for each person to be fully educated, and socially and economically engaged.

It should be clear that these 'generations' are very broad concepts, and that individuals vary widely in every generation. A lot of research has been conducted, and a lot of publications written about the differences between the generations, but I tend to agree with Thomas Koulopoulos and Dan Keldsen when they state: 'Generational thinking is like the Tower of Babel: it only serves to divide us. Why not focus on the behaviours that can unite us?' This is the essence of their book 'The Gen Z Effect: The Six Forces Shaping the Future of Business'[14].

There is also an interesting video on TED called 'Closing the Gap – A millennial proposal for a happy multigenerational workplace'[15] by Patrice Thompson, a recently graduated millennial.

Staff demographics[16] reveal that men and women are more or less equally represented in the Commission's staff, as seen in Figure 2.3 on the next page.

It is interesting to note that in the younger population of the Commission staff there are more women than men. This will undoubtedly influence the overall mentality over time, as the older generation of male baby boomers gradually disappears (retire) and are replaced (by promotion and internal mobility) by Gen. X, Y and eventually Z female colleagues.

In the Commission – and the other EU institutions by extrapolation – the gender issue is also interconnected with the cultural issue. Because of the relatively recent enlargements the older, and higher ranking men are mainly Western European, while the younger, and lower ranking females have a heavily Eastern European origin.

The Juncker Commission is very serious about the gender balance issue, and has set the objective of having 40% female representation at intermediate and higher levels by 2019. In the Commission's 2135th meeting of 15/07/2015 the following measures were decided:

---

14   'The Gen Z Effect – The Six Forces Shaping the Future of Business' (2014) by Tom Koulopoulos and Dan Keldsen.

15   https://www.ted.com/watch/ted-institute/ted-state-street/patrice-thompson-closing-the-gap-a-millennial-pro-posal-for-a-happy-multigenerational-workplace

16   http://ec.europa.eu/civil_service/docs/europa_sp2_bs_sexe_x_age_en.pdf

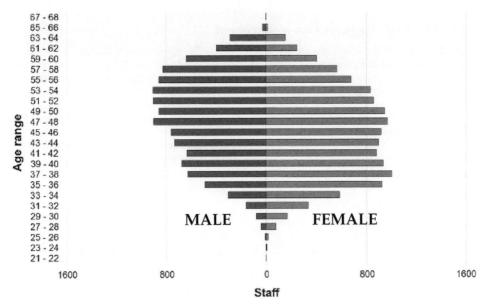

Figure 2.3: Gender distribution by age in European Commission

- DG HR and Security will follow up on the candidacies for management positions and can extend the vacancy periods if there are not sufficient female candidates.

- The composition of pre-selection juries will have to respect gender equality, and jury members can only be appointed after approval from the nomination committee.

- DG HR and Security can ask to re-examine the observations of the pre-selection jury if valid female candidates have not been proposed in the final report.

Furthermore, starting from spring 2016, a yearly progress report has to be submitted to the College of Commissioners.

Article 1d of Staff Regulations[17]

1. In the application of these Staff Regulations, any discrimination based on any ground such as sex, race, colour, ethnic or social origin, genetic features, language, religion or belief, political or any other opinion, membership of a national minority, property, birth, disability, age, or sexual orientation shall be prohibited.

2. With a view to ensuring ensure full equality in practice between men and women in working life, which shall be an essential element to be considered in the implementation of all

cont...

17 http://eur-lex.europa.eu/LexUriServ/LexUriServ.do?uri=CONSLEG:1962R0031:20140101:EN:PDF

Article 1d of Staff Regulations – *continued*

aspects of these Staff Regulations, the principle of equal treatment shall not prevent the institutions of the European Union from maintaining or adopting measures providing for specific advantages in order to make it easier for the under-represented sex to pursue a vocational activity or to prevent or compensate for disadvantages in professional careers.

3. The appointing authorities of the institutions shall determine, by agreement, after consulting the Staff Regulations Committee, measures and actions to promote equal opportunities for men and women in the areas covered by these Staff Regulations, and shall adopt the appropriate provisions notably to redress such de facto inequalities as hamper opportunities for women in these areas. (…)

Emotional intelligence

The rules for work have changed. People are being judged differently; not just by how intelligent they are or by their training and expertise, but also by how well they handle themselves and each other.

The New York Times science writer Daniel Goleman argued in his 1995 book 'Emotional Intelligence: Why It Can Matter More Than IQ' that our emotions play a much greater role in thought, decision making and individual success than is commonly acknowledged. He defines 'emotional intelligence'[18] – a trait not measured by IQ tests – as a set of skills that include control of one's impulses, self-motivation, empathy and social competence in interpersonal relationships.

Emotional intelligence (EI) can be described as interpersonal intelligence or, even more simply, as social skills. For the development of the idea of EI, I refer to the related concept of 'Emotional agility' (David & Congleton)[19], based on Acceptance and Commitment Therapy – which advocates recognising patterns of thoughts and feelings, labelling these, accepting them and then choosing to act/behave according to core values/goals.

Daniel Goleman on emotional intelligence

'Academic intelligence has little to do with emotional life. The brightest among us can founder on the shoals of unbridled passions and unruly impulses; people with high IQs can be stunningly poor pilots of their private lives. One of psychology's open secrets is the relative inability of grades, IQ, or SAT scores to predict unerringly who will succeed in life.

At best, IQ contributes about 20 percent to the factors that determine life success. The vast majority of one's ultimate niche in society is determined by non-IQ factors, ranging from social class to luck.

My concern is with a key set of these other characteristics, emotional intelligence: abilities such as being able to motivate oneself and persist in the face of frustrations; to control impulse and delay gratification; to regulate one's moods and keep distress from swamping the ability to think; to empathize and to hope. Emotional intelligence is a new concept (involving) emotional competencies that can be learned and improved upon.'

---

18   'Emotional Intelligence: Why It Can Matter More Than IQ' (1995) by Daniel Goleman.
19   https://hbr.org/2013/11/emotional-agility

In 1998 Goleman took these concepts into the workplace with a new book 'Working with Emotional Intelligence'[20]. He demonstrates that outstanding performers are not defined by their IQs or even their job skills, but by their emotional intelligence. Analyses done in multiple corporations, government agencies, and nonprofit organisations worldwide conclude that *emotional intelligence is the barometer of excellence in virtually any job.* His book details 12 personal competencies based on self-mastery (such as accurate self-assessment, self-control, initiative, and optimism) and 13 key relationship skills (such as service orientation, developing others, conflict management, and building bonds).

EPSO's Assessment Centre and the staff appraisal processes in the EU institutions are now based on the same principles. However as most candidates are screened out by EPSO at pre-selection by tests of reasoning skills – where emotional intelligence is irrelevant – that could turn out to become an issue for long-term staff development.

Motivation

Motivation is the 'inner force' that drives individuals to accomplish personal and organisational goals.

In our very early days – say some fifty thousand years ago – the underlying assumption about human behaviour was simple and true: we were trying to survive. Call this 'Motivation 1.0', and it served us well – until it didn't.

As humans formed more complex societies, and needed to cooperate in order to get things done, a motivation system that was purely based on biological drive was inadequate, so we slowly replaced it with a version more compatible with how we were working and living. At the core of 'Motivation 2.0' was a new and more accurate assumption: humans are more than the sum of biological urges. We also have a second drive: to seek reward and avoid punishment. Harnessing this second drive has been essential to economic progress around the world, and this assumption also served us well, especially during the last two centuries – until it didn't.

There are essentially two types of motivation: intrinsic and extrinsic. *Intrinsic motivation* is related to meeting your personal needs: you do things because you enjoy them, not because you have to. *Extrinsic motivation* is given or controlled by others, such as salary or praise.

Most of us believe that the best way to motivate others and ourselves is with external rewards and punishment: the carrot-and-stick approach. That is a mistake, says Daniel H. Pink[21] in his provocative and fascinating book 'Drive: The Surprising Truth About What Motivates Us'[22]. According to Pink, the secret to high performance and satisfaction – at work, at school, and at home – is the deeply human need to direct our own lives, to learn and create new things, and to do better by our world and ourselves: 'Motivation 3.0'

---

20 'Working with Emotional Intelligence' (1998) by Daniel Goleman.
21 Daniel 'Dan' Pink (1964) is the author of five books about business, work, and management and also former chief speechwriter for vice-president Al Gore.
22 'Drive: The Surprising Truth About What Motivates Us' (2011) by Daniel H. Pink.

Drawing on four decades of scientific research on human motivation, Pink exposes the mismatch between what science knows and what business does, and how that affects every aspect of life. He demonstrates that while carrots and sticks worked successfully in the twentieth century, that is precisely the wrong way to motivate people for today's challenges. In brief, what this means is that you need to have an amount of *autonomy* in your job, to the level where you feel comfortable. Some people need to have a lot of freedom in what they do, whereas others need more guidance. But there is an optimal level of how much freedom you need in order to be satisfied in your job.

Mastery means that what you do teaches you something; you learn every day and you become better at it. According to Pink, this is the number two pre-condition for being happy in your job: learning from it and feeling that you are improving on a continuous basis.

The third pre-condition is *purpose*, and this is a big factor for many people working in the EU institutions. They feel that engagement in EU affairs means there is a purpose to their work. It is not solely about earning money or having a nine-to-five job; there is a higher goal or a more important objective in what they do.

Psychologists Teresa Amabile[23] and Steven Kramer interviewed over 600 managers and found a shocking result. 95 per cent of managers misunderstood what motivates employees. They thought that all that motivated employees was making money, getting raises and bonuses. In fact, Dan Pink found that actually the exact opposite is true: *'The larger the monetary reward, the poorer the performance. – Money doesn't motivate us, at all, instead emotions do.'*[24]

Intrinsic motivation is a stronger predictor of job performance than extrinsic motivation. The more that people focus on their salaries, the less they will focus on satisfying their intellectual curiosity, learning new skills, or having fun, and those are the very things that make people perform best.

I have an important remark to make at this stage. As you can understand from the above, *the motivation of a person varies over time*, depending on whether the conditions of autonomy, mastery, and purpose are fulfilled – and to which extent. This is clearly NOT a 'permanent' trait of the individual, but is to a large extent determined by the working environment – one's colleagues and one's management. It is mainly the direct supervisor who holds the key to these conditions. In fact it is his or her responsibility to motivate their staff. The point is that most – if not all – people can be motivated, given the right environment. Most of us will have periods in our working lives when we are highly motivated, and other periods when our motivation – and hence our performance – is below standard. So does someone only have themselves to blame if and when their motivation is low? Probably not. If you see that one of your colleagues is demotivated, first ask the question why, and you may even find that the solution lies in your hands. As a corollary I would even say that it is rather pointless to 'select' staff based on their motivation (at that given moment in time) since it is so easy to lose that motivation once that person is recruited, and finds himself in less than optimal working conditions. Clearly, of course, this is not true for people who have a career-long record of low motivation. I will come back to this important issue in the chapter about leadership.

---

23   Teresa Amabile (1950) is Professor of Business Administration at Harvard Business School.

24   https://www.youtube.com/watch?v=Y64ms-htffE

Complementary to McGregor's 'Theory X and Theory Y', Dan Pink created the notions of **'Type I and Type X' behaviour**:

- Type I behaviour is a way of thinking and an approach to life built around intrinsic, rather than extrinsic, motivators. It is powered by our innate need to direct our own lives, to learn and create new things, and to better ourselves and improve our world.

- Type X behaviour is fuelled more by extrinsic desires than intrinsic ones and concerns itself less with the inherent satisfaction of an activity and more with the external rewards to which the activity leads.

You can find out about your behaviour on Dan's website:
www.danpink.com/drive.html

My EPSO experience

In 2011 I was asked to be a member of an EPSO selection board for a big competition aiming to establish a reserve list for AD7 IT specialists. I was involved in this competition from the very beginning where the Notice of Competition was drafted until the final reserve list. At the end of 2011, the president of the competition announced that he was retiring, so he could no longer participate in the selection board. Since I knew him pretty well as we had been working together rather intensively as 'source persons' (the originators of the various test scenarios such as the Case Study, Oral Presentation and Group Exercise), I felt compelled to volunteer for this position. As a result, I became the president for that competition.

In hindsight, this was one of the best periods in my career, and even though it represented a lot of work – on top of my regular job – I was highly motivated to bring this project to a successful conclusion.

First of all, I was deeply convinced of the importance for an organisation to be able to rely on high-quality, in-house IT staff. As you may know, in (larger) organisations a lot of the IT work is outsourced, and it is of vital importance that the internal IT staff have excellent 'soft skills' on top of their technical knowledge. The EPSO selection procedure looked like a good way to select people on this basis. In short one could say that this was the *purpose* part of my motivation.

Second, at EPSO, selection boards are largely independent bodies. Once appointed, the selection board has full responsibility for all aspects of the competition, from the validation of the admission criteria, talent screening, scenarios for the exercises, establishing the intermediate thresholds, dealing with complaints, conducting the exercises, writing the competency passports – right up to the establishment of the final reserve list. In all this, EPSO only provides logistic and legal support. This means that – as president of the board – I had a high degree of *autonomy*, and I enjoyed it very much.

Finally, having been involved in IT management during virtually my entire career I had quite some experience in hiring and managing IT people, so I felt relatively at ease in doing this on a larger scale. Nevertheless, during the selection process, I constantly learned new things. This project had a completely different scope than the projects I was used to. I structured – and deepened – my knowledge of human behaviour and emotional intelligence, and I heard a lot of interesting stories from candidates coming from outside my own universe. In other words, the *mastery* condition was also fulfilled.

Exercise

Try to think back over your own career in terms of how motivated and satisfied you were during various periods, working in different positions for your previous or current employers. It is almost certain that there will have been periods when you felt more at ease than usual. There will also have been periods when you were not so motivated, or even frustrated. In short, your career will show a pattern much like the one in Figure 2.4.

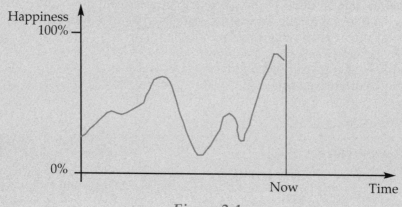

Figure 2.4

Now, think about the (relative) peaks and the reasons why you felt more satisfied during these periods of your career. You will probably come to the conclusion that Pink's conditions of autonomy, mastery and purpose were fulfilled. During these periods of your career you were probably also doing very well professionally. This is because motivated employees tend to give their best.

The Johari Window

The Johari Window was invented by Joseph Luft and Harrington Ingham in the 1950s as a model for mapping personality awareness. In the original version the participant is given a list of 56 adjectives and is asked to choose 5 or 6 of them which best describes their personality. Likewise, peers of the participant are given the same list and each of them is asked to choose 5 or 6 adjectives which best describe the participant. All these are then mapped onto a grid (Figure 2.5).

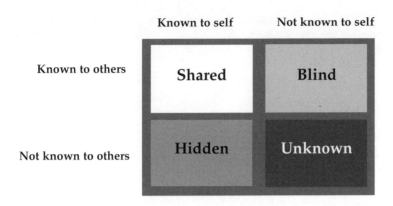

Figure 2.5

The ultimate goal of the Johari Window technique is to enlarge the Shared area in the figure. The Shared area is the most important quadrant, because the more people know about each other, the more productive, cooperative, and effective they'll be when working together. This process is called 'self-disclosure,' and it's a give-and-take process that takes place between yourself and the people that you're interacting with.

The online toolkit that comes for free with this book contains a variant of the original Johari Window: it allows you to ask for – anonymous – feedback on your behaviour and competencies, thus enhancing your self-awareness, and allowing you to set up a realistic development plan.

The toolkit can be found at:

https://www.johnharperpublishing.co.uk/the-ultimate-eu-career-development-toolkit/

Key points to remember

- All human beings are different due to their personality, gender, age, cultural background and education.

- Every person is unique, and has more potential than can be seen at the surface.

- Learning about ourselves gives us the tools to understand others better, and to work better with other people.

Your notes

3.   Analysis and problem solving

Competency definition: 'Identify the critical facts in complex issues and develop creative and practical solutions'.

'Most people spend more time and energy going around problems than in trying to solve them.' – Henry Ford[1]

Problems are at the centre of what most people deal with at work every day; a fundamental part of working life is finding ways to solve them. So being a confident problem solver is really important to your success. Much of that confidence comes from having a good process when approaching a problem.

Some problems are clearly more difficult or complex than others. Unfortunately there is no single, universal way in which all problems can be resolved. There is a universal methodology though, the steps of which are outlined below:

- Identification

- Analysing

- Generating possible solutions

- Making a decision

- Implementation

- Feedback

A somewhat simplified mnemonic for this is IDEAL:

- **I**dentify the problem

- **D**efine the problem

- **E**xamine the options

- **A**ct on a plan

- **L**ook at the consequences.

This methodology is applicable to virtually any kind of problem, including the ones that are regularly encountered in the EU institutions, such as defining a new policy, drafting a new regulation, or in the day to day business when preparing a new IT project, setting up a new evaluation system etc.

We will go over the different steps in more detail in the following pages.

The most prominent difference between an issue and a problem is the solution. When you have an issue, you generally can easily come up with the solution. A problem, on the other hand, is not something that you can solve without serious consideration, and possibly even a certain amount of guesswork.

---

1   Henry Ford (1863–1947) was an American industrialist, the founder of the Ford Motor Company, and pioneer of the development of the assembly line technique of mass production.

How physicians, engineers and scientists approach problems differently

Physicians, scientists and engineers are trained to have different approaches to problem solving. These three types of problem solvers can be seen as archetypes representing the training methods each field is known for. Of course, any individual would use a mix of these problem-solving methods based on their knowledge and experience, but they may never have received formal training in methods other than the ones they are knowledgeable in.

The physician. Medical doctors are trained to think about differences and categories. A patient's presenting signs and symptoms are processed, and then historical information is used to determine the most common diagnosis associated with the collected evidence. This is a categorical approach to problem solving, based on probabilities. This is a very efficient approach when a patient has a problem that has been encountered before. However, when the patient has something not seen before, this is a very inefficient way of treating the problem, as the MD moves to less and less common solutions.

The scientist. In contrast to the physician, the scientist is trained to look at a problem in the abstract and use testable assumptions (models) to isolate all the component parts of a problem and solve them (individually, if possible) in a logical way. Breaking down the problem into its component parts can determine the independent root causes. Then, using those root causes, the scientist can arrive at a solution to the overall problem. Solving problems in this way is more resource- and time-intensive than the physician's method, but if the right hypotheses are posed, this system can handle a broader range of problems and generate new data that are applicable to other problems.

The engineer. One way to think of the engineer's method is as a hybrid of the scientist's and physician's methods. The scientist starts with a new set of hypotheses for each problem, and the physician starts with a set of solutions that can be applied. The engineer is trained to take a known solution and then use that as a starting point to find a solution that applies to the problem. A very simple example can illustrate this. The most common way to find the area of a triangle is to multiply the base and height and to divide the result by two. This rule has been proven by mathematicians, and applies to all types of triangles (right, equilateral, isosceles, obtuse, and acute). So, if an engineer has to calculate the surface of a triangle, he will simply apply this rule, and not try to re-invent the theory behind it.

Problem identification

'A problem well put is half solved.' – John Dewey

Problem identification involves detecting and recognising that there is a problem, and identifying the nature of the problem – in other words, *defining* the problem. Identifying a very clearly defined and specific problem is the first critical step to successful problem solving.

A problem occurs when there is a difference between what 'should be' and what 'is' – a difference between the ideal and the actual situation. A problem is directly or indirectly related to a desired outcome or standard of behaviour.

Is it an issue or a problem?

"All we need to do is rename
'the problem' to 'the solution'
and I think we're done here."

Size often dictates the difference between an issue and a problem. An issue is smaller, and it doesn't present such a degree of difficulty that you have to seek out the advice of others in order to figure out the impact of the issue. A problem is larger in scale; it requires the advice and guidance of those around you in order to solve it.

An issue is something that might only cause you some frustration. On the other hand, a problem can impact people and situations around you, even if they are not directly related to the problem. For instance, forgetting your lunch is an issue, but losing your job is a problem.

At an organisational level, an issue is something that can be handled behind closed doors, impacting no one but the people of highest authority in the situation. A problem involves information that must be available, because there will be cause to involve other employees, other organisations, or citizens, in the solution to the problem.

When confronted with a problem, the natural tendency is to propose possible solutions. Consequently, thinking and discussion focus on the merits of the proposed *solution(s)*, rather than an in-depth discussion of the possible *causes* of the problem itself. Inexperienced problem solvers will soon find out that a great solution isn't worth much, if the problem it resolves was misidentified.

Very often, finding or identifying a problem is more important than the solution. For example, Galileo recognised the problem of needing to know the speed of light, but did not come up with a solution. It took ages of advances in mathematics and science to solve this problem. But Galileo still received credit for identifying the problem.

Sometimes problem identification may be nothing more than the art of asking the right questions at the right time (this is actually the best kept secret of coaching).

Problem analysis

'If I had an hour to solve a problem I'd spend 55 minutes thinking about the problem and 5 minutes thinking about solutions.' – Albert Einstein

Following the problem identification, problem analysis involves gaining more information about the problem and increasing understanding. This phase is all about fact finding and analysis, building a more comprehensive picture of both the goal(s) and the barrier(s). This stage may not be necessary for simple problems – or issues – but it is essential for more complex problems. The following things need to be done in problem analysis:

- Identifying the stakeholders

- Understanding the root causes

- Identifying the constraints

Identifying the stakeholders

A *stakeholder* is anyone who is affected by the problem and its resolution. The following questions can be helpful in identifying the stakeholders:

- Who are the main users?

- Are there any other internal or external users whose needs must be addressed?

- Who are the beneficiaries or customers?

- Who else is affected?

- Is there anyone else who cares?

- Who will evaluate and approve the solution when it is delivered and deployed?

- Who will monitor and provide feedback?

Stakeholder analysis is a process of systematically gathering and analysing qualitative information to determine whose interests should be taken into account when developing and/or implementing a policy or program. An interesting read can be found on the website of WHO[2].

Understanding the root causes

A root cause analysis is a systematic way of uncovering the 'roots' – or underlying causes of an identified problem, or the symptom of a problem. The fishbone (or Ishikawa[3]) diagram identifies the possible causes for an effect or problem. It can be used to structure a brainstorming session. It immediately sorts ideas into useful categories (see Figure 3.1).

'5 Whys' is an iterative question-asking technique used to explore the cause-and-effect relationships underlying a particular problem by repeating the question 'Why?' The '5' in the name derives from an empirical observation on the number of iterations typically required to solve a problem.

2   http://www.who.int/workforcealliance/knowledge/toolkit/33.pdf

3   Kaoru Ishikawa (1915–1989) was a Japanese organisational theorist, and professor at the Faculty of Engineering at the University of Tokyo.

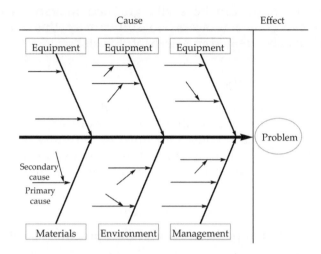

Figure 3.1: A fishbone diagram (Wikipedia)

Not all the root causes are equally important. That is why another way of looking at the root causes is the Pareto[4] diagram (Figure 3.2).

This technique helps to identify the top portion of causes that need to be addressed to resolve the majority of problems. In essence, the problem-solver estimates the benefit delivered by each action, then selects a number of the most effective actions that deliver a total benefit reasonably close to the maximum possible one.

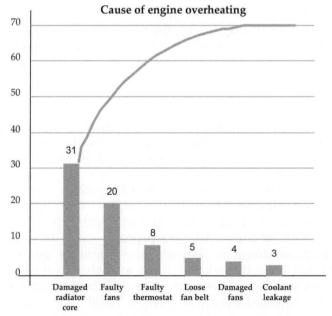

Figure 3.2: A Pareto diagram (Wikipedia)

4   Vilfredo Pareto (1848–1923) was an Italian engineer, sociologist, economist, political scientist, and philosopher.

Although Pareto charts can be easily graphed in various project management applications, not everyone has access to software of this type. Fortunately, these analysis tools can also be created in Microsoft Excel.

Identifying the constraints

Constraints are restrictions on the degree of freedom we have in providing a solution. Constraints have the potential to restrict our ability to deliver a solution as we imagine it. Therefore, each constraint must be carefully considered as part of the problem solving process, and some constraints may even cause us to reconsider the entire approach we initially conceived. Below is a non-exhaustive list of some possible constraints:

- What are the financial or budgetary constraints?
- Do internal or external political issues affect potential solutions?
- Are there environmental or regulatory constraints?
- Are there legal constraints?
- Is the schedule defined, are there deadlines?
- What (human) resources are available?

Kurt Lewin's **Force Field Analysis** is a powerful strategic tool used to understand what's needed for change in both corporate and personal environments. Lewin states: 'An issue is held in balance by the interaction of two opposing sets of forces – those seeking to promote change (driving forces) and those attempting to maintain the status quo (restraining forces)'. What he postulates is that whenever driving forces are stronger than restraining forces, the status quo or equilibrium will change.

This is an interesting idea, especially if we apply it to understanding how people move in response to change and why they resist change. There will always be driving forces that make change attractive to people, and restraining forces that work to keep things as they are; successful change is achieved by either strengthening the driving forces or weakening the restraining forces.

The force field analysis integrates with Lewin's **three-stage theory of change**[5] as you work towards unfreezing the existing equilibrium, moving towards the desired change, and then freezing the change at the new level so that a new equilibrium exists that resists further change.

This point is of particular importance in the EU context, as it differs considerably from a typical private sector situation. For example, an independent publisher can publish what he wants about the EU, he can work with whatever authors, printers, etc. that he chooses without any tendering process. An independent publisher can initiate a project without doing an impact assessment or getting a sign-off from anyone else. He doesn't have to make versions available in multiple languages, can set his own deadlines, budget etc. The range of options for most staff in the EU are much more circumscribed and even a director-general cannot just decide to do his own thing.

---

5   http://www.change-management-coach.com/kurt_lewin.html

Generating possible solutions

'Be passionate about solving the problem, not proving your solution.' – Nathan Furr

During this stage you generate a range of potential solutions, but with little or no attempt to evaluate them at this point. In a group situation this stage is often carried out as a brainstorming session, letting each person in the group express their views on possible courses of action. Different people will have different expertise in different areas and it is useful, therefore, to hear the views of everyone.

During brainstorming, defer judgement on whether solutions are achievable, practical, or reasonable. This is the time for creative thinking, not critical thinking. Creative thinking is like putting your foot on the accelerator of a car. Critical thinking is putting your foot on the brake. There is a time for each but not at the same time, or otherwise the engine will stall.

I invite you to have a look at the TED talk by Tom Wujec[6]: 'Got a wicked problem? First tell me how you make toast.'[7] His books are worthwhile reading too.

"Remember that great idea you had
that we ridiculed and ignored? It
appears that we need it after all.
What was it?"

Making a decision

Following on from the previous stage it is now time to look at each potential solution and carefully analyse it on its merits. Some solutions may have to be eliminated, due to the constraints that were previously identified.

6　Tom Wujec (1959) is the author and editor of several books, and a pioneer in the emerging practice of business visualisation.

7　https://www.ted.com/talks/tom_wujec_got_a_wicked_problem_first_tell_me_how_you_make_toast?language=en

Determine the criteria you are going to use to evaluate the pros and cons of the potential solutions. Agree upon both the criteria and the weighting. Determine whether you will evaluate ideas primarily on the basis of cost, timeframe, and interference with existing operations, or on any other considerations.

For each criterion, assess its importance relative to the other criteria. If the criteria are weighted equally, your evaluation will simply be based on how each potential solution measures up to all the criteria alike. If the criteria deserve different weightings, assign a unique weighting to each.

Since the world around us is constantly changing, solutions don't last as long as people typically think. Also realise that many 'good enough' solutions – or 'quick fixes' – meant for a few months end up in place for a few years, long past their intended lifespan and appropriateness. Reach agreement on the likely lifespan of the alternative solutions before evaluating them.

Finally, you make a decision on which course of action to take. Decisions can be made through either an intuitive or reasoned process. Intuition is a combination of your past experience and your personal values. It is worth taking your intuition into account, especially for simple problems, but complicated decisions tend to require a more formal approach, involving reasoning.

There are a number of reasons that can prevent effective decision-making. These can include (among others):

- Not enough information.

- Too much information.

- Too many stakeholders.

- Emotional attachments, or the lack thereof.

- Incomplete problem definition, analysis or invalid proposed solutions.

- Too many, or contradictory constraints.

- Lack of experience or knowledge of the problem domain.

- (Political) taboos or inability to think outside the box.

The dangers of groupthink

The term *groupthink* was first described in 1972 by social psychologist Irving Janis[8]. It is a phenomenon that occurs when a group makes incorrect decisions because group pressures lead to a deterioration of 'mental efficiency, reality testing, and moral judgment'[9]. Groups affected by groupthink ignore alternatives and tend to take irrational actions that dehumanise other groups. A group is especially vulnerable to groupthink when its members are similar in background, when the group is insulated from outside opinions, and when there are no clear rules for decision-making.

---

8   Irving Lester Janis (1918–1990) was a research psychologist at Yale University and a professor emeritus at the University of California at Berkeley.

9   'Victims of Groupthink: A psychological Study of foreign-policy decisions and fiascoes' (1972) by Irving Janis.

Janis documented eight symptoms of groupthink:

- *Illusion of invulnerability* – Creates excessive optimism that encourages taking extreme risks.

- *Collective rationalisation* – Members discount warnings and do not reconsider their assumptions.

- *Belief in inherent morality* – Members believe in the rightness of their cause and therefore ignore the ethical or moral consequences of their decisions.

- *Stereotyped views of out-groups* – Negative attitudes to those seen as the 'enemy' make effective responses to different opinions seem unnecessary.

- *Direct pressure on dissenters* – Members are under pressure not to express arguments against any of the group's views.

- *Self-censorship* – Doubts and deviations from the perceived group consensus are not expressed.

- *Illusion of unanimity* – The majority view and judgments are assumed to be unanimous.

- *Self-appointed 'mind guards'* – Members protect the group and the leader from information that is problematic or contradictory to the group's cohesiveness, view, and/or decisions.

Clearly, the EU institutions are not immune to the hazards of groupthink, and – in fact – most of these symptoms can be frequently observed. One deep-seated example of groupthink in the institutions is the idea that the only reason people don't like the EU is because they are ignorant and it is just a matter of educating them. This reflects the perspective of the institutions, embedded in the founding treaties themselves, that the EU and indeed further integration are by definition a 'good thing' – and it makes genuine engagement with those outside that consensus uncomfortable and at times impossible.

Adopting some of the following measures may prevent groupthink:

- The leader should assign the role of critical evaluator to each member.

- The leader should avoid stating preferences and expectations at the outset.

- Each member of the group should routinely discuss the group's deliberations with a trusted associate and report back to the group on the associate's reactions.

- One or more experts should be invited to each meeting on a staggered basis. The outside experts should be encouraged to challenge the views of the members.

- At least one articulate and knowledgeable member should be given the role of devil's advocate (to question assumptions and plans).

- The leader should make sure that a sizeable block of time is set aside to survey warning signals from rivals; leader and group construct alternative scenarios of rivals' intentions.

Implementation

'An idea that is developed and put into action is more important than an idea that exists only as an idea.' – Edward de Bono[10]

Implementation means acting on the chosen solution. During implementation new problems may arise, especially if identification or analysis of the original problem was not carried out properly. If this happens one should go back to the previous stages. I will expand on some possible implementation strategies below.

Seeking feedback

The final stage of problem solving is verifying that the implemented solution has been successful. This can be achieved by monitoring and gaining feedback from the stakeholders for any changes that have occurred. It is good practice to keep a record of outcomes and any additional problems that occurred. This is a very important stage, because in this you verify if the stakeholders' expectations were met, and to what extent – in other words this is the 'delivering quality' part of the delivering quality and results competency.

Implementation strategies

In large and complex projects, various implementation strategies can be applied. These can be roughly divided into three categories: waterfall, iterative, and agile.

The more traditional **waterfall approach** is a linear approach in which each stage of the problem-solving project has to be finished before the next one can begin. There is also typically a milestone between the stages; for example, the problem definition must be reviewed and approved by the stakeholders before the analysis and solution generation can begin. Figure 3.3 describes the distinctive phases of this approach. In this figure the horizontal axis is time, and the vertical axis describes the functional dependencies between the phases. For example, you must have a plan before you can start building; the system has to be built before you can test it; you can only review once you have tested; and finally, you can only deploy if it has been reviewed (and accepted).

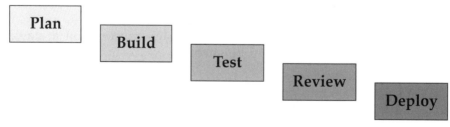

Figure. 3.3: The waterfall approach

10   Edward de Bono (1933) is a Maltese physician, psychologist, author, inventor and consultant.

One of the positive things about this approach is that all agree – in writing – very early in the project on what will be delivered. This makes planning, budgeting and allocating resources more straightforward. Progress is easily measured, as the full scope of the work and the milestones are known in advance. A major potential drawback of the pure waterfall approach, however, is the risk that the stakeholders will be dissatisfied with the implemented solution, once delivered. As all deliverables are based exclusively upon documented requirements, a stakeholder may not entirely understand what solution will be delivered until the project is almost finished. By that time, changes can be difficult (and costly) to implement.

In the **iterative approach**, the problem is split up into a few, more or less independent chunks, and these chunks are then executed separately and consecutively, sometimes even by different teams. In public administrations this technique is frequently used to stay within the constraints of the (annual) budget.

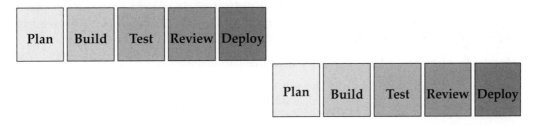

Figure 3.4: The iterative approach

One issue with this approach is linked to the difficulty of making accurate esti-mates of the time and resources needed to complete the work and meet the expecta-tions of the stakeholders. With this approach we implicitly 'fix' the time (e.g. the budget year) and the resources (money, people, etc) but because of the many uncer-tainties it is impossible to guarantee that the deliverables will effectively meet the expectations of all the stakeholders.

Agile is also an iterative approach, but with a much finer granularity, both in terms of timing and deliverables, along with the possibility of adjusting the overall planning on-the-fly. This approach emphasises the rapid delivery of partial solutions, and every partial solution is 'time-boxed'. Each time box has a defined duration with an agreed list of deliverables, planned at the start of the time box. Deliverables are prioritised by business value as determined by the stakeholders. If all planned work for the time box cannot be completed, work is reprioritised and this information is used for future planning. Agile relies on a very high level of stakeholder involvement throughout the project.

The main advantage of the agile approach is easy to see: the stakeholders have fre-quent and early opportunities to see the work being delivered, and to make decisions and changes throughout the project. However, the very high degree of stakeholder involvement may present problems for some of them, because they simply may not have the time or the interest for this type of participation.

Teamwork

'Coming together is a beginning, staying together is progress, and working together is success.' – Henry Ford

In organisations, the individual competency of analysis and problem solving is closely related to the competency of working with others.

A team is a small group of people who regularly meet – in person or perhaps online – to discuss shared agendas, causes, or interests. Each team is unique and draws on the backgrounds and abilities of its members. Depending on the situation, teams can have a different name: task force, work group, study group, commission, committee, or such like. In the EU administration, teamwork is frequently used alongside – and across – the hierarchical organisation.Members of a team can exchange information, personal experiences and the results of individual endeavours and set up physical meetings, online conferences, or any other form of collaborative work. You need three types of people in any team effort:

- *Deciders* - They hold the authority and are the 'bosses'.

- *Doers* - The implementers get the job done.

- *Experts* - They bring the knowledge, expertise and/or charisma to the table.

In order to have really productive problem solving meetings, the best behaviour of all participants is as follows:

Maximize	Minimize
Listening	Criticising
Appreciating	Impatience
Seeking usefuness	Being judgmental
Clarifying	Boredom
Accepting	Rejecting

Table 3.1

Why should we have teams to solve problems?

Firstly, when you are working in a team there is a higher chance that most of the things you are uncertain about will come to the surface and the answers will arise naturally.

Secondly, it is often quite hard to grasp every detail of a problem when you are alone.

Thirdly, through their cooperative but also competitive nature, teams promote both critical thinking and creativity in the form of new questions and explanations within discussions and debates.

Finally, when you are alone, the temptation to procrastinate is much larger than when in an interactive environment. Although taking breaks is important, dipping in and out of your work mood can only make you waste time, and contribute to the build-up of frustration due to being inefficient.

'Too many cooks spoil the broth' is an expression meaning that a team becomes inefficient if too many people are involved, as it becomes more difficult to coordinate, communicate with all members and maintain the necessary discipline. In workplace situations the ideal size of a team tends to be around three to four people, but sometimes more are needed, for example if a variety of specific technical expertise is required.

Critical thinking

'It is the mark of an educated mind to be able to entertain a thought without accepting it.' – Aristotle

Critical thinking is the process we use to reflect on, assess, and judge the assumptions underlying our own and others' ideas and efforts. The Socratic method[11] is at the heart of critical thinking. It is a method of disciplined questioning that can be used to pursue thought in many directions and for many purposes, including: to explore complex ideas, to get to the truth of things, to open up issues and problems, to challenge assumptions, to analyse concepts, to distinguish what we know from what we don't know, and to follow out the logical implications of thought or to control the discussion. The key to distinguishing Socratic questioning from questioning per se is that Socratic questioning is systematic, disciplined, deep and usually focuses on fundamental concepts, principles, theories, issues or problems.

According to authors Richard Paul and Linda Elder there are nine types of Socratic questions:

- Questions of clarification

- Questions that probe purpose

- Questions that probe assumptions

- Questions that probe information, reasons, evidence, and causes

- Questions about viewpoints or perspectives

- Questions that probe implications and consequences

- Questions about the question

- Questions that probe concepts

- Questions that probe inferences and interpretations

11 Named after the classical Greek philosopher Socrates.

You can find out more about this method in their book 'The Thinker's Guide to the Art of Socratic Questioning.'[12]

Creative thinking

'The significant problems we face cannot be solved at the same level of thinking we were at when we created them.' — Albert Einstein

Creative thinking uses very different approaches from critical thinking; it involves a much more relaxed, open, and playful approach. *Thinking outside the box* is a metaphor that means to think differently, unconventionally, or from a new perspective; it refers to creative thinking.

When thinking creatively we are looking for many possible solutions, rather than just one. We allow ourselves to make wild and crazy suggestions, make mistakes, and we do not judge ideas early in the process. We allow ourselves to doodle, daydream or play with a theory or a suggestion.

Creative thinking is more about attitude and self-confidence than it is about talent. Creativity is often disorderly, unstructured, and unpredictable. Strong emotional self-control is needed to allow creative thinking states to arise, as it is important to be able to cope with risk, confusion, disorder and the feeling that you are not progressing.

In hindsight, every great idea seems obvious. But how can you be the person who comes up with those ideas? In his book 'Thinkertoys'[13], Michael Michalko unveils the secrets of creative genius and brings creative techniques within everyone's reach. This book presents dozens of field-tested, immediately usable tools for generating ideas and stimulating creativity, and provides an understanding of many creativity techniques that can be applied to problems, opportunities, or situations. The principles and methodologies include a variety of options developed by Michalko, and the strategies are easily adapted to specific needs or industries.

"Come on, people. We need a
creative epiphany right now.
Who has one?"

12   'The Thinker's Guide to the Art of Socratic Questioning' (2007) by Richard Paul and Linda Elder.
13   'Thinkertoys – A Handbook of Creative Thinking Techniques' (2006) by Michael Michalko.

Left brain or right brain?

Maybe you think you are 'right-brained': creative, artistic, an open-minded thinker. Or perhaps you are more of a 'left-brained' person: a critical thinker, analytical, good at tasks that require attention to detail, and more logically minded.

It is true that some brain functions occur in one or the other side of the brain; language tends to be on the left, attention more on the right. But in reality people don't tend to have a stronger left- or right-sided brain network.

Researchers from the University of Utah looked for something called 'lateralisation,' which is the idea that certain mental processes occur mainly in either the right or left hemisphere of the brain. They divided the brain into 7,000 regions, to see if any brain connections between regions were left-lateralised or right-lateralised, and found no patterns where the whole left-brain network is more connected or the whole right-brain network is more connected in some people. The conclusion was that being 'right-brained' or 'left-brained' is more a figure of speech than anything else. Our personality seems to be determined more connection by connection, than by the side of our brain we are using for any particular behaviour.

Lateral thinking

'Everyone has the right to doubt everything as often as he pleases and the duty to do it at least once. No way of looking at things is too sacred to be reconsidered. No way of doing things is beyond improvement.' – Edward de Bono

Dr Edward de Bono coined the term *lateral thinking* in his book called 'The Use of Lateral Thinking'[14]. De Bono is widely regarded as one of the leading experts in the fields of creativity and lateral thinking. He was the first person to propose that the human brain is a self-organising system. It was from this understanding that he developed his thinking tools and creativity methods that have helped people and organisations transform their thinking by avoiding the normal thought-blocks that inhibit their everyday thinking.

According to De Bono, lateral thinking deliberately distances itself from standard perceptions of creativity as either 'vertical' logic (the classic method for problem solving: working out the solution step-by-step from the given data) or 'horizontal' imagination (having many ideas but being unconcerned with the detailed implementation of them).

De Bono defines four types of thinking tools:

- Idea-generating tools intended to break current thinking patterns – routine patterns, the status quo.

- Focus tools intended to broaden where to search for new ideas.

- Harvest tools intended to ensure more value is received from idea generating output.

14 'The Use of Lateral Thinking' (1967) by Edward de Bono.

- Treatment tools that promote consideration of real-world constraints, resources, and support.

One famous technique that is promoted by de Bono is his 'Six Thinking Hats'; you can read more about this in the chapter on working with others.

Strategic thinking

Strategic thinking is a mental process that is applied by an individual in the context of achieving success in a game or other endeavour. General André Beaufre[15] wrote in 1963 that strategic thinking 'is a mental process, at once abstract and rational, which must be capable of synthesising both psychological and material data.' The work of Henry Mintzberg[16] and other authors, points towards the conclusion that the critical strategic question is not the conventional 'What?' but 'Why?' or 'How?' So strategic thinking is closely related to the leadership competency.

Strategic thinking is the ability to come up with effective plans in line with an organisation's objectives within a particular economic or political situation. Strategic thinking helps managers review policy issues, perform long term planning, set goals and determine priorities, and identify potential risks and opportunities. Clearly, within the EU institutions, strategic thinking is important.

Strategic thinking involves developing an entire set of critical skills:

- Strategic thinkers have the ability to use both the logical and the creative capabilities of their brain.

- They have the ability to balance their tremendous amount of creativity with a sense of realism and honesty about what is achievable in the longer term.

- They have the ability to develop a clearly defined and focused vision for the organisation, and a personal vision.

- They have the ability to clearly define their objectives and develop a strategic action plan with each objective broken down into tasks and each task having a list of needed resources and a specific timeline.

- They have the ability to design flexibility into their plans by creating some benchmarks in their thinking to review progress.

- They are remarkably aware and perceptive. They will listen, hear and understand what is said and will read and observe whatever they can so that they have very helpful and strategic information to guide them.

- They are committed lifelong learners and learn from each of their experiences. They use their experiences to enable them to think better on strategic issues.

15   André Beaufre (1902–1975) was a French general and military strategist, well known as an exponent of an independent French nuclear force. He was also chief of staff at SHAPE, the NATO headquarters in Europe.

16   Henry Mintzberg (1939) is a renowned academic and author on business and management.

- They are committed to and seek advice from others. They may use a coach, a mentor, a peer advisory group or some other group that they can confide in and offer up ideas for feedback.

- They have the ability to be non-judgmental and they do not allow themselves to be held back or restricted by judging their own thinking or the thinking of others when ideas are initially being developed and shared.

- They have the ability to be patient and not rush to conclusions and judgments. Great ideas and thoughts require time to develop into great successes in the future to reach their vision.

You can also have a look at Michael Porter's[17] TED Talk[18] 'Why businesses can be good at solving social problems'. This is what strategic thinking is about.

Developing your analysis and problem solving skills

How to develop your analysis and problem solving skills is a problem on its own. You may have realised that the GROW[19] model I propose in this book is nothing else than the IDEAL[20] methodology applied to the problem of performance development.

Please refer to Chapter 1 (methodology) and Annex 1 for further development of this competency, have another look at the current chapter to find out about your options, and remember: YOU are responsible for your own development, not your manager, your colleagues, or your mentor.

The online toolkit that comes for free with this book can be used to follow-up on your development in this area. The toolkit can be found at:

https://www.johnharperpublishing.co.uk/the-ultimate-eu-career-development-toolkit/

Your notes

---

17 Michael Porter (1947) is an economist, researcher, author, advisor, speaker and teacher at Harvard Business School.
18 http://www.ted.com/talks/michael_porter_why_business_can_be_good_at_solving_social_problems?language=en#t-864545
19 See Chapter 1.
20 As discussed at the start of this chapter.

4. Communicating

Competency definition: 'Communicates clearly and precisely both orally and in writing'.

Good communication skills are a ticket to success in the working environment.

Communication can be broken down into two major categories: rhetorical and relational. The focus of *rhetorical* communication is primarily on the study of influence; the art of rhetorical communication is based on the idea of persuasion. The *relational* approach examines communication from a different perspective; two or more people coexist to reach an agreed upon perspective.

As Herta A. Murphy and Herbert W. Hildebrandt observed in their book 'Effective Business Communications[1]', good communication should be complete, concise, clear, concrete, correct, considerate, and courteous (the 'seven C's'). More specifically, this means that communication should answer basic questions like *who, what, when, where*; be relevant and not overly verbose; focus on the receiver and his or her interests; use specific facts and figures and active verbs; adopt a conversational tone in written texts for readability; include examples and visual aids when needed; be tactful and friendly; and be accurate and non-discriminatory. Unclear, inaccurate, or thoughtless communication, on the other hand, can waste valuable time, push away employees or customers, and destroy goodwill toward individuals or the overall organisation.

Information theory

'The fundamental problem of communication is that of reproducing at one point either exactly or approximately a message selected at another point.' – Claude Shannon

In his ground-breaking paper 'A Mathematical Theory of Communication', Claude E. Shannon[2] introduced a qualitative and quantitative model of communication as a statistical process. Shannon developed his theory to find the fundamental limits on signal processing operations such as compressing data and on reliably storing and communicating data. Since its inception the theory has broadened to find applications in many other areas, including statistical inference, natural language processing, cryptography, neurobiology, the evolution and function of molecular codes, model selection in ecology, thermal physics, quantum computing, linguistics, plagiarism detection, pattern recognition, anomaly detection and other forms of data analysis.

---

1   'Effective Business Communications' (1997) by Herta A. Murphy et al.

2   Claude Shannon (1916-2001) was an American mathematician, electronics engineer, and cryptographer known as 'the father of information theory.'

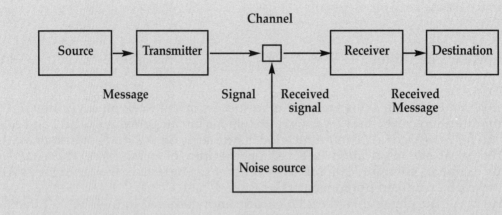

Figure 4.1

Clearly, it is not my intention to go into the mathematical intricacies of information theory, but simply to make you aware of its implications for human communication.

Before being transmitted, the original message (idea, concept, statement) has to be transformed (coded) into a signal. It is then pushed through the channel during which another transformation takes place (i.e. addition of noise, or deformation). The received signal is finally transformed (decoded) resulting in the received message. All the transformations are inevitably imperfect, meaning that the destination will 'understand' a different message than the one that was originally intended.

Things get even worse in the advent of multiple – parallel or sequential – channels and multiple receivers, each with their own transformation mechanisms in place. This is the main concept behind Shannon's theory.

The number of transformations and hence distortions of the messages in human communication is important. Think of confusion in the sender's mind, poor language mastery, and unclear expression of ideas, limited vocabulary, translation errors, and other things that can go wrong when humans communicate with each other. This leads to failed communication, misunderstandings, conflicts, catastrophes and even war.

It is crucial at this point to observe that all communication should be adapted to the audience. The same message needs to be wrapped differently according to the audience: a lunchtime conference, a presentation to stakeholders or a note to the management on the same topic will have different content and key messages.

Oral communication

Oral communication can be either formal or informal: conversations and discussions taking place at meetings are often informal while inteviews and public speaking opportunities are more formal.

With advances in technology, new forms of oral communication continue to develop: video conferencing combines audio and video so that workers in distant locations can both see and speak with each other. Other modern forms of oral communication include Podcasts (audio clips that you can access on the internet) and Voice over IP (VoIP), which allows callers to communicate over the internet. Skype is an example of VoIP.

There are many situations in which it makes sense to choose oral over written communication. Oral communication is more personal and less formal than written communication. If time is limited and a matter requires quick resolution, it may be best to have a face-to-face or telephone conversation. Oral communication can be especially effective in addressing conflicts or problems. Talking things over is often the best way to settle misunderstandings or disagreements. Finally, oral communication is a great way to give individual feedback and inspire or motivate a team.

Conversations

Milton Wright wrote 'The Art of Conversation'[3], a comprehensive treatment of the subject, in 1936. The book deals with conversation both for its own sake, and for political, sales, or religious ends. It might be considered a self-help book – one that most of us might like to take advantage of and read.

More recently, Catherine Blyth wrote another interesting book with a similar title[4]. Every day we use cell phones and computers to communicate, but it's easy to forget that we possess a communication technology that has been in research and development for thousands of years. Catherine Blyth points out the state of disrepair that conversation has fallen into – and then, taking examples from history, literature, philosophy, anthropology and popular culture, she gives us the tools to rebuild.

Most people are not good listeners, they just wait their turn to speak, and once they have the floor they follow their own agenda. Try to remember how you felt the last time someone 'listened' to you in this way. Do you want to do this to others?

Research suggests that we only remember between 25 and 50 per cent of what we hear. That means that when you talk to your boss, your colleagues, or spouse for 10 minutes, they 'hear' less than half of what you say. Now turn this around and it reveals that when you are being presented with information, you aren't hearing the whole message either. You can hope that the important parts are captured in your 25-50 per cent, but what if they are not?

Interviews

In an interview situation the first impression you make is of the utmost importance – 'you only get one chance to make a first impression'. Until we get to know someone, our brain relies on snap judgments to try to categorise the person, predict what they will do, and anticipate how we should react. According to research done by Alex Todorov[5], this is an evolutionary survival mechanism.

3   'The Art of Conversation' (1936) by Milton Wright.
4   'The Art of Conversation – A guided Tour of a Neglected Pleasure' (2009) by Catherine Blyth.
5   Alex Todorov is Professor of Psychology at Princeton University.

The dangerous 'why question'

Why is a powerful, yet dangerous, question; it seeks not after efficiency, effectiveness, or value, but rather, the truth, which is most elusive of all.

Why is powerful because, more than any other question, it challenges us to question our priorities, and to re-examine what we hold most dear. It seeks to uncover the truths about life, meaning, purpose, and the world that we live in, and – perhaps the most frightening subject of all – ourselves. Why is the question behind all other questions. It gets us thinking about the reasons behind just about everything we do, see, and experience.

The danger of the 'why question' is that it is a passive – not active – question; it focuses on the past, not the future. It allows you to stay stuck, worrying and hypothesising, without making the change necessary to get out of the situation in which you are stuck. Why questions can also put you in a victim position, subtly admitting that you accept your destiny and injustice. Why questions often reiterate what isn't working and allow for an intellectual re-examination of the cause of the trouble. In this way, asking 'why?' can be an invitation for a fight. The danger of a why question is that it doesn't lead to a solution!

It is not always wise to insist on knowing the 'why's'. If you want to change, ask any of the other five questions (Who?, What?, When?, Where?, How?) and you will see the steps necessary to make progress.

Figure 4.2

Your brain decides from the information it has – in other words, from how someone looks – whether they are trustworthy, threatening, competent, likeable and many other traits. Being mindful of our body language can influence the other person's perception of us and thereby the outcome of the situation.

A particular form of interview is the **Competency Based Interview (CBI)** as is used in the EPSO Assessment Centre. During a CBI, the interviewers are trying to assess your competencies through the observation of your self-declared behaviour in the past. In this context it is relevant to mention the STAR model, an interesting way of structuring your answer. STAR is the acronym for **S**ituation, **T**ask, **A**ctions, **R**esults:

- *Situation* – what was the challenge or situation in which you found yourself?

- *Task* – what did you have to achieve? What was expected of you?

- *Actions* – what did you do? How did you do it? How did you respond to the situation?

- *Results* – what was the outcome of your actions? What did you achieve? Did you meet your objectives? What did you learn from this experience and have you used this learning since?

A trained interviewer will immediately recognise this structure when you are using it, and he will be grateful for that, because you are making his life a lot easier.

Application of the STAR model

The following example came to me from one of my coachees while preparing for her structured interview in an EPSO competition for (Greek) translators. The question went like this:

'Can you give an example of a situation where you had to face unforeseen obstacles to complete a task?.'

Her answer was:

(Situation and Task)

Back in 2010, I was working as a free-lance translator. Being a freelance, I usually worked from home. One day, I was contacted by one of my main customers, a project manager at an Athens-based translation agency, who offered me a 2000-word (some four pages) document to be translated from Greek into Spanish.

(Actions)

Because this assignment was rather unusual for me (I normally translate into Greek) and urgent (the deadline was in less than a week) I put my other, ongoing work on hold and started right away. This was an important customer for me, and I didn't want to disappoint him by not meeting his expectations – or missing the deadline.

I began with the pre-translation part and used my memory tools in the Cloud. All went well until, at some point, the power went off in the eastern part of Athens, which meant that I had no computer, no internet connection, and consequently I would not be able to finish the work on time.

The first thing that came to my mind was that I could not ask for an extension because I had no idea how long the blackout would last. In addition to that, the translation agency was based in the centre of Athens, which was not affected by the power outage.

cont...

continued from the previous page

This meant that they would probably not be aware of my problem as they were not experiencing such problems themselves. I did some quick thinking and remembered that there was an internet cafe – about 1 km away from where I live – that used a backup generator. I took my laptop, where my memories were kept intact, and went over there to finish my job. I had to stay out late, beyond my usual working hours, but that was not a problem since the internet café was open until midnight.

(Result)

I managed to finish on time and the project manager congratulated me for the 'job well done' after I had explained to him what had happened.

Please note in this answer the concern for meeting expectations, the prioritising and organising actions, the personal responsibility and initiative, and the quick 'thinking outside the box'. Also note the STAR approach of this reply.

A similar method is known as the SHARE model. In this instance the acronym stands for **S**ituation, **H**indrances, **A**ctions, **R**esults and **E**valuation.

Public speaking

'If I am to speak for ten minutes, I need a week for preparation; if fifteen minutes, three days; if half an hour, two days; if an hour, I am ready now.' – Woodrow T. Wilson

The first step in preparing a public speech is to decide on the essence of the communication, the 'big idea'. Public presentations tend to have one of three general purposes: to persuade, to inform, or to entertain. Out of the purpose will come the main ideas to be included in the presentation. These ideas should be researched carefully and adapted to the needs of the audience.

"This information is so exciting I feel obliged to tone it down a little with these boring slides."

The ideas are then organised to include an introduction, a main body, and a summary or conclusion. Or, as the old adage about giving speeches goes, 'Say what you're going to say, say it, and then say what you have said.' The introduction should grab the audience's interest and establish the theme of the remainder of the presentation. The main body should concentrate on points of emphasis. The conclusion should restate the key points and summarise the overarching message that is being conveyed.

Visual aids can be a useful component of oral presentations, but you should not consider them as unavoidable. Visual aids have to be meaningful, creative, and interesting in order to help the speaker get a message across. Visual aids should help to illustrate and strengthen your points, not be a distraction from what you are saying. The key to successful use of visual aids is that they should support the theme of the presentation; support its transmittal but do so without being chaotic, complicated, or even too entertaining. Visual aids should not be the presentation! Too many speakers just read aloud what's on the PowerPoint slides. Your audience could have done that themselves in the comfort of their office, or at home.

Steve Jobs put it even more strongly: *'People who know what they are talking about don't need PowerPoint.'*

Why bullet points are bad for presentations

You have probably heard this advice before: *don't use bullet points in your presentations*. The reason for this is that bullet points make information more difficult to remember when the bullet point lists are accompanied by spoken information.

In 2014, the International Journal of Business Communication published the results from 'The Use of Visualisation in the Communication of Business Strategies'[6], a study designed to gather empirical evidence regarding whether the use of visualisation is superior to text in the communication of business information. The results of that experiment confirmed that lists of text are ineffective for presentations. Slides with visuals are undeniably more effective than slides with text. In other words, when your slides contain lists of text, your audience will struggle to pay attention to your slides, they will find it difficult to agree with your message, and they will retain less information.

Dr Chris Atherton[7] discovered that the limits of our working memory are to blame for this phenomenon. By actively processing the information instead of attempting to simultaneously read the slides as well as listen to the presenter, audience members are more likely to retain the meaning of the presentation. Dr Atherton recommends creating slides with minimal text to limit the cognitive load of your presentation. In addition, she also recommends using visuals to communicate complex concepts. Since the area of the human brain that processes visuals has a working memory capacity that is separate from the short-term memory limit of the linguistic and auditory processing areas of the brain, you expand the amount of information that audience members can process by utilising visuals on your slides.

---

6   http://job.sagepub.com/content/early/2014/04/01/2329488414525444.abstract

7   http://finiteattention.net/

The **delivery of an effective speech** requires the speaker to consider his or her vocal pitch, rate, and volume. It is important to incorporate changes in vocal pitch, to add emphasis, and to avoid monotony. It is also helpful to vary the pace at which you speak and incorporate pauses to allow the audience to reflect upon specific elements of the overall message. Your voice is multitalented; it can sound assertive, cautious, critical, humorous, motivational, sympathetic, or neutral, and it does all this through pitch, tone, volume and enunciation. Taking emotions out of your voice will bore your audience.

Non-verbal elements such as posture, gestures, and facial expressions are important factors as well. Some movement may be helpful to hold listeners' attention or to increase emphasis, but constant shifting or pacing should be avoided. Likewise, hand and arm gestures can be used to point, describe, or emphasise, but these too should be varied, carefully timed, and adapted to the audience. Now, I am not saying that you always have to act and behave like Steve Ballmer in his famous 'Monkey Boy Dance'[8], but using all your body is definitely a good thing if you want to capture your audience's attention. Finally, good speakers make frequent eye contact with their audience, let their facial expressions show their own interest in the ideas they are presenting, and dress in a way that is appropriate for the occasion.

Public speaking anxiety is one of the most common fears. A little bit of anxiety as you prepare for a presentation is normal. Even the best speakers get anxious before they get on stage or speak in front of a large group. You should never expect yourself to be completely anxiety free. What you need is to turn that anxiety into energy for giving a great presentation, not holding you back from speaking. Although the 'stress hormone' cortisol is linked to many health detriments it is also our 'get up and do things hormone.' Just like we have 'eustress' (good stress) and 'distress' (bad stress), we need cortisol to stimulate our sympathetic nervous system and kick-start our bodies into action.

Fear of public speaking – also known as *glossophobia* – comes from our fear of being judged or the fear of forgetting what we need to say. Doubts over our own ability, combined with the knowledge that others are obliged to pay attention to what we are saying, create a feeling of fear that is difficult to overcome. On top of that, our mind tends to focus on the mistakes we make, and our fear is then confirmed. Instead, you should think of the idea that your audience is not there to judge you, but because they believe you have something interesting to say. So you should make it interesting!

There are literally hundreds of books and other resources about delivering presentations and speaking in public so I will limit myself to pointing out just a few.

First, I warmly advise you, if you understand French, to read the book 'Prendre la Parole en public'[9] by Bernard Blein as it contains a wealth of very practical ideas.

There is also an interesting slide deck called 'Death by PowerPoint'[10] available on SlideShare. It explains the dos and don'ts if you want to use PowerPoint anyway.

Another book worth mentioning is 'HBR Guide to Persuasive Presentations'[11] by Nancy Duarte. There are, by the way, many other Harvard Business Review Press (HBR) books and publications covering the topics of the present book.

8   https://www.youtube.com/watch?v=edN4o8F9_P4
9   'Prendre la parole en public' (2009) by Bernard Blein.
10   http://www.slideshare.net/itrimble/death-by-powerpoint-51110764
11   'HBR Guide to Persuasive Presentations' (2012) by Nancy Duarte.

TED is a nonprofit organisation devoted to spreading ideas, usually in the form of short, powerful talks (18 minutes or less). TED began in 1984 as a conference where Technology, Entertainment and Design converged, and today covers almost all topics — from science to business to global issues — in more than 100 languages. You can watch some of the masters at work and learn from them on their website[12], but if there's one you must absolutely see, it is Dan Pink's 'The Puzzle of Motivation'[13] – but maybe wait until you have read the rest of this chapter and try to figure out which 'best practices' Dan is using.

'American Rhetoric – Top 100 Speeches'[14] is another great resource.

Finally, I would like you to know about Toastmasters[15]. Toastmasters International is a world leader in communication and leadership development. Their membership is 313,000 strong. Members improve their speaking and leadership skills by attending one of the 14,650 clubs in 126 countries that make up a global network of meeting locations. There are Toastmasters clubs in both Brussels and Luxembourg.

Body language

'The body is the unconscious mind.' – Candace Pert[16]

It is often claimed that only 7% of our oral communication is conveyed by what we actually say, 38% is attributed to the tone and speed of our voice, while 55% of our message is passed through our non-verbal communication, our body language. These figures go back to the work of Professor Albert Mehrabian[17] at UCLA, as explained in his book 'Silent Messages', originally published in 1971. However, many trainers and non-verbal communication gurus forget to mention that Mehrabian based his findings on studies that only dealt with the communication of positive and negative emotions via single spoken words. He was trying to understand the mechanisms of feelings of like and dislike. He did not intend this 'rule' to apply across the board to all communication; so, unless a communicator is talking about his or her feelings or attitudes, these numbers are not applicable.

A more accurate set of statements is used by Pamela Thorne[18] in her dissertation 'Debunking the Body Language Myth':

- Words are only part of a message, but they are a vital part. We also communicate through body language and tone of voice.

- Non-verbals support the words by conveying the speaker's feelings.

---

12   https://www.ted.com/playlists/77/11_must_see_ted_talks

13   http://www.ted.com/talks/dan_pink_on_motivation?language=en

14   http://www.americanrhetoric.com/top100speechesall.html

15   https://www.toastmasters.org/

16   Dr Candace Pert (1946–2013) was an internationally recognized pharmacologist who discovered endorphins; she was the author of – amongst other works – the book 'Molecules of Emotion'.

17   Albert Mehrabian (born 1939 in an Armenian family in Iran), is Professor Emeritus of Psychology, UCLA.

18   Pamela Thorne, founder and consultant at Viva Training

- When speaking about feelings and attitudes, and there is a mismatch between the words and the body language, we tend to put more trust in the non-verbals.

- If we have only words, as in emails, it is possible to misunderstand the emotion behind the words.

Body language has been observed and discussed for centuries, going back at least as far as ancient Greece and Rome. However, scientific studies first appeared only in the 1950s, and truly took off in the 1960s.

In the earliest days of the scientific study of body language, there was widespread agreement that it was nothing more than a series of individual, isolated actions, each with a different and specific meaning. However, over time we have come to understand that body language is far more complex and varied. Because of this, even defining the difference between non-verbal communication and verbal communication remains an area of disagreement among experts.

Non-verbal and verbal components of communications are inevitably intertwined and can't be completely drawn apart into separate components. This does not mean, however, that you can't learn to interpret the body language of others and – to some extent – control your own. I can only suggest you read as much as you can about body language and its applications, from the academic and scientific perspective as well as from the real world, practical, perspective. But keep in mind that understanding body language and applying this knowledge is an inexact science. Body language comes in clusters of signals and postures, depending on internal emotions and mental states. Recognising a whole cluster is far more reliable than trying to interpret individual elements, but even the most intuitive and attentive people can misinterpret or misunderstand body language messages.

A simple tip: our hands are a nonverbal way to show and build trust. Studies have found that when we see someone's hands, we have an easier time trusting them.

A rather exhaustive overview of our body language signals can be found in the book 'Ces gestes qui vous trahissent'[19] by Joseph Messinger. I further suggest you have a look at CreativityWorks[20]; they have a short animated video where these ideas are clearly expressed. Another must-see is Amy Cuddy's[21] TED talk[22]; I am sure you will be inspired!

Written communication

One advantage of written communication compared with oral communication is that written messages do not have to be delivered on the spot; instead, they can be

---

19   'Ces gestes qui vous trahissent' (2011) by Joseph Messinger.

20   http://www.creativityworks.net/

21   Amy Joy Casselberry Cuddy (1972) is an American social psychologist known for her research on stereotyping and discrimination, emotions, power, nonverbal behaviour, and the effects of social stimuli on hormone levels.

22   http://www.ted.com/talks/amy_cuddy_your_body_language_shapes_who_you_are

edited and revised several times before they are sent so that the content can be moulded to maximum effect. Another advantage is that written communication provides a permanent record that can be saved for later. Since they are permanent, written messages also enable recipients to take more time in reviewing the message and providing more appropriate feedback. For these reasons, written forms of communication are often considered more suitable for complex messages and contexts where traceability is key. In the context of misunderstandings or faced with a colleague whose unclear expression or reception of ideas is a constant source of concern, having a written record of what was said/agreed or instructed is very important in a working context. Depending on oral communication in this situation can be detrimental to one or both parties involved (peer colleagues or colleague/manager).

However, there is also a potential downside associated with written communication. Unlike oral communication, the sender of a written communication does not generally receive immediate feedback to his or her message. In addition, written messages often take more time to compose, both because of their content-rich nature and the difficulty that many individuals have in composing such communications.

EU staff have to write many different types of documents. Whatever the type — legislation, a technical report, minutes, a press release or speech — a clear document will be more effective, and more easily and quickly understood. A very good guide to how to write clearly can be found on the Commission's website[23].

Structuring documents

Authors make decisions about how to present information to their readers. They choose from a variety of structures to organise their texts:

- *Chronological/Sequence.* Chronological texts reveal events in a sequence from beginning to end. Words that signal chronological structures include: first, then, next, finally, and specific dates and times.

- *Cause/Effect.* Informational texts often describe cause and effect relationships. The text describes events and identifies or implies causal factors.

- *Problem/Solution.* The text introduces and describes a problem and presents solutions.

- *Compare/Contrast.* Authors use comparisons to describe ideas to readers. Images, metaphors, and analogies are used in compare/contrast structures.

- *Description.* Descriptive details help readers visualise information.

- *Directions.* How-to texts frame the information in a series of directions.

If the gist of a text cannot be taken in at one glance, it is a good idea to add an introduction (abstract, management summary) and possibly a conclusion. Aristotle put it that: 'A whole is what has a beginning and middle and end'; technically, the *protasis,*

23 http://ec.europa.eu/translation/writing/clear_writing/how_to_write_clearly_en.pdf

epitasis, and *catastrophe* (a word which survives in modern English but with a rather different meaning!). The introduction is intended to grab the reader's interest and establish the theme of the remainder of the text. The conclusion restates the key points and summarises the main message that is being conveyed.

Identifying the structure of a text helps readers to read efficiently. Readers select specific comprehension strategies that fit a particular text based on knowledge of how the information is organised. Readers can anticipate what information will be revealed in a selection when they understand the text structure. Understanding the pattern of the text also helps readers organise their ideas for synthesising and summarising.

Grammar, spelling and punctuation

Correct grammar, spelling and punctuation are key in written communications. The reader will form an opinion about you, the author, based on both the content and the presentation, and errors are likely to lead them to get a negative impression.

Some employers state openly that any CV or résumé containing spelling or grammatical mistakes will be rejected immediately, while a BBC news article[24] quotes research that calculates spelling mistakes cost online businesses 'millions' in lost sales.

Checking for poor writing and spelling mistakes should be seen as showing respect for your readers, since it will take them much longer to understand what you are trying to say if they have to struggle with and interpret the text. You have to make their life easy.

All written communications should therefore be re-read before sending to print, or hitting the 'Send' button in the case of emails, as it is likely that there will be errors. Do not assume that spelling and grammar checkers will identify all your mistakes for you: words can be spelled correctly but misused, and whole words may be missing, wrecking the sentence and the entire message. If at all possible, take a break before re-reading and checking your writing, because you are more likely to notice problems when you read it afresh.

Even if you know spelling and grammar rules, you should still double-check your work or, even better, have it proofread by somebody else. Our brains work faster than our fingers can type and accidental typographical errors inevitably sneak in.

---

24   http://www.bbc.co.uk/news/education-14130854

Using tables and pictures

A table is a way of arranging data in rows and columns. Any time you have lots of related facts and figures to present, a table is a useful approach to organising them so that the audience can quickly see and understand how they relate to each other.

Tables can be used to supplement your text to help convey the information being presented. Tables should be used for essential information only, adding to, and not just repeating identical material already in the text. A table should not just appear out of nowhere: you need to introduce the reader to the table by referring to it in the text, ideally before the table is presented. Use the text to draw the reader's attention to the significance and key points of the table, but don't repeat details as this defeats the very purpose (efficiency and clarity) of having a table.

Make sure that your tables are self-explanatory. Some readers may be speed-reading: they turn their attention to the tables (and figures) before they read the entire text, so these items should be self-contained.

Give clear and informative titles. Table titles should describe concisely the purpose or contents of the table and should ideally draw the reader's attention to what you want them to notice. In addition, ensure that column heads are clearly and appropriately labelled, as in Table 4.1.

Number of EU civil servants compared with other administrations

Administration	Population	Civil Servants	Ratio
Birmingham	1,036,900	60,000	5,78%
Paris	2,257,981	50,000	2,21%
Helsinki	601,035	40,000	6,66%
Latvia	2,200,000	184,000	8,36%
EU	500,000,000	55,000	0,011%

Table 4.1

A word of caution on the use of tables

There is of course much more to tables than their design. The meaning of the data is critical – and misleading data presented in a table will tend to draw attention to itself. Superficially, Table 4.1 is an example of clarity but actually it is an example of muddying the waters by comparing apples with oranges.

There are not 60,000 'civil servants' in the city of Birmingham in the sense that there are 55,000 EU 'civil servants'. There are 60,000 workers in various areas of the public administration in Birmingham, only a very small number of whom are civil servants in the EU administration sense. Even those who are categorised as 'civil servants' in Birmingham are mostly people involved in things like tax or social security offices, who are also very much front-line staff. The EU administration does not collect taxes and run job centres. The more valid comparison is with the UK central administration in Whitehall and that gives a very different picture!

When using tables you should not underestimate the intelligence of your audience. Otherwise you may end up with the opposite effect from what you intended.

Ensure consistency between values or details in a table (e.g., abbreviations, group names, units of measurement such as thousands and millions ...) and those in the text.

Tables that present repetitive information will impair communication rather than enhance it. Examine the titles of all your tables and check if they talk about the same or similar things. If they do, rethink the presentation and combine or delete some tables. The concept of *normalisation* comes from relational database theory. Normalisation is the process of taking data from a problem and reducing it to a set of relations while ensuring integrity and eliminating repetition. The same ideas can be readily applied when conceiving the tables you intend to use in communicating large amounts of interrelated pieces of information.

When presenting large amounts of information, divide the data into clear and appropriate categories and present it in columns titled accurately and descriptively. If the data you have to present is extensive and would make the tables too cluttered or long, consider making the tables a part of an appendix or add-on material. Also, ensure that there is sufficient spacing between columns and rows and that the layout does not make the table look too disorganised or crowded.

Finally, bear in mind that, sometimes at least, a picture may be worth a thousand words. While tables have to be used where you need to show a lot of precise numerical values, figures (graphics) can frequently be used in professional texts to show trends, patterns, and relationships between and across sets of data, especially when the general pattern is more important than the exact data values. Graphs, plots, maps and pie charts are all different ways of conveying a better understanding of what might otherwise remain hidden in a lengthy text or complex set of tables: how much more attention-grabbing Figure 4.3 is, for instance, than the same data would be just listed in a table!

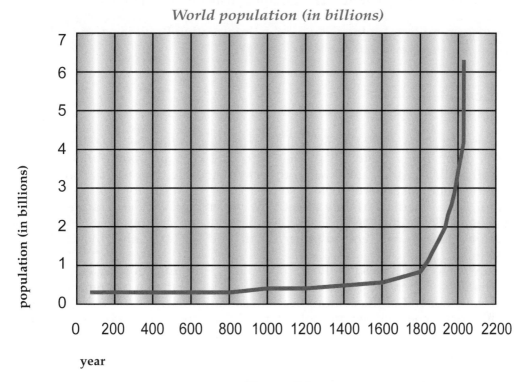

Figure 4.3

Style guides

A style guide is a set of standards for the writing and design of documents, either for general use or for a specific publication, organisation, or field.

Non-native speakers often write in a foreign language, such as English, as if it was their own written language just dressed up in foreign words. For example, you may find that a German colleague writes very long convoluted sentences with lots of commas, parentheses, dashes and asides (comments on what he is saying). A sentence can take up a whole paragraph. Perfectly acceptable German style perhaps, but totally frustrating for those of us not used to this kind of writing – and making it really hard for our German colleague to get his message across. Taking a course in written English style would benefit many, I feel.

The EU publishes an 'Interinstitutional Style Guide'[25] covering official languages across the European Union. This manual is 'obligatory' for all those employed by the institutions of the EU who are involved in preparing EU documents.

Detailed information on in-house conventions for English spelling, punctuation and usage is in the 'English Style Guide'[26] produced by the Commission's DG Translation. Clear writing guides and style guides for several other official languages are also on the DG Translation's website[27].

25   http://publications.europa.eu/code/en/en-000100.htm
26   http://ec.europa.eu/translation/writing/style_guides/english/style_guide_en.pdf
27   http://ec.europa.eu/translation/language_aids

Guidance on drafting Community legislation in all official languages is in the 'Joint practical Guide'[28.]

For advice on writing for the web, see the 'Information Providers Guide'[29.]

Social media

Scan around a restaurant and you will be struggling to find people who don't have their heads down using their cell phones to text, Tweet, or update their Facebook statuses – all while sharing a meal with others at their table. The effect of social media is visible throughout all areas of society, so what does this mean for interpersonal communication? Social media certainly affect how we engage with others across all settings and ages. There has been a shift in the way we communicate; rather than face-to-face interaction, we tend to prefer email, and we text rather than talk on the phone.

There are three key issues involved in people's communication styles when using social media. First, when we communicate through social media, we tend to trust the people on the other end of the communication, so our messages tend to be more open. Second, our social connections are not intensified as much through social media as they are face-to-face, so we don't tend to deepen our relationships. Last, we tend to follow and interact with people who agree with our points of view, so we are not getting the same diversity of viewpoints as we had in the past.

In the workplace too, the use of electronic communication has by and large overtaken face-to-face and voice-to-voice communication. This shift has been driven by two major forces: globalisation and the geographic dispersion of more and more of our activities, and the lack of comfort with traditional interpersonal communication among a growing segment of our employee population; the people who grew up in the internet age, Gen Y and Gen Z. Studies show that these generations – which will comprise more than 50% of the workforce by 2020 – prefer to use instant messaging or other social media than stop by an office and talk with someone. With these two trends at play, leaders must consider the impact on relationships in the workplace and outside, and the ability to effectively collaborate, build trust, and create employee engagement and loyalty.

Further, because most business communication is now done via emails, texts, instant messaging, intranets, blogs, websites and other technology-enabled media – all without body language – the potential for misinterpretation is growing. Rushed and stressed, people often do not take the time to consider the nuances of their writing. Conflicts detonate over the tone of an email, or that all-important cc-list. When an older person writes a text in all capital letters, does it mean that he is shouting? Are short responses, without the traditional politeness formulae, a sign that the person doesn't want to engage? On the other hand, does a smiley really mean they're bought in and aligned? Nowadays, conclusions are drawn on shockingly little information.

---

28   http://eur-lex.europa.eu/en/techleg/index.htm
29   http://ec.europa.eu/ ipg/content/tips/index_en.htm

In the EU administration, social media are taken very seriously as a way to communicate with citizens. For example, in the Commission there is a team in DG COMM who take care of the corporate social media presence and coordinate the Commission's Social Media Network (the network of colleagues in other DGs who have an official role on the social media platforms). They have also developed and published, in collaboration with DG HR and Security, guidelines to staff advising on the pitfalls involved in communicating via these channels, in particular where it can be difficult to draw a clear line between personal and professional use of social media and the internet. The Commission has also adopted Yammer[30] as a tool to facilitate and encourage communication amongst colleagues, beyond and across organisational barriers – so even for internal use social media are seen as a means to improve the flow of information and, thus, efficiency. The other institutions have similar initiatives.

Social media will likely continue to become increasingly integrated into the normal human experience, like most of the technologies that came before. As social media becomes more normalised, we will stop seeing it as something new, and start seeing it as what it really is, just another form of communication.

Context matters

In his film 'The Lord of the Rings – The Fellowship of the Ring', director Peter Jackson devotes the first seven minutes to the story of the creation of the One Ring and the war against Sauron. Without this historical perspective, the audience would have no background for any of the events in this epic trilogy. *Context matters*.

Without context, your audience may not understand your message. On the other hand, you may not understand your audience either.

I very much liked the example given by Dan Pink in his thought-provoking book 'A Whole New Mind'[31]:

'Suppose that one night you and your spouse are preparing dinner. Suppose too, that midway through the preparations, your spouse discovers that you forgot to buy the dinner's most important ingredient. Suppose then that your spouse grabs the car keys, curls a lip, glares at you, and hisses, 'I'm going to the store.' Nearly everyone with an intact brain would understand two things about the words your spouse just uttered. First, your spouse is heading to Safeway[32]. Second, your spouse is pissed.'

This has to do with how our brain works. To oversimplify a bit, the left hemisphere handles *what* is said; the right hemisphere focuses on *how* it's said. However tempting it is to talk of right and left hemispheres in isolation, they are actually two half-brains, designed to work together as a smooth, single integrated whole in one entire, complete brain. The manner in which you deliver your message, from the words you say to how you say them, relies on the situational context – what is appropriate in that situation

30 Yammer is a private social network that helps employees collaborate across departments, locations, and business apps.
31 'A Whole New Mind – Why Right-Brainers Will Rule the Future' (2006) by Daniel Pink.
32 Replace as appropriate by any grocery store!

and that particular environment. For example, the broad smiles and good humour that you might show at a friend's wedding are unlikely to be appropriate at a colleague's funeral.

The key then to understanding your context is to develop a habit of **situational awareness**. Situational awareness refers to your perception of your environment and situation around you on a moment-by-moment basis. In being situationally aware, you can anticipate changes to your environment. In this way, you're always thinking just one step ahead in any given situation or environment, and you are able to adapt accordingly. Cultivating this skill (and it does take time and a keen awareness of your surroundings) is especially helpful when your context may shift or change in subtle or major ways, or in an instant.[33]

Remember that your perception only exists within the context of your life. Without proper definition your vision can get lost in fragmented versions of other people's view of you.

You must never assume that people understand your point of view and understand your vision. Don't cut corners on educating someone about what you do and why you do it. When you are communicating with someone, be it online, in a textbook, or in the real world never forget the critical pieces that will allow people to understand you.

Keep it simple

'If you can't explain it to a six year old, you don't understand it yourself.' – Albert Einstein

KISS is an acronym for 'Keep it simple, stupid', a design principle adopted by the US Navy in the early 1960s. The KISS principle states that most systems work best if they are kept simple rather than made complicated; therefore simplicity should be a key goal in design and unnecessary complexity should be avoided. Variations on the phrase include 'keep it short and simple' and 'keep it simple and straightforward'.

Applied to human communication, the KISS principle actually attempts to control the context of the conversation, by reducing it to its simplest form, hopefully making it a common denominator between the sender and his audience.

The idea of simplicity is implemented by applying a clear and straightforward structure to the message, if possible linear and using a chronological order. Clearly, long sentences, over-sophisticated vocabulary and jargon are to be avoided, and complex ideas and concepts ought to be explained in their simplest possible form, preferably by using metaphors, analogies or real-life examples.

When you convey a message in this way you make life easier for your audience. They don't have to make an effort to understand what you're saying and the probability that your message will come across becomes significantly higher.

---

33 'Situational and Environmental Context', Boundless Communications. https://www.boundless.com/communications/textbooks/boundless-communications-textbook/introduction-to-public-speaking-1/elements-of-speech-communication-21/situational-and-environmental-context-103-4186/

Keeping it simple doesn't mean that you are stupid; quite the contrary. The best proof of someone's intelligence – and mastery of a subject – is their ability to simplify the complex. People who are confident in their knowledge won't hesitate to share it with others in terms that are easily understood. In contrast, people who attempt to talk over people's heads through the use of overly complex terms and descriptions are typically those who lack a true understanding of the subject themselves and are trying to mask that fact.

Too often, people over-complicate things in an attempt to display their intelligence, when all that happens is that they end up pushing people away and ultimately losing credibility. They come across as elitists, rather than team players. Truly intelligent people are not afraid to share their knowledge because they don't view other people gaining knowledge as a threat to their own. Rather, they take pleasure in sharing and in teaching others. As a result they become builders of people, and they contribute tremendously to an organisation's overall success.

Obviously, when you are talking to your peers, who understand the topic perfectly well (or in other words, who share the same context) you don't have to treat them like six-year-olds. You adapt the level of your conversation to the audience.

We can all benefit if we recognise that we don't have to talk like a super genius to be seen as intelligent. There is tremendous virtuosity in our ability to keep it simple. Don't ever forget that many of the world's most difficult problems have been solved with the simplest solutions.

Keep it short

'Being brief is an essential 21st-century skill,' says Joseph McCormack, author of 'Brief: Make a Bigger Impact by Saying Less.'[34] People are buried with information, and the average attention span is now eight seconds. You can't hold anyone's attention if you're not brief.

Acronyms

Acronyms are everywhere, and for a good reason: they speed up conversations by eliminating the need to repeat multi-word phrases everyone knows already, and they make documents shorter and visually more attractive. Acronyms are a sort of metaphor.

On the other hand, indiscriminately littering a document with acronyms serves only to turn it into alphabet soup and guarantee that readers will remember nothing substantive, only how hard it was to read.

Over-use of acronyms in written communication is bad, lazy writing, but at least with a document readers set their own pace and can pause to check what the acronyms refer to. Actually *speaking* in acronyms is a major turnoff. Anyone who works in the EU environment can easily slip into using practically nothing but acronyms. Maybe this is fine when you are with immediate colleagues who share your jargon, but for other people who are not familiar with the acronyms it can be off-putting or even seem hostile.

---

34   'Brief: Make a Bigger Impact by Saying Less' (2014) by Joseph McCormack.

When you are writing a document, answering questions or doing anything that has to do with communicating, assume that your audience doesn't know what any particular acronym means. Use words and phrases anyone can understand. A good practice when you make use of acronyms is to explain every acronym at least once (except the most obvious: like 'EU') at the start of your document or otherwise have a list of acronyms as annex to the body of your text.

By the way, do you know what a TLA[35] is?

Repetition

Human communication mechanisms are anything but perfect. Besides the distortions at the level of the transmitter and the transmission channel, we only receive part of the message because we are simply not listening all the time. It is often a good idea therefore to build some redundancy into your message by repeating the same information.

People rate statements that have been repeated as more valid or true than things they've heard only once. And when we think something is truer, we also tend to be more persuaded by it. Simply said, people are more influenced when they hear statements of opinion and persuasive messages more than once.

Psychological studies clearly suggest that *moderate* repetition has a positive effect on someone's reception of, and agreement with a persuasive argument. John Cacioppo and Richard Petty[36] were two pioneers in this field in the late 1970s and early 1980s. They concluded that low to moderate levels of repetition within a message tend to create greater agreement with the message, along with greater recall. However, their work also suggested that *too much* repetition has an adverse impact and can lead to stronger disagreement with the argument being made.

The use of moderate repetition can be effective if the argument is constructed in such a way that the repetition is spread out over time. The use of repetition over the long course of an argument, written or spoken, creates a greater familiarity with the message and leads to gradual agreement if the intensity of repetition is gradual itself. Too much repetition in a short span of time or space can defeat the purpose of gradual acceptance by creating a stronger aversion to the argument.

In speeches, or other spoken arguments that are highly emotional in nature, frequent repetition of key emotionally charged phrases (*pathos* – see next section) can be effective. Martin Luther King[37] Jr.'s 'I Have a Dream' speech[38] is often cited as one of the prime examples of the success of such repetition. However, it may be effective in messages of this nature only because of the already emotional nature of the issue. Applying this technique in the wrong context (*ethos, logos*) may have the opposite effect of turning off the audience.

---

35   Three Letter Acronym.

36   'The Elaboration Likelihood Model of Persuasion' (1984) by John Cacioppo and Richard E. Petty, in 'NA – Advances in Consumer Research' Volume 11, ed. Thomas C. Kinnear, pp. 673-675.

37   Martin Luther King, Jr. (1929–1968), leader in the African-American Civil Rights Movement.

38   http://www.americanrhetoric.com/speeches/mlkihaveadream.htm

Although repetition can be fruitful as a persuasion strategy, subtlety can be as important as the frequency and intensity of the message. Rather than repeating the same words and phrasing throughout the course of an argument, finding more than one way to make the same argument repeatedly can be a more effective approach. The reader or listener is likely to respond more positively to the same argument stated in several ways rather than having the same message shoved down their throat over and over.

This is what psychologists call the 'illusion of truth effect' and it arises at least partly because familiarity breeds liking. As we are exposed to a message again and again, it becomes more familiar. Because of the way our minds work, what is familiar is also true. Familiar messages require less effort to process, and that feeling of ease unconsciously suggests to us that they *are* true.

Ethos, pathos and logos

No, these are not the three musketeers (their names were Athos, Porthos and Aramis). These are Aristotle's[39] 'ingredients for persuasion' in his treatise on rhetoric[40]. For Aristotle, the goal of argumentative speaking or writing is to persuade your audience that your ideas are valid – or more valid than someone else's. He divided the means of persuasion, into three categories: *ethos, pathos* and *logos*.

Ethos

According to Aristotle, our perception of a speaker or writer's character influences how acceptable or convincing we find what that person has to say. This projected character is called the speaker or writer's *ethos*. We are more likely to be persuaded by a person who, we think, has personal warmth, consideration of others, a good mind and erudition. People whose education, experience, and previous performances qualify them to speak on a certain issue earn the special *ethos* of authority. But whether or not we know anything about the speaker or writer, the actual text we hear or read, the way it is written or spoken and what it says, also conveys an impression of the author's character. This impression created by the text itself is known as the *intrinsic ethos*.

Institutions, public personalities and publications also project an *ethos* or credibility. We may assume, for example, that The Economist is a more credible source than our daily newspaper or that BBC News is more reliable than our national broadcast organisation. And we usually assume that a person selected for a public position of responsibility is more credible than someone without official sanction.

An example may clarify this concept:

'As an environmental scientist who has dedicated the last 25 years of my life studying the earth's climate, I believe that man-made global warming is a serious problem.'

---

39 Aristotle, Greek philosopher and scientist (384-322 BC).
40 Rhetoric is the art of speaking or writing effectively.

Pathos

'Effective communication is 20% what you know and 80% how you feel about what you know.' – Jim Rohn[41]

The influential appeal of *pathos* is a call to the audience's sense of identity, their self-interest, and their emotions. Appeals to our sense of identity and self-interest exploit common biases; we naturally bend in the direction of what is advantageous to us, what serves our interests or the interests of any group we believe ourselves a part of. Even when advantage is not an issue, writers who belong to groups we identify with, or create groups we can belong to, often seem more persuasive. We also naturally find more convincing the speaker or writer who flatters us (especially indirectly) instead of insulting us. Thus skilful speakers or writers create a positive image in their words of the audience they are addressing, an image their actual readers can identify with.

An example:

'Like an oncoming freight train, global warming threatens the noble and beautiful polar bear with extinction. As the ice melts, these magnificent, iconic creatures will face the devastating, painful realities of hunger and starvation. No longer will the mother cub be able to care for her once frolicking and playful little pups.'

This example illustrates at the same time the use of metaphors and the power of images.

Logos

Finally, we come to the arguments themselves – the explicit reasons the arguer provides to support a position, or *logos*. There are many ways to describe the support provided in an argument, but a simple way to begin is to consider all the principles the author seems to supply. These can be scattered throughout the argument and expressed indirectly, so identifying premises is a judgement call in itself.

Next ask which of the premises are presented as objects of agreement that the arguer considers as given, elements of the argument taken for granted. Objects of agreement are basically either facts or values. Of course, the facts may not be facts at all and readers may not agree with the values assumed. Some of the premises will be supported further, but fundamentally every argument has got to come down to certain objects of agreement that it presents as shared between arguer and audience.

41   Jim Rohn (1930–2009) was an American entrepreneur, author and motivational speaker.

You can also classify premises into the following categories:

- *Arguments based on definition*; in other words, making claims about the nature of things, about what terms mean, what features things have.

- *Analogies or comparisons*, citing parallel cases.

- *Appeals to cause and consequences.* This is especially common when policy issues are debated.

- *Reliance on testimony or authority* by citing the received opinions of experts, or creating some kind of authoritative reference group, citing public opinion on what most people think as support for a particular position.

Example:

- America has had a 20% increase in carbon dioxide emissions from the burning of fossil fuel since 1990.

- Another 15% increase in carbon dioxide emissions is predicted by 2020.

- 2006 was the hottest year in recorded history in the continental United States (Environmental Defence Fund).

- According to NOAA, the global warming rate in the last 25 years has risen to 3.5° F per century (Braasch).

Please note that in this example the credibility of the figures was established by citing the source.

(Examples are taken from

http://www.slideshare.net/guest484cbf/pathosethoslogos-presentation)

An icon of rhetoric

'Friends, Romans, countrymen, lend me your ears!
I come to bury Caesar, not to praise him.
The evil that men do lives after them,
The good is oft interred with their bones;
So let it be with Caesar.'

(Marc Antony, in 'Julius Caesar' by William Shakespeare.)
This speech is a famous example of the use of emotionally charged rhetoric in which Marc Antony skilfully manipulates the crowd. You may find it interesting to read more about how he does this[42.]

---

42   https://en.wikipedia.org/wiki/Friends,_Romans,_countrymen,_lend_me_your_ears

Metaphors

According to Oxford Dictionaries a metaphor is 'A figure of speech in which a word or phrase is applied to an object or action to which it is not literally applicable.' For example, when we speak of 'gene maps' and 'gene mapping', we use a cartographic metaphor. In English, the word was adopted in the late 15th century from the French 'métaphore', via Latin from the Greek 'metaphora', from 'metapherein' meaning 'to transfer.'

Metaphors make for effective communication because *analogy* – a process of finding the properties of a thing by comparing it to another thing – is fundamental to thought. 'Human thought processes are largely metaphorical,' write Lakoff and Johnson[43]. 'The human conceptual system is metaphorically structured and defined. Metaphor is as much a part of our functioning as our sense of touch, and as precious.'

We use metaphors all the time. As Lakoff and Johnson point out, we compare:

- *Arguments to war.* (Attack your position, claims are indefensible, criticisms were right on target, shoot down arguments.)

- *Time to money.* (Spending time, wasting time, saving time, investing time, costing time.)

- *Computers to offices.* (Desktops, files, folders, documents, notepads.)

In our minds, 'love is a journey', 'problems are puzzles' and 'the EU is a family' (possibly).

When you give information in the form of a metaphor, you effectively pre-process it for your audience. They don't have to invest the mental effort of finding an analogy in their inventory. When you use a metaphor, then, you are coming about as close as you can to placing a thought directly into the mind of your audience. Speaking of effective communication!

Metaphors are therefore powerful methods of persuasion, because they allow you to convey not just the information, but *how your audience should think* about that information. Scientific American reported a study[44] in which a group of subjects read a passage that said, 'Crime is a beast'. Another group read a passage that said, 'Crime is a virus'. In subsequent surveys, those who had read the beast passage were more likely to prescribe punishment as a means to control crime, while those who read the virus passage were more likely to prescribe treatment. Thus a good metaphor goes beyond effective communication to something approaching thought control. So pick your metaphors carefully and use them responsibly.

The 'bottom line' is: if you are communicating complicated, technical, or scientific information, use metaphors. And this is, of course, another metaphor.

---

43   'Metaphors we live by' (1980) by George Lakoff and Mark Johnson.
44   http://www.scientificamerican.com/article/figurative-speech-sways-decisions/

The European Dream Is Based On an 'Equals Around a Table' Metaphor

by Rune Kier Nielsen (Source: http://www.socialeurope.eu/2013/11/european-dream/)

When receiving the Nobel Peace Prize on behalf of the European Union, José M. Barroso and Herman van Rompuy spoke about the Union as a means to end war on a war torn continent. I have argued that this rhetoric has equated the union with 'a drain plug' with the sole purpose of avoiding further harm. That is not an engaging story or a positive dream for the future. It only rests on the fear of a Hobbesian nightmare – at the very bottom of the Maslow pyramid of needs.

Yet *The Passage to Europe*[45] describes how something else happened. The leaders might have met to talk trade but the fact that they met at all created something more. Because when people sit around a table they don't fight and when they don't fight they might trade. And when they trade, they might see that sitting around a table can do much more than stop a future war. In between the trade talks European leaders came to see that they had something in common besides the name of the table at which they sat. They formed a group independent of its members. Indeed *The Passage to Europe* dedicates extensive space to 'the crisis of the empty chair'[46] showing that the table is more than the people around it.

On this foundation I propose that 'equals around a table' should be the governing analogy and the founding myth behind any new narrative or 'European Dream'. The slogan of the European Union is 'united in diversity' and in the words of Hannah Arendt in *The Human Condition*[47]:

'To live together in the world means essentially that the world of things is between those who have it in common, as a table is located between those who sit around it: the world like every in-between, relates and separates men at the same time.'

A 'table'-metaphor further has a strong mythology in the European context. Jesus sat around a table, predicted his demise and forgave his traitors depicted on 'The Last Supper'. King Arthur and his 'Knights of the Round Table' is a common legend of valour, righteousness and equality. Martin Luther King Jr. might not be European, but his 'I have a dream' speech has resonated strongly with many Europeans over the last 50 years. He too talked about 'the table of brotherhood' as the central meeting place in his dream about equality and racial justice. Even the idea of a European continent in the very physical and geological sense rests on the idea of a tableau – or table.

The 'European Dream' needs concrete and vivid imagery

These myths are powerful because they are shared and they derive their power from the concrete, vivid and sensual imagery that all of us connote to the idea of 'a table'. It is where we eat our dinners as a family; it is where we gather when seeing good friends. It is enjoyment, closeness and reconciliation. At a table the seat is active in its productive sociality. We do something when we sit at a table – and everybody knows that sitting there is more than just sitting. That is also the force of the European Union and would be a powerful idea to associate with EU bureaucracy.

The dynamics of the 'European Dream' is what happens when people come together around a table and come to see the humanity in each other's eyes. Therefore, it cannot be an individualistic liberalistic dream like the American 'working from scratch to success'. The 'European Dream' is born from commonality and moves towards what people only desire when they can work together. It is social. In fact, it is entirely at the top of Maslow pyramid and rests firmly in the social contract. We do not have a European Union because we do not want to be killed; we have a European Union because it makes our lives better.

---

45   'The Passage to Europe' (2009) by Luuk van Middelaar.

46   The 'empty chair' crisis of 1965–1966 was when President Charles de Gaulle withdrew France from the workings of the Council of Ministers.

47   'The Human Condition' (1958) by Hannah Arendt.

Storytelling

'Audiences forget facts, but they remember stories.' – Ian Griffin

Many people have discovered the power of storytelling – they have observed how compelling a well-constructed narrative can be. Recent scientific work explains just how stories change our attitudes, beliefs, and behaviours.

Storytelling evokes a strong neurological response. Professor Paul Zak's[48] research indicates that our brains produce the stress hormone cortisol during the tense moments in a story, which allows us to focus, while the cute factor releases oxytocin, the feel-good chemical that promotes connection and empathy. Other neurological research tells us that a happy ending to a story triggers the limbic system, our brain's reward centre, to release dopamine, which makes us feel more hopeful and optimistic.

As social creatures, we depend on others for our survival and happiness. Professor Zak discovered that a neurochemical called oxytocin is a key 'it's safe to approach others' signal in the brain. Oxytocin is produced when we are trusted or shown a kindness, and it motivates cooperation with others. It does this by enhancing the sense of empathy, our ability to experience others' emotions. Empathy is important for social creatures because it allows us to understand how others are likely to react to a situation, including those with whom we work.

These findings on the neurobiology of storytelling are relevant to workplace settings. For example, character-driven stories with emotional content result in a better understanding of the key points a speaker wishes to make and enable better recall of these points many weeks later. When you want to motivate, persuade, or be remembered, start with a story of human struggle and eventual triumph. It will capture people's hearts – by first engaging their brains. Why should a person on the street care about the project you are proposing? How does it change the world or improve lives? How will people feel when it is complete? These are the components that make information persuasive and memorable.

In his book 'Things That Make Us Smart'[49], Don Norman accurately summarises the power of storytelling:

> 'Stories have the felicitous capacity of capturing exactly those elements that formal decision methods leave out. Logic tries to generalize, to strip the decision making from the specific context, to remove it from subjective emotions. Stories capture the context, capture the emotions … Stories are important cognitive events, for they encapsulate, into one compact package, information, knowledge, context, and emotions.'

Storytelling may seem like an old-fashioned tool. But that is exactly what makes it so powerful. Life happens in the narratives we tell one another. A story can go where quantitative analysis is denied admission: our hearts. Data can persuade people, but it doesn't inspire them to act; to do that, you need to wrap your vision in a story that fires the imagination and stirs the soul.

---

48   Paul J. Zak is a professor at Claremont Graduate University and President of Ofactor, Inc.
49   'Things That Make Us Smart' (1994) by Don Norman.

The use of large numbers

Our brain is not so good at grasping the meaning of large numbers. Whether describing the vastness of the universe or the microscopic intricacies of the human body, the need to use large numbers is often inevitable. When we consider the estimated 200,000,000,000 (200 billion) stars in the Milky Way Galaxy or the estimated 150,000,000,000 (150 billion) galaxies in the universe or the estimated 100,000,000,000,000 (100 trillion) cells in the human body, we are forced to use numbers so large we cannot comprehend their meaning.

In the EU administration we often have to deal with large numbers: billions of euros, millions of people, thousands of staff, etc. When communicating about EU matters it is often difficult for our audience to understand the true meaning of these numbers. There are a few techniques that can be used to overcome this problem:

- *Comparing side by side by side.* A common way to put things in perspective is to literally line them up, side by side. We're visual creatures. We like to see, not imagine abstract numbers.

- *Rescale and resize.* Instead of looking up at the 'big numbers', we can shrink them to our level. Imagine the average person makes 50.000 euros per year, while Bill Gates earns around 5 billion euros per year. What's the difference? To understand Bill Gates' scale, don't think of 5 billion/year income — it's just another large number – but try to imagine having things cost 100,000 times less. A laptop would cost less than a eurocent, a Porsche around 60 cents, and a nice villa merely 5 euros.

- *Use what we know: time and distance.* Sometimes, a different type of scale may be useful. We know time and distance, which cover a surprisingly broad range of sizes. A well-known example is the compression of Earth's history into one year. Life would appear in the oceans around the first of April and half the year would go by with still no life on the land. Around 31 December, still no sign of humans. With about one hour to go before the year-ends the Neanderthal shows up, and only around 23:55 does civilisation begin.

Humour

'If you're going to tell people the truth, you'd better make them laugh. Otherwise, they'll kill you.' – George Bernard Shaw

The important thing to remember is that humour is beneficial at work as in life. Office humour makes our work more enjoyable, and humour outside the office – at home or with friends – will benefit our resilience, as it allows us to see things from a different perspective. As Dale Carnegie, author of 'How to Win Friends and Influence People'[50] said: 'People rarely succeed unless they have fun in what they are doing.'

---

50 'How to win Friends and Influence People' by Dale Carnegie, first published in 1936 and a big seller ever since.

One reason why we suppress humour at work is the fear of what others might think. While it is of course important to consider your image and reputation, many people become preoccupied with what their peers, managers, and direct reports think of them. To laugh at something is a revelation of our personality. It tells others what we think is funny, and that scares people. If you are in a meeting involving your Head of Unit or Director and someone makes a joke, the tendency is to glance at your superior to see if they think it's funny – if they laugh, then surely it's OK for you to laugh also. The problem is that your manager is doing the same thing: checking how other people in the room are reacting; after all, managers are normal people too, and they have the same insecurities as the rest of us.

Our daily communications at work consist of much more than the information we give and receive. Emotional tone (*pathos*) is just as important. Think back to conversations you have had with people you met in the past. Chances are you remember your emotional reaction to that person and the general feeling of the conversation much better than you remember what was actually said. Shared amusement and laughter help ensure that both participants in the conversation will remember the good feeling they had long after the content is forgotten.

This is especially important in situations where the initial mood of the conversation is hostile or confrontational. Research has shown that humour helps reduce hostile feelings among co-workers. The better mood that shared laughter creates puts you in a better position to resolve conflict and get on with your job. The fact is that humour is incompatible with anger and other negative emotions, and that makes it such a great tool for conflict management. Since conflict and stress are so common in the workplace these days, the savvy manager will cultivate appropriately timed humour as a means of keeping tensions, frustration and upset from escalating.

Laugh at your mistakes

A senior EU official once made a mistake that he knew he would have to explain in the press conference that was about to take place. After presenting his defence as well as he could, he said: 'That concludes my prepared evasion. I will now evade questions from the audience.' This melted some of the negative feelings in the room, and allowed everyone to focus more clearly on how to best deal with the circumstances they were now in. Once a mistake is made, it is important to acknowledge the error and move on. The ability to laugh at your mistakes helps to reduce the tensions resulting from them and focus on moving forward.

The pitfalls of technology

'*The more elaborate our means of communication, the less we communicate.*' – Joseph Priestley[51.]

The impact of technology on communication, in particular, has been extensive and largely positive. Organisations use websites, email, text messages, chatting and other forms of technological communication channels to transfer information to managers, employees and the public at large. But while technology has enhanced the way organisations conduct business, a number of disadvantages exist.

A first significant disadvantage of technology in business communication is the perception of communication being impersonal. Employees may perceive electronic communication as impersonal if they only receive messages from managers or other employees through email. Email can also create confusion, requiring employees to seek more feedback than normal compared to more personal communication methods.

Second, technology such as text messages and email allows us to communicate in short, carefully edited sentences that lack proximity and completely remove the contextual information provided by tone of voice and body language. As a result, people who connect with others primarily through technology can find it difficult to engage in a normal conversation, since they may have issues understanding non-verbal cues due to lack of practice with face-to-face interaction that cannot be paused, edited or filtered.

Also, many users of technology pay little attention to basic rules of grammar and format when composing their texts. This careless correspondence style reflects a lack of professionalism and may communicate to the recipient a view of the organisation behind the message as equally unprofessional. Much has been written on the vocabulary and peculiarities of online and text messaging jargon. This jargon, usually derived from English, can be extremely confusing for people who are not native English speakers, making it harder to detect the meaning of a sentence; people who regularly text or chat online may end up using it, out of habit, even in situations where it is inappropriate or out of place, such as in business messages or professional texts. The ease and informality of the medium should not be confused with the quality of writing necessary to use it properly.

Next, because communicating through technology creates an obstacle between people that isn't there when speaking face to face, some may find it easier to be rude and aggressive. Sherry Turkle[52], professor at the Massachusetts Institute for Technology, suggests that this happens because technology keeps us from having to see the reaction of the person on the receiving end of the message, making it harder to empathise with them.

---

51   Joseph Priestley (1733–1804) was an 18th-century English scientist, religious dissenter and political theorist.

52   Sherry Turkle is Professor of the Social Studies of Science and Technology at MIT and the founder (2001) and current director of the MIT Initiative on Technology and Self.

"No. Add some words to make that sound like maybe, and email it to everyone."

Yet another pitfall of technology is the permanent risk of information overload (also known as 'infobesity' or 'infoxication'). According to Lucy Jo Palladino, a psychologist and author of 'Find Your Focus Zone[53]', information overload occurs when a person is exposed to more information than the brain can process at one time. Obviously, technology has had a major effect on our minds in this respect.

Finally, technology allows us to always be reachable if we want to be, no matter where we are or what we are doing. Although this can be beneficial, it may also lead to a vicious cycle of stress and anxiety in which people feel pressured to immediately check and answer any incoming messages, emails or phone calls regardless of whether it is appropriate, for fear of being seen as incompetent or inattentive. In turn, this can potentially cause the breakdown of the very same relationships the person is trying to maintain.

Besides the potential negative effects on the quality of our communications, these last two weaknesses of technology may also affect our resilience and our prioritising and organising competencies – but these are the subjects of two other chapters of this book.

Developing your communication skills

One of the key aspects of good communication is *awareness*. Awareness, not only of your own strengths and weaknesses in this area, but first and foremost awareness of the environment and the audience:

53   'Find Your Focus Zone' (2011) by Lucy Jo Palladino.

- What is the context of the communication?

- Who is my audience?

- What is the level of the audience?

- What are the needs of the audience?

- Do I have the audience's attention?

- Do I really get my message across?

Especially in oral communication, stress is a major inhibitor of good performance. The trick is to convert this stress into positive energy. Daily practice is the best way to achieve this.

It is also important to select the appropriate communication channel(s); for communication that involves emotions, usually oral communication is best, while complex and factual communication is better done in writing.

Please refer to Chapter 1 (methodology) and Annex 2 for further development of this competency, have another look at the current chapter to find out about your options, and remember: YOU are responsible for your own development, not your manager, your colleagues, or your mentor.

The online toolkit that comes for free with this book can be used to follow-up on your development in this area. The toolkit can be found at:

https://www.johnharperpublishing.co.uk/the-ultimate-eu-career-development-toolkit/

Key points to remember

- Being able to communicate clearly, both orally and in writing is a key competency for all.

- The most important aspect of communication is the ability to listen and understand what the other person is saying. Focus your energy on being *interested*, not *interesting*.

- Besides the words that are spoken or written the surrounding emotions are of paramount importance.

- Stay aware of the dangers of using technology when communicating.

Your notes

5. Delivering quality and results

Competency definition: 'Take personal responsibility and initiative for delivering work to a high standard of quality within set procedures.'

Time now to come to the nub of the matter: the quality of the work we produce. Delivering work of good quality, in a timely manner, is after all what we are paid for. All our behaviour at work, whether it is analysing and solving problems, communicating, prioritising and organising, or any of the other 'core' competencies, should ultimately contribute to the same goal: doing what we are paid to do, in the best possible way.

Does one bad apple spoil the barrel?

Unfortunately, in the EU institutions, there are some people who think differently. They believe that they are paid simply because they are so good. They think that being selected out of thousands and thousands of candidates by EPSO, or their seniority, gives them the right to their salary. The fact that they are 'established' officials – they believe – secures a life-long employment, without the necessity to actually produce results. These people think that they only have rights and no obligations. That is probably why they refer to their professional activity as a 'position' and not as a 'job'. I am happy to say that, in my experience, these 'bad apples' only form a small minority of EU staff; but nevertheless they sometimes spoil the barrel for others, or give the EU institutions a bad reputation.

What is work?

'*In 1880, about nine out of 10 workers made and moved things; today, that is down to one out of five. The other four are knowledge people or service workers.*' – Peter Drucker[1]

A formal definition of work could be:

'*Any activity involving mental or physical effort done in order to achieve a result.*'

- A *task* is a unit of work, that is, a set of activities needed to produce some result.

- A *result* is the final consequence of a task that can be expressed qualitatively or quantitatively.

- A *job* is a collection of tasks and responsibilities that an employee is responsible to conduct; jobs have titles.

- A *role* is a set of responsibilities or expected results associated with a job. A job usually includes several roles.

- A *career* is something that someone wants to pursue for the rest of their (working) life.

---

1   Peter Drucker (1909–2005) was an Austrian-born American management consultant, educator and author.

Usually, the concept of work is related to the concept of being paid; most people work to get a salary or revenue. Intuitively, one would think that higher pay should produce better results, but scientific evidence indicates that the link between compensation, motivation and performance is much more complex; why else would people have hobbies, do sports, or be volunteering – and be highly motivated and well-performing – without any financial compensation?

"Are we supposed to eliminate quality or improve waste?"

Behavioural scientists usually divide work into two categories: 'algorithmic' and 'heuristic'. An algorithmic task is one in which you follow a set of pre-established instructions, down a single pathway to one conclusion. That is, there is an algorithm for solving it. A heuristic task is the opposite; because there is no algorithm you have to experiment with possibilities and find a novel solution. During the twentieth century, most work was algorithmic, but today, in much of the Western world algorithmic work is disappearing, as it is offshored to wherever it can be done cheaper.

In the EU institutions, most of the employees are so-called 'white collar' workers whose job entails largely heuristic work. The term white collar used to simply characterise non-manual workers, but now it refers to employees or professionals whose work is knowledge-intensive, non-routine, and mostly unstructured. Historically, in the West, clerical workers wore white shirt collars and manual workers wore blue, hence the denomination.

According to Professor Russell Ackoff[2], the content of the human mind can be classified into five categories:

- *Data* – symbols. Data is raw; it simply exists and has no significance beyond its existence. It can exist in any form, usable or not. It does not have meaning of itself.

- *Information* – data that is processed to be usable. Answers to 'who', 'what', 'where', and 'when' questions. Information is data that has been given

---

2   Russell Ackoff (1919–2009) was an American organisational theorist, consultant and professor at the Wharton School, University of Pennsylvania.

meaning by way of relational connection. This meaning can be useful, but does not have to be.

- *Knowledge* – application of data and information. Answers the 'how' question; knowledge is information organised in a way that makes it useful.

- *Understanding* – appreciation of 'why'. For example, elementary school children memorise knowledge of the times table. They can tell you that 2 x 2 = 4 because they have amassed that knowledge (as it is in the times table). But when asked what 123 x 456 is, they cannot respond correctly because that calculation is not in their times table. To correctly answer such a question requires understanding.

- *Wisdom* – evaluated understanding. Unlike the previous categories, wisdom deals with the future because it incorporates vision and design.

White-collar work is about the exchange of data, information, knowledge, understanding and wisdom. This is what working as an EU official involves – though some may imagine differently (Figure 5.1)!

Figure 5.1

The inner game of work

In his book 'The Inner Game of Work'[3] Tim Gallwey defines work in terms of a triangle with the words performance, learning and enjoyment at the points. He stresses that all three of these are important and that, therefore, if enjoyment is decreased, performance is also decreased. This has obvious implications for many traditional work cultures; he says:

> 'When either the learning or the enjoyment side is ignored, performance will suffer in the long run. When it does, management feels threatened and pushes even harder for performance. Learning and enjoyment diminish even further. A cycle ensues that prevents performance from ever reaching its potential.'

In the same book Gallwey also introduces the concept of mobility, which he defines as: 'the ability to move or adapt, change or be changed. It also means the ability to reach one's objectives in a fulfilling manner – to reach goals at the right time and in a way we feel good about. Therefore, mobility is not only change but fulfilment and harmony with one's progress.'

What is quality?

'Quality in a service or product is not what you put into it. It is what the client or customer gets out of it.' – Peter Drucker

Joseph Juran[4] defined quality as 'fitness for use' but this is – to say the least – somewhat simplistic. Allow me to use a very practical example to illustrate this.

Say that we are talking about smartphones. We all know that there are hundreds of different models and brands out there, and that there is a constant evolution going on, almost forcing people to buy a new smartphone every two years or so. Unless you were really ripped off, or your smartphone recently broke, you can definitely say that the model you are using today is 'fit for use'; you can use it for what it's intended, that is to communicate with others.

But does that mean that it is of 'good' or 'excellent' quality? Or, inversely, that the 'fitness for use' of an older model has dropped over time? Of course not, because we all have different needs – or call it expectations, and these needs evolve over time. Technology freaks will 'need' the most recent, fancy model to show off to their friends, while elderly people will probably be satisfied with the simplest, cheapest, and even out-dated model. In fact, our 'needs' and 'expectations' are to a large extent driven by the market and the outrageous competition between the manufacturers of smartphones. In order to survive, they have to produce – and sell – new models at an ever-increasing pace. Manufacturing costs are dropping constantly, and so are the profit

---

3   'The Inner Game of Work: Overcoming Mental Obstacles for Maximum Performance' (2000) by Timothy Gallwey.
4   Joseph Moses Juran (1904–2008) was a Romanian-born American engineer and management consultant.

margins. This can only be compensated for by selling higher volumes. The bottom line is that 'fitness for use' is not 'fit for use' as a comprehensive definition of quality; we have to take the expectations of our clients into account.

The notion of quality

Defining the notion of quality is not straightforward, at least if one wants to define it in general terms, without the context. For example, when assessing the quality of a translation, you really cannot do so without introducing subjectivity, which is the enemy of fairness. There tends to be an agreed consensus on what quality is NOT (the negatives are more objective: e.g. poor grammar, bad spelling, incorrect terminology, wrong tone, etc.) because the bad can be assessed against an agreed set of common, external standards. What is 'good' however, is often the subjective view of the reader.

For assessment purposes, therefore, once you remove 'the bad', the remainder is, by definition, 'the good' – or at the very least, the tolerable. Take the example of water: what won't kill you is actually perfectly fine. Bottled water may make claims of 'quality' – but tap water won't do you any harm either. Ultimately which one is 'better' is down to personal preference, which is not a valid assessment criterion for an objective yardstick. The trick in assessing quality is to identify all the negatives, quantify them (the more there are, the lower the quality) but don't try to judge the positive – it'll speak for itself through the absence of negatives. Obviously, it's a bit subtler than that: there are usually some commonly agreed positives as well, but this is a generalisation that works in many cases.

The ISO[5] definition of quality goes as follows: 'The totality of features and characteristics of a product or service that bear on its ability to satisfy stated or implied needs.'

More directly, one can say that a product or service has good quality when it complies with the requirements specified by the client. A *requirement* is a singular, documented physical and functional need that a particular design, product or process must be able to perform. In the business world, requirements are also called *specifications*.

"Go tell the workers that I'm serious about this quality crap."

---

5   ISO – International Organisation for Standardisation.

In the context of office work, quality can be seen as a measure of the degree to which the expectations of your client (your boss, your institution, or the general public) are met. However, 'expectations' are deeper and broader than 'requirements' or 'specifications'. *Expectations* are your client's vision of a future state or action, usually unspoken but nevertheless critical to your success. These expectations are not always clear and obvious. Your Head of Unit may want a piece of work to be 'quick and dirty,' or to be personally 'involved in all the details' or 'not involved at all,' or expect that your work is of 'high quality' without giving any further details as to what that means in practice.

In conclusion, the quality of your work is determined by the person who asked for it, not by society in general. It is not related to cost, and adjectives or descriptors such as 'high' and 'poor' are not applicable as such.

Bureaucracy

In the definition of delivering quality and results it is also said that the results have to be delivered 'within set procedures'; clearly, what is meant here are the procedures as imposed by the working environment, the EU institutions in our case.

The EU institutions are *bureaucracies* – and there is nothing wrong with that, since a bureaucracy is the administrative system governing virtually every large institution.

Professor Henry Mintzberg[6] labelled a highly bureaucratic organisation as being like a 'machine.' The machine organisation is defined by its standardisation. Work is very formalised, there are many routines and procedures, decision-making is centralised, and tasks are grouped by functional departments. Jobs are clearly defined; there will be a formal planning process with budgets and audits; and procedures are regularly analysed for efficiency.

Bureaucracies have a tight vertical structure. Functional lines go all the way to the top, allowing top managers to maintain centralised control. These organisations can be very efficient, and they rely heavily on economies of scale for their success. However, the formalisation leads to specialisation and, quite often, functional units may have conflicting goals that can even be inconsistent with overall objectives.

The term bureaucracy is French in origin, and combines the French word *bureau* – desk or office – with the Greek word *kratos* – rule or political power. It was coined sometime in the mid-18th century and was a satirical pejorative from the outset.

Bureaucracies have been criticised as being too complex, inefficient, or too inflexible. The dehumanising effects of excessive bureaucracy became a major theme in the work of Franz Kafka[7]. Others have defended the necessity of bureaucracies. The German sociologist Max Weber[8] argued that bureaucracy constitutes the most efficient and rational way in which one can organise human activity, and that systematic processes and organised management levels are necessary to maintain order, max-

---

6   Henry Mintzberg (1939) is an internationally renowned academic and author on business and management.

7   Franz Kafka (1883–1924) was an Austrian-Hungarian German language writer, considered to be one of the most influential authors of the 20th century.

8   Max Weber (1864–1920) was a German sociologist, philosopher, jurist, and political economist.

imise efficiency and eliminate favouritism. But Weber also saw unrestricted bureaucracy as a threat to individual freedom.

In the EU, the debate is open. Even Pope Francis has publicly voiced his discontent with the European Union's bureaucracy, widely seen as wasteful, elitist and self-serving. Europe, he declared, has lost its way, its energies sapped by economic crisis and a remote, technocratic bureaucracy.

It has to be said that the EU institutions are very much aware of these criticisms. The 2015 Work Programme reflects the Commission's strengthened commitment to Better Regulation, building on the **Regulatory Fitness Programme (REFIT)**, which seeks to cut red tape and remove regulatory burdens, contributing to an environment conducive to investment. The institutions are working hard on transparency, efficiency, and effectiveness and more and more focus is put on the internal debate on ethics and integrity.

What is REFIT?

REFIT is the European Commission's Regulatory Fitness and Performance programme. Action is taken to make EU law simpler and to reduce regulatory costs, thus contributing to a clear, stable and predictable regulatory framework supporting growth and jobs.

To do this successfully, REFIT requires a joint effort between the European Parliament, the European Council, the European Commission, Member States and stakeholders. Every level of government should be involved to ensure that the benefits are realised at least cost for citizens and business.

(http://ec.europa.eu/smart-regulation/refit/index_en.htm)

An interesting book to read in this context, if you understand German, is 'Der europäische Landbote'[9] by Robert Menasse. Menasse writes about the future of Europe and the EU, criticising tendencies of re-nationalisation and anti-European integration, which are a reaction to the financial crisis and its aftermath, the euro-crisis.

To end on a lighter note on bureaucracies, I'd recommend you to read 'The Peter Principle', as mentioned in Chapter 1. The first edition of this book by Laurence J. Peter and Raymond Hull was published in 1969, but the main ideas still hold true today. It is a very funny book that will for sure deepen your understanding of how life in an organisation really works.

Ethics and integrity

In the Commission, Ethics and Integrity is now a compulsory one-day course, classified under the heading 'internal procedures' and not under any of the general competencies. The focus is on 6 key principles: independence, impartiality, objectivity, loyalty, responsibility and circumspection[10]. It is about maintaining 'a healthy balance

9   'Der Europäische Landbote: die Wut der Bürger und der Friede Europas' (2012) by Robert Menasse.

10   Circumspection: the quality of being wary and unwilling to take risks; prudence.

between duty, obligation and personal values within an organisation' and also to prevent conflicts of interest. It is growing in importance, I think, because of the way the EU is perceived these days by the media and by the general public. The situation was somewhat different in the past.

The training covers everything from leisure activity to unpaid work and from competitive advantage to delivering speeches, etc. The key reference documents are standard: guidelines on gifts and hospitality, guidelines on social media, guidelines on whistleblowing, and of course the Staff Regulation's Title II on rights and obligations of officials.

Time management

The competency of delivering quality and results is closely related to the competency of prioritising and organising, better known as *time management*. The modern concept of time management really began with Frederick Taylor's[11] scientific management techniques. His goal was to increase worker productivity (see Table 5.1). To do this, he conducted time and motion studies and began to focus on the best ways for jobs to be performed to maximise the work completed in a given amount of time.

Effectiveness	Efficiency	Productivity
Effectiveness is about doing the right task, completing activities and achieving goals.	Efficiency is about doing things in an optimal way, for example doing it the fastest or in the least expensive way.	Productivity is an average measure of efficiency. It can be expressed as the ratio of output to inputs used, i.e. output per unit of input.

Table 5.1

Time management has also been employed as a tool for increasing the productivity of white-collar workers, for whom work output may be hard to measure. In this respect, modern managers in these areas look for ways to monitor worker productivity in terms of time use.

In the specific context of the Commission, new provisions on working time were introduced with the revision of the Staff Regulations in 2014. In a flexible approach to working time, staff can adjust their working hours as long as this is compatible with the Commission's needs.

The Commission adopted a new decision to make *flexitime*[12] the default working arrangement for all staff (with a few exceptions) from 1 June 2014. It also confirmed the increase in working hours, from 37.5 to 40 hours per week, and required that all

---

11   Frederick Winslow Taylor (1856–1915) was an American mechanical engineer who sought to improve industrial efficiency.

12   Meaning flexible working hours for each individual employee.

staff members record their daily working hours. Another flexible time management tool is telework. *Telework* practices vary greatly across the EU institutions and even across the Commission's DGs. Furthermore, a considerable number of staff members make use of part-time working, parental leave and family leave.

Obviously, this flexible approach to working time requires a lot of self-discipline and responsibility from EU staff, and good leadership skills from their managers.

Performance management

Performance management is a process by which managers and employees work together to plan, monitor and review an employee's work objectives and overall contribution to the organisation. More than just an annual performance review, performance management is a continuous process of setting objectives, assessing progress and providing on-going feedback to ensure that employees are meeting their objectives and career goals.

One of the cornerstones of performance management is the employee's *job description*. Through their job description an employee will know in general terms what is expected without having to refer to more detailed instructions for a task at hand. Complex positions in the organisation can include many tasks, which are sometimes called functions.

Job descriptions are lists of the general tasks, or functions, and responsibilities of a position. Typically, they also include who the position reports to, and specifications such as the qualifications needed by the person in the job, salary range for the position, etc. It is important to make a job description practical by keeping it dynamic, functional and current. A well-written job description will help the manager avoid hearing a refusal to carry out a relevant assignment because 'it isn't in my job description.' A poor job description will keep employees from trying anything new and from learning how to perform their job more productively. Good job descriptions will help them to grow within their position and make larger a bigger contribution to the organisation.

Do refer back to Chapter 1, where the notion of performance management in the EU institutions is described in more detail.

Expectation management

'Always give people more than what they expect to get.' – Nelson Boswell[13]

Expectation management is very valuable. Managing expectations proactively will increase your chances of success, a great performance review, and ultimately have a positive effect on your career progression.

Obviously, the first thing to do is to make sure you understand exactly what is expected of you. Understanding your job description and learning about the procedures that are to be followed for your particular role or job is clearly a first step in

---

13   US author of self-help books.

understanding what is expected. People often get into hot water when they assume that somebody else knows what they expect or even what they are talking about. Don't fall into the trap of assuming that someone else has the same understanding of a situation, project, deadline, or task to accomplish. When you have a team to supervise, make sure to share your expectations with them. Giving others a picture of what you think success looks like for the team and each individual will give them a way to move forward. The SMART[14] model can be a useful tool in this respect.

"Meeting my expectations will be easy. Just be better than you are, and smarter than you are, and work harder than you can."

One of the best ways to manage expectations is to make sure you communicate with everyone on a frequent basis. To keep in control of your performance, constant dialogue provides opportunities to measure progress, assess risks, and adjust actions. By keeping your boss in the loop, you also ensure that they are aware of your progress and successes along the way. If you are a manager yourself, share with the people you manage how you expect them to tackle potential issues, so that these can be dealt with in a timely manner and don't become obstacles to your own success.

Finally, *plan for contingencies.* When objectives are set, 'what if?' questions are rarely part of the conversation. Some tasks will be easier than others and some are more dependent on circumstances beyond your control. The landscape can change quickly if a critical assumption does not end up holding true. Assess the risks and identify potential options for addressing the most likely scenarios. That way you will be less likely to be caught by surprise. Speak to your team about the risks they perceive and how you can help them mitigate these risks to achieve their objectives. Also, being honest about a delay is a thousand times better than promising to deliver and then missing your deadline.

---

14   Specific, Measurable, Achievable, Realistic and Time-framed (see Chapter 1).

Exceeding expectations

A former colleague who worked at that time in DG TRADE once told me a story about exceeding the expectations of her superiors. She was appointed to be the head of a trade delegation that was sent on a mission to one of Europe's trading partners, in Asia.

Before the mission she had carefully prepared the possible 'landing positions' for the negotiation: a list of possible outcomes, ordered from 'most desirable' through 'acceptable' down to the 'red line' beneath which the outcome should not go. In discussing this list with her Head of Unit, he expressed his doubts about whether even the 'red line' was achievable, and suggested to her to lower the worst, but still acceptable, outcome of the negotiations.

Clearly, the Asian counterparts had done their homework too. They were aware of all the timing constraints (flight plans, travel time, etc.) on the EU delegation, and effectively tried to exploit this information by wasting time, and coming up with a first concrete proposal only towards the end of the meeting – hoping that the EU delegation would quickly give in for the sake of not missing their flight home. (In the chapter on working with others I explain the reasons behind this manoeuvre that is sometimes used in intercultural negotiations.)

As an experienced negotiator, however, she was aware of what was going on, and didn't let herself be put under pressure by this. So, she didn't give in and managed to get the 'most desirable' outcome after all. In doing so, she exceeded by some measure the expectations of her Head of Unit.

Personal responsibility

'The power behind taking responsibility for your actions lies in putting an end to negative thought patterns. You no longer dwell on what went wrong or focus on whom you are going to blame. You don't waste time building roadblocks to your success. Instead, you are set free and can now focus on succeeding.' – Lorii Myers[15]

Personal responsibility is the willingness to both accept the importance of standards for individual behaviour, and to make active personal efforts to live by those standards. But personal responsibility also means that when individuals fail to meet expected standards, they do not look around for some factor outside themselves to blame.

Our brain is inclined to flatter and shield our ego from blame when we make mistakes. Despite how difficult it is to counter the mechanisms of our ego defence system we must make the effort. In doing so, you will find that striving to take responsibility for your actions and ownership of your mistakes is worthwhile for many reasons:

- *It allows you to make better decisions.* Self-justifications distort reality. The more you use them, the more you create an alternative universe for yourself. This leads to a decreased ability to make good choices, as the information you're using to do so is distorted. Most dangerously, one self-justification leads to another, setting off a domino effect that sends you more and more off track. Once you justify one decision, you're deeper into it, and you'll make a decision that digs you even further into it … and so the cycle continues.

---

15 'Targeting Success' (2011) by Lorii Myers.

- *It keeps little problems from turning into big ones.* If you can own up to a mistake as soon as you make it and do your best to correct it or make it right, you can prevent it from turning into a huge problem that's going to be difficult to solve.

- *It allows you to learn from your mistakes.* You can't learn from your mistakes if you can't acknowledge you've made them! And if you don't learn from your mistakes, you're destined to repeat them. That's a recipe for quickly going nowhere.

- *It engenders the respect of others.* We often hide our mistakes from other people because we worry they will think less of us once they've seen that we've messed up. But, frankly acknowledging your mistakes, apologising for them, and then earnestly working to make things right almost always has the opposite effect: people will respect you for it.

There are two ways to explain things we get wrong: someone did something because of the *situation*, or, because of *who they are*. We typically use the former explanation for what we do ourselves – 'I forgot we had agreed to discuss this beforehand because I just have so much on my mind right now.' We tend to use the second explanation about others' behaviour: 'He totally forgot we had agreed to discuss this beforehand because he is self-centred and couldn't care less about others.' In the second case we don't evaluate their behaviour, but their personality – they don't do bad stuff, they are bad. The person is stupid, useless, selfish, immature, evil, lazy, etc. We judge them to be failed human beings. This kind of criticism is called a 'global label.' Global labels are rarely accurate, but your brain finds them very satisfying to develop. They allow you to see the other as deliberately hurting you. It is their fault, and you are the victim, so you feel entitled to punish and attack them.

Initiative

'Initiative is doing the right thing without being told.' – Victor Hugo

Initiative is all about taking charge. An initiative is the first in a series of actions. A person with initiative is motivated to do things. If you take the initiative, you are willing to get things done on your own. However, taking the initiative can be risky; if you do something on your own initiative, then there is nobody else you can blame if it goes wrong.

When you show initiative, you do things without being told; you find out what you need to know; you get going when the going gets tough; and you identify and take advantage of opportunities that others pass by. You act, instead of react.

Initiative has become increasingly important in today's workplace. Organisations want employees who can make quick decisions and take action without waiting for someone to tell them what to do.

The good news is that initiative is a skill that you can develop. The first step is to develop your own career plan. Research has shown that people who have a long-term career plan are more likely to take the initiative. The next step is to build your self-confidence. It takes courage to show initiative, especially if you fear that people may disagree with your actions or suggestions. Set yourself small goals so you can achieve some quick wins. Then push yourself to do bigger things. Have another look at the GROW model as introduced in Chapter 1; you will find it to be a good tool to develop your self-confidence.

Unforeseen obstacles

'The greater the obstacle, the more glory in overcoming it.' – Molière

Sometimes, things are not working out as expected, or we have to overcome an unforeseen obstacle. For sure, these are situations of high stress, and we have to deal with them.

Anticipating the various potential outcomes and/or reactions that others may have in a situation is extremely helpful in many ways. Thinking about all the possible actions and reactions of others to a situation makes your planning process more complete. What you ultimately piece together will likely not only have a solid plan 'A', but it may have a plan 'B', 'C', etc. as well.

When you take the time to anticipate, you are less likely to be surprised when and if what you thought *might* happen actually *does* happen. When you are less surprised you are less likely to be destabilised and you will be in better control of your emotions. When you are in control of your emotions you have the upper hand. You never know precisely what's around the corner, but you don't allow that to throw you off your game. Train yourself to anticipate possible challenges, to be prepared.

Of course, not everything can be anticipated, and really unforeseen – or unforeseeable – obstacles can block your way. You will have to find a workaround. You may be forced to 'think outside the box'. This means approaching problems in new, innovative ways; conceptualising problems differently; and understanding your position in relation to any particular situation in a way you have never thought of before. Thinking outside the box, like any skill, is one that can be developed through practice; you may find some ideas on WikiHow[16].

Finally, you should see these unexpected situations as learning opportunities. Being pushed out of your comfort zone creates a learning opportunity, as long as you are not drawn into your panic zone.

Quality management

'It is not necessary to change. Survival is not mandatory.' – W. Edwards Deming

'Kaizen'[17] is a Japanese word which has given its name to a management technique referred to as '**continuous improvement**'. When applied to the workplace, it refers to activities that continuously improve all functions and involve all employees, from the top executives to those at entry-level.

---

16   http://www.wikihow.com/Think-%27Outside-of-the-Box%27
17   'Kaizen: The Key to Japan's Competitive Success' by Masaaki Imai.

Kaizen was first implemented in several Japanese businesses after the Second World War, influenced by the ideas of the American quality guru W. Edwards Deming[18]. It has since spread around the world and been adopted in a wide range of environments, including government and business.

Deming provided a simple, yet highly effective technique that serves as a practical tool to carry out continuous improvement in the workplace. This technique is called the PDCA Cycle or simply Deming Cycle. PDCA is acronym of Plan, Do, Check and Action. The Deming Cycle provides a conceptual as well as practical framework while carrying out Kaizen activities by the employees – see Figure 5.2. Notice the similarities to the GROW model.

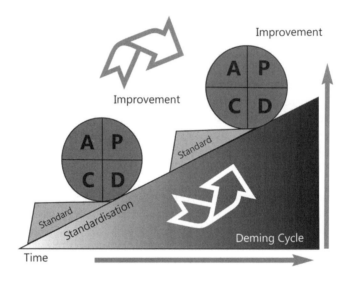

www.totalqualitymanagement.wordpress.com

Figure 5.2

Kaizen is continuous improvement that is based on certain guiding principles:

- Good processes bring good results
- Go see for yourself to grasp the current situation
- Speak with data, manage by facts
- Take action to contain and correct root causes of problems
- Work as a team
- Kaizen is everybody's business

18   William Edwards Deming (1900–1993) was an American engineer, statistician and management consultant.

One of the most notable features of kaizen is that big results come from many small changes accumulated over time. However, this has been misunderstood to mean that kaizen equals small changes. In fact, kaizen means everyone being involved in making improvements.

In Europe, the concepts of quality management through continuous improvement are promoted by the European Foundation for Quality Management (EFQM), a not-for-profit membership foundation in Brussels, established in 1989 to increase the competitiveness of the European economy. EFQM provides networking, education, and awards, using a framework called the EFQM Excellence Model.

The **Common Assessment Framework (CAF)** is the common European quality management instrument for the public sector. The CAF helps organisations to perform a self-assessment with the involvement of all staff, to develop an improvement plan based on the results of the self-assessment and to implement the improvement actions. CAF is being used by many public sector administrations, including most of the EU institutions and agencies.

Developing your skills in delivering quality and results

For this competency, it is necessary to be fully committed to and immersed in the concept of quality. Quality is the degree to which you meet and exceed the expectations of your 'customers'. It is therefore important to have a good understanding of one's own job description and the wider working environment – and to proactively understand and manage the expectations of your colleagues, superiors, and clients.

The competency of delivering quality and results is closely related to the competency of prioritising and organising, otherwise known as time management. The Commission organises training for this on a regular basis.

Please refer to Chapter 1 (methodology) and Annex 3 for further development of this competency; review the current chapter to find out about your options, and remember: YOU are responsible for your own development, not your manager, your colleagues, or your mentor.

The online toolkit that comes for free with this book can be used to follow-up on your development in this area. The toolkit can be found at:

https://www.johnharperpublishing.co.uk/the-ultimate-eu-career-development-toolkit/

Key points to remember

- Quality is the degree to which a product or service meets the expectations of the customer.

- Expectation management, personal responsibility and taking initiative are key for delivering quality and results.

- Taking the initiative, and the capability to overcome unforeseen obstacles, are important features.

- Bureaucratic rules are there for good reasons but they should be applied with insight and common sense.

- Quality management by continuous improvement is a responsibility for all.

Your notes

6. Learning and development

Competency definition: 'Develops and improves personal skills and knowledge of the organisation and its environment.'

'At each stage of human existence the adult man is off on his quest of his holy grail, the way of life he seeks by which to live. At his first level he is on a quest for automatic physiological satisfaction. At the second level he seeks a safe mode of living, and this is followed in turn, by a search for heroic status, for power and glory, by a search for ultimate peace; a search for material pleasure, a search for affectionate relations, a search for respect of self, and a search for peace in an incomprehensible world. And, when he finds he will not find that peace, he will be off on his ninth level quest. As he sets off on each quest, he believes he will find the answer to his existence. Yet, much to his surprise and much to his dismay, he finds at every stage that the solution to existence is not the solution he has come to find. Every stage he reaches leaves him disconcerted and perplexed. It is simply that as he solves one set of human problems he finds a new set in their place. The quest he finds is never ending.' – Clare W. Graves[1]

Is there a difference between learning and development?

In her article 'Making the Case for a Developmental Perspective'[2] Susanne Cook-Greuter[3] distinguishes between two directions of human development: horizontal growth and vertical transformation.

Horizontal growth refers to the gaining of new knowledge and skills within a particular stage of development. In doing so, the learner becomes better equipped to perform in their environment.

Vertical transformation is much more subtle. Rather than expanding capability within the same stage of development, the learner promotes their intellect to a higher stage of development.

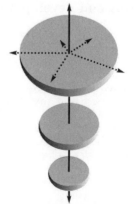

Horizontal = expansion at same stage (developing new skills, adding information & knowledge, transfer from one area to another)

Up = Transformation, vertical development, new more integrated perspective, higher centre of gravity

Down = temporary or permanent regression due to life circumstances, environment, stress and illness

Figure 6.1

---

1   Clare W. Graves (1914–1986) was an American professor of psychology and originator of a theory of adult human development.
2   http://www.cook-greuter.com/Making%20the%20case%20for%20a%20devel.%20persp.pdf
3   Susanne Cook-Greuter is as a leading expert in mature ego development and self-actualization.

This bidirectional model of development can represent the two sides of the learning and development equation:

- Horizontal growth represents the 'learning' – improving your competence.

- Vertical transformation represents the 'development' – maturing your mind.

In my classroom training and coaching sessions I use a somewhat simpler, less sophisticated, way to explain the difference between learning and development:

- Learning is about hard skills, development about soft skills.

- Learning is about the acquisition of knowledge and know-how, development about changing your behaviour.

- Learning is a process that takes a certain amount of time (and effort), and one can usually demonstrate the effect by passing a test or an exam. Development is an on-going process (you start developing when you are born, and stop when you die), and your behaviour can only be observed, or assessed, but not measured with high precision.

Both learning and development are important, but they occur at different rates. Learning happens via many channels; school, professional training, self-directed and life-long learning, practice, or simply through the exposure to life. Development is much rarer, especially in adults. It refers to how we learn to see the world through new eyes, how we change our interpretations of experience, and how we transform our views of reality. It describes our increasing awareness, and therefore what becomes part of our understanding and behaviour.

Learning and development

In Chapter 8 (Resilience) I use the example of how I taught my daughter to drive a car, in order to explain the notion of the 'comfort zone'. I explain how I passed on knowledge and know-how, and how I gradually increased the challenges so that she would learn how to drive a car. Her learning experience was successfully concluded by the driver's exam.

From that moment on, however, her 'development' started. Mainly by further practice, exposure to various traffic situations, some near misses and a fine, she became more aware of what driving a car is about, and adapted her behaviour accordingly. She has developed 'vertically', and continues to do so.

The Leadership Development Profile

The Leadership Development Profile (LDP) was originally created by Susanne Cooke-Greuter and Bill Torbert[4], and is based on the Leadership Development

---

4   http://www.williamrtorbert.com/

Framework (LDF) that describes nine sequential changes – or 'action logics' – in how a person interprets events, or makes meaning.

Torbert and Cook-Greuter adapted this instrument for professionals and explored it in managerial populations in the 1980s and 1990s. Harthill[5] has continued with improvements and created the Leadership Development Profile (LDP) so that it now provides a unique and highly validated tool for understanding personal and organisational development, and is being used with leading organisations across the world. Only the seven most commonly encountered action logics in the corporate world are referred to in the LDP. These range from the Opportunist, through the Diplomat, Expert and Achiever, to the stages of Individualist, Strategist and Magician (or Alchemist):

- *Opportunist* – focuses on own immediate needs, desires and opportunities. Seeks short-term concrete advantage and what is good for them personally. They often display sarcasm and hostility, resisting feedback and manipulating events to make themselves look good.

- *Diplomat* – seeks approval through socially expected behaviour. Seeks conformity, belonging and pleasant low stress relationships in order to gain approval from others. Diplomats avoid conflict and focus on preserving their status or membership of a group. They will argue to ensure they do not lose face.

- *Expert/Technician* – believes in the 'right way' to do things, seeking to display own skills and expertise in a dogmatic way, following procedures and behaving in ways expected of their role. They admire efficiency, consistency, incremental improvement, quality and perfection, but can get stuck in the details and their need for perfection.

- *Achiever* – seeks effectiveness through logical application of objectives, plans and controls, in order to deliver results and goals that will secure success within the system. They are proactive and use scientific problem solving techniques to assert their views and set high standards for others. Successful managers will have this logic in their psyche.

- *Individualist* – enjoys being appreciated for their own uniqueness, working through diverse relationships, experimenting with own power, developing increased spontaneity and pursuing new ideas. They tend to focus on the interactions between self and system, which means they understand the consequences of specific actions and are able to question assumptions. As a result they can adjust and adapt what they do to fit the context they find themselves in.

- *Strategist* – sees the world as a dynamic of inter-related processes and relationships, playing many roles in these. Sees the big picture and holds long-term perspective. Values integrity, principles and freedom in creating positive change. Strategists understand that reality is a social construction, which is what makes it complex with many interacting elements and factors.

5   http://harthill.co.uk/

They are tolerant of difference, seeing diversity as a resource for finding win-win solutions.

- *Magician/Alchemist* – committed to transformation of self, organisations and society. Seeks common good. Enjoys interplay of purposes, actions and results. Is elusive, chameleon-like and powerful. They have the ability to make meaning by combining practical, ontological, systemic and spiritual practices.

Once an action logic has been assimilated it remains a part of the person's meaning-making capability, even as later and more integrated logics are adopted (just as when a child learns to run it doesn't cease to be able to walk). People may be in transition from one action logic to another or rooted firmly in one central logic. In stressful times adults often revert to behaviour associated with earlier action logics because of unconscious patterns. People may choose to act from earlier action logics if the situation demands it. In contrast, behaviours associated with action logics beyond a person's current logic cannot be reliably drawn on.

"I'm sorry, I don't understand what you're talking about when you criticize me."

In general, every bit of information or topic that can be considered, is viewed and acted upon differently by people at different stages. For example, here is how someone's understanding and response to the concept of 'feedback' changes with increasing development (Table 6.1):

Magician	View feedback (loops) as a natural part of living systems; essential for learning and change; and take it with a grain of salt.
Strategist	Invite feedback for self-actualization; conflict seen as inevitable aspect of viable and multiple relationships.
Individualist	Welcome feedback as necessary for self-knowledge and to uncover hidden aspects of their own behaviour.
Achiever	Accept feedback especially if it helps them to achieve their goals and to improve.
Expert	Take it personally; defend own position; dismiss feedback from those who are not seen as experts in the same field (general manager).
Diplomat	Receive feedback as dissaproval, or as reminder of norms.
Opportunist	React to feedback as an attack or threat.

Table 6.1

It is important to understand that this framework is not a guide to increased happiness (or even wealth). Each action logic has its own merits and difficulties, beauties and shadows. There is no evidence that later stages bring more joy or greater satisfaction from life, only that the nature of what delights and what causes suffering changes. However, the framework does give some very reliable pointers as to the qualities and types of leadership capability an individual may have.

If you are interested to see where you stand you can take an assessment at https://leadershipcircle.com/assessment-tools/, though please note that these tools are not for free.

Hard skills and soft skills

I frequently get asked what exactly the difference is between hard skills and soft skills.

Hard skills are teachable abilities or skills that are easy to quantify. Examples of hard skills include proficiency in a foreign language, a degree or certificate, typing speed, machine operation, computer programming, etc.

Soft skills, on the other hand, are subjective skills that are much harder to quantify. Also known as 'people skills' or 'interpersonal skills,' soft skills concern the way you relate to and interact with other people, to the way you behave. Obviously, the 'core competencies' as described and detailed in this book are soft skills, and, in most cases, your 'professional competencies' are hard skills (even though, for example for press officers, communicating is a hard skill too).

"People skills? What's wrong with my #@&!*#! people skills?"

Hard skills are skills where *the rules stay the same* regardless of which organisation, circumstance or people you work with. In contrast, soft skills are skills where *the rules change* depending on the organisational culture, the circumstances and the people you work with. For example, computer programming is a hard skill. The rules for how you can be good at creating a computer program are the same regardless of where you work (provided you know the company's internal standards). Communication skills are soft skills. The rules for how to be effective at communicating change and depend on your audience and on the content you are communicating.

Hard skills can be learned at school, from books, or the internet. There are usually designated levels of proficiency and a direct path to how to excel with each hard skill. For example, accounting is a hard skill. You can take basic accounting and advanced accounting courses. You can then work to get experience and take an exam and be certified as a professional accountant, etc. In contrast, there is no simple path to learn soft skills. Most soft skills have to be learned on the job, by trial and error. There are many books and guides on soft skills (including this one), but they only help to a certain extent, because there aren't any easy step-by-step instructions on how to master a soft skill.

EU careers can roughly be classified into 3 categories:

- Careers that need many hard skills and relatively few soft skills (example: certain AST and AD 'specialists'). This is where you see brilliant people who may not easily work well with others. In the EU institutions however, a minimum level of soft skills is required for all. That is why, even for specialists, all candidates are assessed on their soft skills in the EPSO Assessment Centre.

- Careers that need both hard and soft skills (example: AST and AD 'generalists'). They need to know the rules and procedures of the EU very well, but dealing with their colleagues, the public, and the politicians also requires excellent soft skills.

- Careers that need mostly soft skills and relatively few hard skills (example: senior EU officials and politicians). They don't really need to know that much about the technicalities, just a little more than the public, or the press; they are more dependent on their ability to read public opinion, communicate their messages, persuasion skills, and negotiation skills.

For the EU and for the EU staff alike, life-long learning is definitely a must. The world is changing at a growing pace, so new topics arise and new departments are added to the Commissioners' portfolios all the time. Globalisation and technology shifts only add to this equation.

How we learn

'The genius of our brain's construction is not that it contains a lot of hardwiring, but that it doesn't' – Nicholas Carr

The basic building block of our brain is the neuron or nerve cell. A neuron is a cell that processes and transmits information by electro-chemical signalling. These signals between neurons occur via synapses, specialised connections with other cells. Neurons can connect to each other to form neural networks (Figure 6.2).

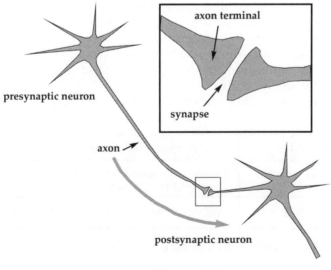

Figure 6.2

It is widely accepted that the synapse plays a role in the construction of memory. The strength of two connected neural pathways is thought to result in the storage of information, resulting in memory. There is an interesting video on Youtube[6] that explains in a very lively fashion the way in which this works.

The average human brain has about 100 billion neurons. Each neuron may be connected to up to 10,000 other neurons, passing signals to each other via as many as 1,000 trillion synaptic connections, equivalent by some estimates to a computer with a 1 trillion bit per second processor. Estimates of the human brain's memory capacity vary wildly from 1 to 1,000 terabytes.

Unlike other cells, neurons never divide, and neither do they die off to be replaced by new ones. By the same token, they usually cannot be replaced after being lost, although there are a few exceptions.

At the most basic level, we remember because the connections between our brain's neurons change; each experience primes the brain for the next experience. Memory also represents a change in who we are because it is predictive of who we will become. What we remember from the past has a lot to do with what we can learn in the future. Our behaviour, our habits, our ideologies, our hopes and fears are all influenced by what we remember of our past.

An understanding of memory is an understanding of the role of experience in shaping our lives, a critical tool for effective learning and development.

Scientists divide memory into categories based on how long the memory lasts: the shortest memories lasting only a few milliseconds are called immediate memories, memories lasting about a minute are called working memories, and memories lasting anywhere from an hour to many years are called long-term memories.

Another way to categorise memory is to divide memories about what something is from those about how something is done. Skills like walking, swimming, or riding a bicycle are called non-declarative memories because we perform those activities with no conscious recollection of how we learned the skills. Declarative memories, on the other hand, are memories of facts and events that we can consciously recall and describe verbally.

The end result is that we are good at remembering complex lumps of information while we are not so good at remembering large amounts of simple items of information; it is a lot easier for a person to remember a photograph in great detail than it is to remember a list of telephone numbers. Mnemonic strategies, contextual learning, repetitive rehearsal, and emotional arousal are all good ways to ensure that we remember the things that really matter.

Table 6.2 summarises some other recent brain research findings and their implications for learning.

Recent Brain Research Finding	Implications for Learning
Frequency and recency of neuron synapses increase memory	Increase frequency through practice and maintain fluency through use
Emotions strengthen memory	Appeal to and engage emotions while learning

Table 6.2 – continued on the next page

Table 6.2 – continued on the next page

---

6   https://www.youtube.com/watch?v=BEwg8TeipfQ

Recent Brain Research Finding – *cont...*	Implications for Learning – *cont...*
Learning causes changes to the physical structure of the brain	Engaging in learning increases our ability to learn throughout our lives
Memories are stored in multiple parts of the brain	Engage all senses when learning
Our brains are programmed to focus on new and unusual inputs	Learning should tap into the brain's natural curiosity and intrinsic motivation

Table 6.2 - continued

Learning styles

Learning and development is about remembering things, and how to do them. It is believed that on average we actually remember around:

- 10% of what we read

- 20% of what we hear

- 30% of what we see

- 50% of what we see and hear

- 70% of what is discussed with others

- 80% of what is experienced personally

- 95% of what we teach to someone else

These are only averages, because each person prefers different techniques and ways of learning.

Learning styles group common ways that people learn. Everyone has a mix of learning styles. Some people may find that they have a dominant style of learning, with far less use of the other styles. Others may find that they use different styles in different circumstances. There is no right mix. Nor are your styles fixed. You can develop ability in less dominant styles, as well as further develop styles that you already use well.

Generally speaking there are seven learning styles:

- *Visual* (spatial) – you prefer using pictures, images, and spatial understanding.

- *Aural* (auditory-musical) – you prefer using sound and music.

- *Verbal* (linguistic) – you prefer using words, both in speech and writing.

- *Physical* (kinaesthetic) – you prefer using your body, hands and sense of touch.

- *Logical* (mathematical) – you prefer using logic, reasoning and systems.

- *Social* (interpersonal) – you prefer to learn in groups or with other people.

- *Solitary* (intrapersonal) – you prefer to work alone and use self-study.

By recognising and understanding your own learning styles, you can use techniques better suited to you. This improves the speed and quality of your learning.

A learning secret: don't take notes with a laptop[7]

New research by Pam Mueller and Daniel Oppenheimer demonstrates that students who write out their notes on paper actually learn more.

Across three experiments, Mueller and Oppenheimer had students take notes in a classroom setting and then tested students on their memory for factual detail, their conceptual understanding of the material, and their ability to synthesise and generalise the information. Half of the students were instructed to take notes with a laptop, and the other half were instructed to write the notes out by hand. As in other studies, students who used laptops took more notes. In each study, however, those who wrote out their notes by hand had a stronger conceptual understanding and were more successful in applying and integrating the material than those who used took notes with their laptops.

What drives this paradoxical finding? Mueller and Oppenheimer postulate that taking notes by hand requires different types of cognitive processing than taking notes on a laptop, and these different processes have consequences for learning. Writing by hand is slower and more cumbersome than typing, and students cannot possibly write down every word in a lecture. Instead, they listen, digest, and summarise so that they can succinctly capture the essence of the information. Thus, taking notes by hand forces the brain to engage in some heavy 'mental lifting,' and these efforts foster comprehension and retention. By contrast, when typing students can easily produce a written record of the lecture without processing its meaning, as faster typing speeds allow students to transcribe a lecture word for word without devoting much thought to the content. ...

Technology offers innovative tools that are shaping educational experiences for students, often in positive and dynamic ways. The research by Mueller and Oppenheimer serves as a reminder, however, that even when technology allows us to do more in less time, it does not always foster learning. Learning involves more than the receipt and the regurgitation of information. If we want students to synthesize material, draw inferences, see new connections, evaluate evidence, and apply concepts in novel situations, we need to encourage the deep, effortful cognitive processes that underlie these abilities. When it comes to taking notes, students need fewer gigs, more brain power.

Formal and informal learning

Formal learning is planned learning that derives from activities within a structured learning setting. Formal learning is enrolling on a programme of study, attending lectures, preparing coursework, and engaging in seminar/tutorial discussions.

Informal learning is learning that originates from activities external to a structured learning context, or unstructured learning within a structured learning environment.

Benefits of formal learning:

- Large numbers of employees will learn the same information and/or processes at the same time.

- If properly designed, the course content should be accurate and up to date.

- Employees learning through formal training programs come up to speed faster once they start their jobs.

---

7   http://www.scientificamerican.com/article/a-learning-secret-don-t-take-notes-with-a-laptop/

- Properly designed formal training programs can include a variety of methods to appeal to all learning styles.

Benefits of informal learning:

- Creating informal learning situations can be less costly and more time efficient given technology and the social media currently available.

- Learning informally can be more personal and less intimidating for some people.

- Subject-matter experts may be more willing to share their knowledge with others this way.

- Since learning this way happens more naturally during the workday, employees may be more enthusiastic about learning new things.

The four stages of competence

The earliest origins of the 'four stages of competence' theory are uncertain and could be very old indeed. Noel Burch, a former employee of the US organisation Gordon Training International, formalised the theory in the 1970s[8]. Burch suggested that individuals are initially unaware of how little they know, or unconscious of their incompetence. As they recognise their incompetence, they consciously acquire a skill, and then consciously use it. Eventually, the skill can be operated without it being consciously thought through: the individual is said to have acquired *unconscious competence* (Figure 6.3).

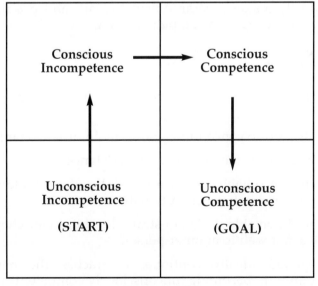

Figure 6.3

8   http://www.gordontraining.com/

Unconscious incompetence

- The person is not aware of the existence or relevance of the skill area.
- The person is not aware that they have a particular deficiency in the area concerned.
- The person might deny the relevance or usefulness of the new skill.
- The person must become conscious of their incompetence before development of the new skill or learning can begin.
- The aim of the trainer or teacher is to move the person into the 'conscious competence' stage, by demonstrating the skill or ability and the benefit that it will bring to the person's effectiveness.

Conscious incompetence

- The person becomes aware of the existence and relevance of the skill.
- The person is therefore also aware of their deficiency in this area, ideally by attempting or trying to use the skill.
- The person realises that by improving their skill or ability in this area their effectiveness will improve.
- Ideally the person has a measure of the extent of their deficiency in the relevant skill, and a measure of what level of skill is required for their own competence.
- The person ideally makes a commitment to learn and practise the new skill, and to move to the 'conscious competence' stage.

Conscious competence

- The person achieves 'conscious competence' in a skill when they can perform it reliably.
- The person will need to concentrate and think in order to perform the skill.
- The person can perform the skill without assistance.
- The person will not reliably perform the skill unless thinking about it – the skill is not yet 'second nature' or 'automatic'.
- The person should be able to demonstrate the skill to another, but is unlikely to be able to teach it well to another person.
- The person should ideally continue to practise the new skill, and if appropriate commit to becoming 'unconsciously competent' at the new skill.
- Deliberate practice is the single most effective way to move to the next stage.

Unconscious competence

- The skill becomes so practised that it enters the unconscious parts of the brain – it becomes 'second nature'.

- Common examples are driving, sports activities, typing, manual tasks, listening and communicating.

- It becomes possible for certain skills to be performed while doing something else, for example, knitting while reading a book.

- The person might now be able to teach others in the skill concerned, although after some time of being unconsciously competent the person might actually have difficulty in explaining exactly how they do it – the skill has become largely instinctual.

- This arguably gives rise to the need for long-standing unconscious competence to be checked periodically against new standards.

Our body is constantly creating new neural stem cells, or embryonic brain cells, by a process known as neurogenesis. Here is the catch: if you don't learn something so new that you fire those new neurons, they get digested. And it's only in the phases of conscious incompetence and, a bit, of conscious competence, that you are actually learning something new.

So the advice to stick to what you are good at is terrible from the perspective of putting your hard-won new baby neurons to work. Better advice would be to start learning something new, and stick with it as long as it feels uncomfortable and you know that you haven't mastered it. As soon as you are good at it, start something new.

Several elements, including helping someone 'know what they don't know' or to recognise a blind spot, can be compared to some elements of a Johari Window (see Chapter 2), although Johari deals with self-awareness, while the four stages of competence deals with learning stages. Also, the GROW model that is used in this book relies for an important part on the same ideas.

Learning and development in the EU

'Live as if you were to die tomorrow. Learn as if you were to live forever.' – Mahatma Gandhi

The EU institutions depend on the expertise of their staff to achieve their goals, as EU staff are mostly knowledge workers. For staff with short-term contracts, the priority is to learn rapidly what they need to be effective. However, the biggest element of the EU staff is the permanent officials, who stay with the institutions for an average of 27 years or more. The EU needs to respond to constant change in the technological, economic, and political environment, and the resulting policy priorities of the EU. Staff cannot do the same job, in the same way, throughout their careers. With recruitment reduced, the institutions' future development depends very considerably on the learning capacity of current staff.

Learning and development is not an end in itself, it is only a means to an end. The goal of the (Commission's) strategy is therefore to ensure that staff:

- Have the knowledge and the skills they need to do their job effectively.

- Have the flexibility to adapt, to learn and to lead change.

- Work effectively together, in networks across the institutions, and with partners outside.

To enable staff to develop, it is necessary for them to have access to appropriate training and opportunities to move jobs. The EU institutions offer a wide range of opportunities for staff to develop. To give you an idea of the extent, Figure 6.4 shows the number of 'participant days' and 'trainer days' delivered in 2014 (Commission only).

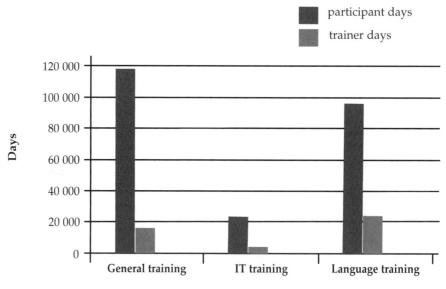

Source: Human Resources and Security DG

Figure 6.4: Training in the European Commission

The Human Resources and Security DG (HR.B.3)[9] organises language training centrally for all Commission staff. It also aims to organise general training (e.g. on HR policies, personal development and financial procedures) where this is the most cost-effective or appropriate approach.

In addition, DGs organise training locally, mainly for their own staff. In each DG or department, the 'Coordinateur en matière de Formation' (COFO), or training coordinator, is responsible for training at the DG level for the Commission. The other institutions also have their own learning and development policy (usually in coordination at interinstitutional level).

9   http://myintracomm.ec.europa.eu/hr_admin/fr/training/Pages/index.aspx

The central IT training courses are provided by DIGIT at the Digit Training Services (DTS)[10]. A team of informatics training managers organises the courses and manages the enrolments.

The Learning Centre[11] is an assisted self-tuition centre installed in a welcoming, quiet environment conducive to study. The range of different learning aids enables everyone to find the most suitable formula.

Syslog Formation[12] covers all needs concerning the treatment of information for the Commission's management of training. It facilitates the exchange of information between the different user groups on central and local level. The purpose of Syslog is to plan and organise training activities for the whole of the Commission staff, as well as staff of other institutions and agencies.

The **European School of Administration (EUSA)** is responsible for training in induction, certification and management. It was founded in 2005 with the aim of improving and extending the range of learning opportunities available to staff of the European civil service. By bringing staff of different institutions together the School also contributes to the spread of common values, promotes better inter-institutional understanding and cooperation, and facilitates the creation of valuable networks at various levels in the institutions. The School's training offer, which concentrates on skills and behaviours that are needed across the European civil service, is complemented by the individual institutions' own programs to meet their specific needs.

In the Commission, *internal mobility* is considered to be an important tool for staff to diversify their experience and for the acquisition of competencies within the organisation. Internal mobility is facilitated by the sheer number of policy domains and the variety of competences and tasks exercised by the Commission. It is generally accepted that officials should stay at least two years in a given post to ensure a degree of stability and to give a return on learning experience. Furthermore, a rule of five to seven years as a maximum in post applies for sensitive positions. Limiting the number of years a person can occupy a sensitive post is one way of reducing the risk that the person concerned may benefit from misuse of their discretionary powers.

In the other institutions, bodies and agencies, internal mobility possibilities are more limited because of the smaller size of these organisations, and (in agencies) the even more specialised profiles of many of the people working there. However, it is sometimes possible to move to another institution, even though the Staff Regulations explicitly favour internal mobility (Article 29).

The institutions can also support the investment staff make in learning in their own time. Where a personal initiative is relevant to the current job, or the future career, but is not essential and/or would not be cost-effective to be fully financed by the employer, staff can apply for partial reimbursement of costs. In addition, special leave can be awarded.

In its 2012 Special Report N° 10[13], the Court of Auditors made some recommendations on how to improve and further optimise this offering. As a consequence certain things will change over the coming years. For a more detailed and up-to-date overview of these possibilities you can always consult the Annual Activity Reports from DG HR and Security, and EPSO (which covers EUSA as well).

---

10   http://myintracomm.ec.europa.eu/serv/en/digit/training_help_and_support/Pages/index.aspx
11   http://myintracomm.ec.europa.eu/hr_admin/en/training/learning_center/Pages/index.aspx
12   http://www.cc.cec/di/syslog_formation/catalogue/catalogue.cfm
13   The Effectiveness of Staff Development in the European Commission (2012), European Court of Auditors.

Seeing the bigger picture

Motivation is an important factor in learning and development. From Chapter 2 we learned that *purpose* is a necessary condition for motivation. Purpose is not just about earning money, it is not just about having a nine-to-five job; it means having a higher goal, or a more important objective in what you do.

Onge good way to build motivation and purpose is by learning and understanding all you can about the EU and its institutions.

You can start by reading about the EU on the web. Some examples worthwhile exploring:

- http://europa.eu/legislation_summaries/institutional_affairs/treaties/
- http://www.europarl.europa.eu/aboutparliament/en/007c895f4c/Powers-and-procedures.html
- http://www.europedia.moussis.eu/books/Book_2/2/4/3/?all=1
- http://europa.eu/eu-law/

Of course, there are also some very good books that have been written about this topic. I will limit myself to a few titles from my own publisher, John Harper[14], who specialises in EU affairs:

- 'The European Commission – A Practical Guide'[15] by Manuel Szapiro
- 'The European Parliament'[16] by Richard Corbett et al.
- 'How the EU Institutions Work and How to Work with the EU Institutions'[17] by Alan Hardacre and Erik Akse

Recent information on the institutions can also be found in their Annual Activity Reports, and on their intranet and public websites.

Furthermore, it is important that you keep informed about the EU 'hot topics'. For this, of course, the specialised press is the place to be:

- http://europa.eu/rapid
- http://euobserver.com
- http://www.euractiv.com
- http://www.presseurop.eu
- http://www.politico.eu

---

14   https://www.johnharperpublishing.co.uk/books/
15   ISBN: 978-0-9571501-3-3
16   8th edition 2011, 9th edition June 2016.
17   2nd edition, 2015. ISBN: 978-0-9929748-8-6

The perfect Commission official's toolkit

The European Union is first and foremost a legal construction. This very much influences the Commission staff, who anchor their work to a framework of rules. Commission staff activities are framed by some basic rules/guidelines which can be found in a set of basic documents (always at hand's reach of most staff):

- The treaties – these define for staff the limits of the competences attributed to the EU and the procedures to be followed (material and procedure competences).
- The Commission's rules of procedure, implementing rules and manual of procedures that give a core set of rules for organising the internal decision-making and relations with external actors.
- The Code of Good Administrative Behaviour
- The Internal Control Standards.

At DG level we also have:

- Programming and reporting documents of the DG Commission work programme, EU budget, DG annual management plan, annual report, synthesis report.
- The DG's organisational chart.
- List of contacts (name, function, phone numbers) from the Directorate/unit.
- For staff dealing with the budget: the Financial Regulation (general and Commission) and its implementing rules.
- For staff dealing with or interested in human resources issues: the Staff Regulation and implementing rules.
- For staff dealing with policy-making
  - The basic rules relevant to the field of activity of each official including legislative acts, delegated acts and implementing measures.
  - Any other document (consultative documents including white papers, green papers, communications, etc).

(Source: 'The European Commission: A Practical Guide', by Manuel Szapiro)

Learning another language

Article 45, point 2 of the Staff Regulation stipulates:

'Officials shall be required to demonstrate before their first promotion after recruitment the ability to work in a third language among those referred to in Article 314 of the EC Treaty. The institutions shall adopt common rules by agreement between them for implementing this paragraph. These rules shall require access to training for officials in a third language and lay down the detailed arrangements for the assessment of officials' ability to work in a third language, in accordance with Article 7(2)(d) of Annex III.'

This effectively means that mastering three languages is considered to be 'normal' for an EU official, as it is a requirement for the first promotion. Upon recruitment, proficiency in only two languages (mother tongue plus one of the three 'working languages' – English, French, or German) is required. The EU institutions also provide a lot of facilities (classroom training, online language courses ...) to make this happen. I have known former EU colleagues – not translators or linguists – who mastered up to six different languages, so it is possible!

Mastering multiple languages is not only about hard skills; it enables a better understanding of the different cultural backgrounds of your colleagues, and hence develops your interpersonal – or soft – skills.

As a Dutch (Flemish[18] actually) native speaker, I consider it to be particularly important to point out that Brussels is not only the capital of Europe, but also of Belgium and the Flemish Community alike. Both French and Dutch are commonly spoken languages in Brussels. So, in my opinion it makes sense that an EU official, who spends the better part of his or her life in Brussels, acquires at least the basic notions of both these languages, so that they can step outside of the 'European bubble'. This can only benefit the image of the EU and its institutions.

The **Common European Framework** divides language learners into three broad divisions that can be divided into six levels; for each level, it describes what a learner is supposed to be able to do in reading, listening, speaking and writing. These levels are described in Table 6.3.

Basic User	A1	• Can understand and use familiar everyday expressions and very basic phrases aimed at the satisfaction of needs of a concrete type • Can introduce him/herself and others and can ask and answer questions about personal details such as where he/she lives, people he/she knows and things he/she has. • Can interact in a simple way provided the other person talks slowly and clearly and is prepared to help.
	A2	• Can understand sentences and frequently used expressions related to areas of most immediate relevance (e.g. very basic personal and family information, shopping, local geography, employment). • Can communicate in simple and routine tasks requiring a simple and direct exchange of information on familiar and routine matters. • Can describe in simple terms aspects of his/her background, immediate environment and matters in areas of immediate need.
Independent User	B1	• Can understand the main points of clear standard input on familiar matters regularly encountered in work, school, leisure, etc. • Can deal with most situations likely to arise while travelling in an area where the language is spoken. • Can produce simple connected text on topics that are familiar or of personal interest. • Can describe experiences and events, dreams, hopes and ambitions and briefly give reasons and explanations for opinions and plans.
	B2	• Can understand the main ideas of complex text on both concrete and abstract topics, including technical discussions in his/her field of specialization. • Can interact with a degree of fluency and spontaneity that makes regular interaction with native speakers quite possible without strain for either party. • Can produce clear, detailed text on a wide range of subjects and explain a viewpoint on a topical issue giving the advantages and disadvantages of various options.

Table 6.3 – continued on the next page

Table 6.3 – continued on the next page

18   https://www.smartling.com/2014/08/03/top-differences-flemish-dutch/

Proficient user	C1	• Can understand a wide range of demanding, longer texts, and recognise implicit meaning. • Can express ideas fluently and spontaneously without much obvious searching for expressions. • Can use language flexibly and effectively for social, academic and professional purposes. • Can produce clear, well-structured, detailed text on complex subjects, showing controlled use of organisational patterns, connectors and cohesive devices.
	C2	• Can understand with ease virtually everything heard or read. • Can summarise information from different spoken and written sources, reconstructing arguments and accounts in a coherent presentation. • Can express him/herself spontaneously, very fluently and precisely, differentiating finer shades of meaning even in the most complex situations.

Table 6.3 – continued

Mnemonic strategies

A mnemonic (pronounced: ne-mo-nic) is any learning technique that aids information retention in the human memory. Mnemonics aim to translate information into a form that the brain can retain better than its original form. Typically the initial letter of each word gives us the mnemonic.

In Chapter 1 we discussed the 'SMART' mnemonic which stands for Specific, Measurable, Achievable, Realistic, and Time-bound. Likewise in Chapter 3 we had the IDEAL mnemonic for analysing and problem-solving and in Chapter 4 the STAR mnemonic for Situation, Task, Action, Results.

There are many types of mnemonics, and I am sure you are sometimes use them as well. Just be aware that this is a simple, but powerful technique that can improve your learning skills.

Deliberate practice

'What we hope ever to do with ease, we must learn first to do with diligence.' – Samuel Johnson

Repetition is perhaps the most intuitive principle of learning, traceable to ancient Egyptian and Chinese education. In ancient Greece, Aristotle commented on the role of repetition in learning by saying 'it is frequent repetition that produces a natural tendency' and 'the more frequently two things are experienced together, the more likely it will be that the experience or recall of one will stimulate the recall of the other'[19].

Repetition is one of the most basic learning techniques. Children use it to learn to speak. Athletes use it to perfect their athletic skills. Repetition is sometimes seen as boring, or looked down upon as an attempt to simply memorise rather than understand. However, repetition is essential, because it effectively creates the neural pathways in our brain needed for remembering and understanding new information and skills.

19 'Aristotle' (2004) by Sir David Ross.

Deliberate practice is not the same as mere repetition, or 'drill and kill'. Simply repeating a task will not by itself improve performance. Deliberate practice involves awareness, attention, rehearsal and repetition, and leads to new knowledge or skills that can later be developed into more complex knowledge and skills. Although other factors such as intelligence and motivation affect performance, practice is necessary, but not sufficient, for acquiring expertise.

Research suggests that several conditions must be in place in order for practice activities to be most effective:

- Building on existing knowledge

- Repeated opportunities

- Encouragement

- Timely and descriptive feedback

Trial and error

'Mistakes are a fact of life. It is the response to the error that counts.' – Nikki Giovanni[20]

Trial and error is a method of learning in which various responses are tentatively tried, and some discarded, until a valid solution is reached.

Edward Thorndike[21] was the chief exponent of the theory of *connectionism* or trial and error. He conducted Stimulus – Response (S-R) theory experiments with the help of animals. Thorndike was the first to study the subject of learning systematically using standardized procedures and tools. All learning, according to Thorndike, is the construction of bonds or connections between Stimulus and Response.

If circumstances permit, learning from our mistakes is a very powerful way of learning. That is why it is advised to managers and leaders to create a 'safe' environment for those who work under them. A safe environment is an environment where

---

20   American poet and activist (1943).

21   Edward Lee 'Ted' Thorndike (1874–1949) was an American psychologist.

people are not afraid to make mistakes, where they can learn and develop, and are supported rather than punished for whatever goes wrong.

Trial and error in the EU

It is rather atypical for the EU institutions to accept trial and error as a learning model. Very few, if any, of them have 'Research and Development' or 'Innovation' departments, which goes hand in hand with the concept. However, the Joint Research Centre (JRC) is the European Commission's in-house science service. It provides independent scientific and technical advice to the European Commission to support a wide range of EU policies. It has seven scientific institutes, located at six different sites in Belgium, Germany, Italy, the Netherlands, and Spain. The Directorate-General of the JRC is located in Brussels.

Mind mapping

A *mind map*, as in Figure 6.5, is a powerful graphic method that provides a universal key to unlock the potential of your brain. It exploits the full range of cortical skills – word, image, number, logic, rhythm, colour and spatial awareness – in a single, powerful manner. In so doing, it gives you the freedom to explore all the areas of your mind.

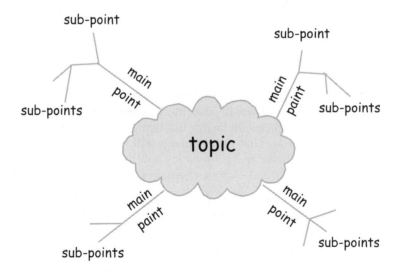

Figure 6.5

A mind map is basically a diagram that connects information around a central topic. At the centre is your main topic, and the branches are related points. Greater levels of detail branch out to sub-points from there, and branches can be linked together. Mind maps link and group concepts together through natural associations. This helps to generate more ideas and find deeper meaning in your subject, and also prompts you to fill in more or find what you are missing. Mind mapping is a very intuitive way to organise your thoughts, because mind maps imitate the way your brain thinks.

Mind maps can be used for pretty much any thinking or learning task, from studying a subject (such as a new language) to planning your career or even building better habits. They are great for teams to use as well, for brainstorming and interactive presentations.

70-20-10 model

The 70-20-10 model is a learning and development model, usually credited to Morgan McCall and his colleagues, Lombardo and Eichinger, working at the Centre for Creative Leadership[22] (CCL). In their 1996 book, 'The Career Architect Development Planner'[23], they published the results of a survey asking nearly 200 executives to self-report on how they believed they learned. These results were that lessons learned by successful and effective managers are roughly:

- 70% from tough jobs

- 20% from people (mostly the boss)

- 10% from courses and reading

Lombardo and Eichinger expressed their rationale behind the 70-20-10 Model like this:

> 'Development generally begins with a realization of current or future need and the motivation to do something about it. This might come from feedback, a mistake, watching other people's reactions, failing or not being up to a task – in other words, from experience. The odds are that development will be about 70% from on-the-job experiences – working on tasks and problems; about 20% from feedback and working around good and bad examples of the need; and 10% from courses and reading.'

This model is used in the Commission's learning and development strategy, which is built around the ideas of 'lifelong learning' and 'lifewide learning'. Although the exact percentages vary from person to person, and job to job, this model points to the importance of on-the-job learning, alongside formal training.

22   www.ccl.org
23   'The Career Architect Development Planner' (2000) by Michael Lombardo and Robert Eichinger.

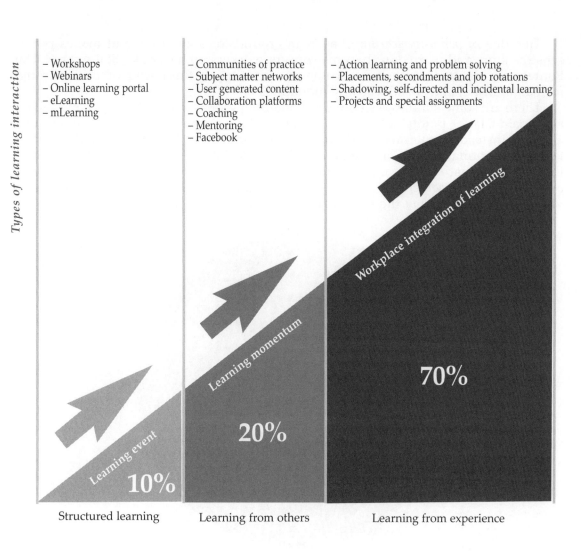

Figure 6.6: the 70-20-10 model

Pervasive learning

Daniel Pink's[24] book 'A Whole New Mind'[25] first describes how our society has gone from agricultural to industrial to the information age. But then, he describes how we have moved on to a new age where the dominant value for most organisations is created by high-end knowledge workers – concept workers. For concept workers, work and learning merge.

24 Daniel Pink (1964) is the author of books about business, work, and management and also former chief speechwriter for vice-president Al Gore.
25 'A Whole New Mind: Why Right-Brainers will rule the Future' (2006) by Daniel Pink.

The idea of *pervasive learning* has been around for some time and makes perfect sense as more and more of us become concept workers. In his book, 'Flat Army'[26] Dan Pontefract[27] defines pervasive learning as 'learning at the speed of need through formal, informal and social learning modalities'.

There are some similarities between Pontefract's ideas and the 70-20-10 model, but as Donald Clark[28] points out, the 70-20-10 model may not be universally applicable to all staff. Instead, Pontefract's **3-33 model** often fits better. In the 3-33 model, 33% of learning is formal, 33% is informal, and 33% is social (see Figure 6.7). What is most interesting is that the research behind this model revealed that when learners were asked to give the percentages for how they thought they learned, the numbers were very different from what the researchers actually found to be the case.

Figure 6.7: the 3-33 model

One of the other major flaws of the 70-20-10 model is that it places reading in formal learning. This error is probably due to the limited survey amongst managers who viewed writers as part of the elite, while learning and development was seen as less important.

---

26   'Flat Army: Creating a Connected and Engaged Organisation' by Dan Pontefract.

27   Dan Pontefract on his website describes himself as author, speaker and chief envisioner.

28   http://www.nwlink.com/~donclark/hrd/media/70-20-10.html

Teaching others

'While we teach, we learn' – Seneca[29]

Most people are familiar with learning through books, or in classes, but many overlook perhaps the most comprehensive learning experience of all – *teaching*. The best test of whether or not you really understand a concept is trying to teach it to someone else. Teaching others calls for thorough understanding of the concept yourself.

Students teaching other students work harder to understand the material, recall it more accurately and apply it more effectively. Scientists have called this 'the protégé effect.' Student teachers score higher on tests than pupils who are learning only for their own sake. The benefits of this practice were indicated by a pair of articles published in 2007 in the journals Science[30] and Intelligence[31]. These studies concluded that first-born children are more intelligent than their later-born brothers and sisters and suggested that their higher IQs result from the time they spend instructing their younger siblings.

Teaching also forces you to communicate your thoughts clearly and precisely. As our society becomes ever more interconnected and interdependent, cooperation becomes more and more important. This cooperation requires communication. However, being heard is not enough; you must also be understood. Your ideas will never be more effective than your ability to make others comprehend them. Teaching helps you develop the extremely important skill of describing your ideas well enough for others to use them.

Teaching others is not limited to a simple transfer of information between individuals, be it in a formal or an informal setting. Teaching others is also coaching and mentoring them for the purpose of learning and development (Figure 6.8).

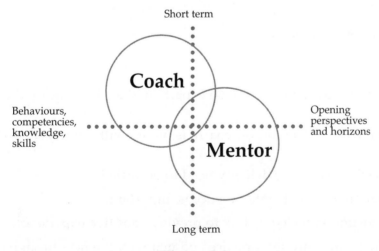

Figure 6.8

29   Seneca (c. 4 BC–AD 65) was a Roman philosopher, statesman, and dramatist.
30   http://www.sciencemag.org/content/316/5832/1717.abstract
31   http://www.sciencedirect.com/science/article/pii/S0160289607000062

For sure, my activities, as a coach and author of books about the topic of personal development, are part of my own learning and development strategy.

Developing your learning and development skills

Learning and development bring about changes in the way we act, think and/or feel about ourselves, about other people, and about the world around us. These changes may be permanent or temporary depending on our own perceptions of the importance and relevance of the knowledge gained.

Both learning and development are important, but they occur at different moments and rates. Learning happens via many channels – school, professional training, self-directed and life-long learning, practice, or simply through exposure to life. Development refers to how we learn to see the world through new eyes, how we change our interpretations of experience, and how we transform our views of reality. It describes our increasing awareness, and therefore what we can integrate and influence.

Please refer to Chapter 1 (methodology) and Annex 4 for further development of this competency, have another read of the current chapter to find out about your options, and remember: YOU are responsible for your own development, not your manager, your colleagues, or your mentor.

The online toolkit that comes for free with this book can be used to follow-up on your development in this area. The toolkit can be found at:

https://www.johnharperpublishing.co.uk/the-ultimate-eu-career-development-toolkit/

Key points to remember

- When possible learners should take part in the planning of their learning activities.
- Interaction with a mentor or coach is vital, with timely and descriptive feedback.
- Learning activities and/or delivery need to be varied.
- Self-evaluation and deliberate practice is important.
- Build on existing knowledge, link to previous positive experience.
- Increase frequency through practice and maintain fluency through use.
- Appeal to and engage emotions while learning.
- Engaging in learning increases our ability to learn throughout our lives.
- Engage all senses when learning.

- Learning should tap into the brain's natural curiosity and intrinsic motivation.
- Enhance your motivation by seeing the bigger picture.
- For EU staff, mastery of multiple languages is a must.
- Teaching others is the most comprehensive learning experience.

Your notes

7. Prioritising and organising

Competency definition: 'Prioritises the most important tasks, works flexibly and organises own workload efficiently.'

Prioritising and organising is more commonly known as *time management*, but what is time management? Time itself can't be managed. It is constant and it always goes forward, never backwards. Everyone has the same amount of time in an hour, a day, and a week. Therefore, time management does not mean that you are trying to manipulate time, but that you are trying to make the best use of your time.

Time management is the act of taking conscious control (*awareness and responsibility*, remember) over the amount of time you spend on specific activities. Time management is about goal setting, effective scheduling of your time, prioritising and choosing what to do and what not to do, delegating tasks, analysing and reviewing your spent time, organising your workspace, keeping your concentration and focus on your work, and motivating yourself.

You exercise time management (your prioritising and organising comnpetency) to increase your effectiveness, efficiency, and ultimately your productivity. You practise skills and use tools and techniques to aid you when accomplishing tasks, projects or are working towards goals and deadlines.

---

1   Peter Drucker (1909–2005) was an Austrian-born American management consultant, educator and author.

The most significant problem in today's working world is not competition, lack of skilled employees or an uncertain economy, but an *attention deficit*. Put simply, with all the noise from constant meetings, and deluges of voice mail and email, it's hard to get anyone's undivided attention anymore. In their book 'The Attention Economy'[1], authors Thomas Davenport and John Beck state that the organisations and individuals that succeed in the future will be those that focus their efforts on this problem, instead of on conventional approaches to time management. Attention, they say, is 'the new currency of business.'

Tasks

Ever since Adam and Eve were expelled from the Garden of Eden most of us have had to work for a living. But even though we have to work in exchange for a financial reward, there is nothing wrong with actually enjoying our work. After all, we spend a big slice of our waking hours at work, and spending that time in an enjoyable and productive way is part of what makes life worth living. Agreed, your boss, your colleagues, or the work you have to do are not always exciting, but 'feeling in control' of what you do – and how you do it – will at least give you some degree of job satisfaction and happiness.

The most elementary building block of work is a *task*. A task is an activity that needs to be accomplished within a defined period of time (or by a deadline) to reach work-related goals.

A task is an (abstract) three-dimensional object: input, output and time. The *input* is what you do; the efforts, knowledge, energy, focus or whatever other contribution you make to get the work done. The *output* is the result; it can be a message, a report, a presentation or any tangible or intangible deliverable of your work. The *time* is the difference between the moment you started working on the task and when your work was complete. It is important to be aware that these three dimensions are interrelated; they influence each other.

Figure 7.1

1   The Attention Economy: Understanding the New Currency of Business' (2002) by Thomas H. Davenport and John C. Beck.

I sometimes use the metaphor of a balloon, filled with air. This is a three-dimensional object too, right? When you squeeze the balloon (thus modifying one dimension) this will influence the other two dimensions. By analogy, when you change one 'dimension' of a task this will also have an impact on the other dimensions. Say your manager changes the (expected) output; you will then be forced to either change your input or the time it takes to complete the task. If you reduce your input then either the output will have to be less or it will take you more time to complete the task (or both).

There is another nice use of this metaphor. What happens if you squeeze a balloon too hard? It will burst. Well, the same thing happens with tasks. Say the deadline (or the time allotted) is too tight: you will never manage to complete the task. If the (expected) output is too high you will never make it in time and neither will you accomplish the task if your input is too low.

Processes

According to Professor Tom Davenport[2] a process is:
'A specific ordering of work activities across time and place, with a beginning and an end, clearly defined inputs and outputs, a structure for action.'

A simple analogy would be to look at an organisation as a wheel and the individual processes as the spokes of that wheel. Having just one or two spokes loose can make a wheel roll out of balance. The longer a wheel runs out of balance, the more damaging the effect to the wheel. When the wheel becomes so unstable that its primary function fails, you would simply replace the wheel. Obviously, an organisation cannot replace itself – but your stakeholders can, and will do so if the organisation does not perform to their needs and expectations.

The purpose of a process is to transform input into output. This transformation is done through the support of resources (people, money, infrastructure, information …) and according to – formal or informal – specifications.

A process can be broken down into several *steps* and organised in a *workflow*. Each step is performed by an actor (a person or a group of persons) with a given role in the workflow. Very often processes (also known as procedures, or operations) are implemented through an IT system.

The output of a process can be material (a product) or non-material (a service). In fact, often it is a combination of both (e.g. a paper file is the material component, while the content is the service component of a written report).

Most of the tasks we have to do are in some way part of a process: we are 'actors' with a given role, transforming input into output according to some specifications.

The nice thing about this view on matters is that it makes our life easier in terms of prioritising and organising our work. We know the input, what is expected and how much time we have to execute the task. We also have an idea of how important our tasks are. Being aware that we are part of a bigger entity is also an extrinsic motivator.

2   Tom Davenport is the President's Distinguished Professor in Management and Information Technology at Babson College.

A typical process in the EU administration

A good example of a *process* within the EU administrative realm is the implementation of revenue and expenditure as governed by the EU Financial Regulation (Regulation N° 966/2012 of the European Parliament and of the Council).

Each EU institution (or body) is responsible for implementing revenue and expenditure in accordance with the principle of sound financial management and for ensuring compliance with the requirements of legality and regularity. Each EU institution (or body) has an 'Authorising Officer by Delegation' who can sub-delegate his powers by appointing other officials to oversee different budget posts, related to their functional domain of activity. Authorising Officers by (sub)delegation (in short AO) are assisted by Initiating Agents (IA), of which they are the superiors. The Verifying Agent(s) (VA) – who are independent from the AO to ensure autonomy of judgment – assist the AO in ensuring compliance with the requirements of legality and regularity by means of 'ex-ante' and 'ex-post' verification of all the files. While the AO is responsible for the financial transactions it is the Accountant (AC) who executes them (i.e. pays invoices and receives income) and keeps track of them in the accounting system. In most EU institutions and bodies this process is supported by the ABAC system, which enforces the workflow.

The 'actors' in this process are the AO, IA, VA and AC, and they all have limited access rights and permissions on the part of the budget under their control. They perform their tasks and duties in the context of the wider process, and within the time constraints as imposed by the procedure. Each step of the process has well-known inputs and outputs and the actors' tasks come down to transforming the inputs into the outputs. The (formal) specifications are laid down in the Financial Regulation (which applies to all EU institutions and bodies) and the Internal Rules (which are specific to each organisation).

Projects

'Crash programs fail because they are based on the theory that, with nine women pregnant, you can get a baby in one month.' – Werner Von Braun

Projects have always been a part of life, ever since the first groups of humans worked together to gather, plant or hunt. Over the years, the concept of *project management* – planning and directing the activities executed by a group of people with a fixed objective and over a limited period of time – has been refined and formalised into a profession.

The Project Management Institute (PMI), a leading organisation in the development of project management principles and certification standards, defines a project as 'a temporary endeavour undertaken to create a unique product, service, or result.'

Projects and processes differ primarily in that processes are on-going and repetitive, while projects are temporary and unique.

The objectives of projects and processes are fundamentally different. The purpose of a project is to attain its objective and then terminate. Conversely, the objective of an on-going operation (a process) is to sustain the organisation. Projects are undertaken at all levels of an organisation and they can involve a single person or many thousands. Projects can involve one or many organisational units, including joint ventures and partnerships.

The best-known project management methodologies (or frameworks) are **PRINCE2** (Projects In a Controlled Environment) and **PMBOK** (Project Management Body of Knowledge). Table 7.1 lists the main differences:

PRINCE2	PMBOK
Origin: UK	Origin: US
Adoption: worldwide	Adoption: worldwide
A process based methodology	A knowledge based approach
A series of management processes defining what must be done, when and how it must be done and by whom over the life of a project	Describes core practices and a wider range of techniques that can be applied to manage a project
Prescriptive	Non-prescriptive
Defines the roles of everyone involved in a project	Focuses on the project manager's role

Table 7.1

The **PM² (PM square)** methodology that is used by the Commission is built on PMBOK, and is supported by four pillars:

- A project governance model (roles & responsibilities)
- A project lifecycle (project phases)
- A set of processes (project management activities)
- A set of project artefacts (templates and guidelines)

Gantt charts

Henry Gantt[3] developed one of the first project management tools, today known as *Gantt charts*. Gantt charts plot the activities necessary to complete a project on a timeline using a bar or a line, which begins and ends at a definite time (Figure 7.2). The Gantt chart also provides milestones, or markers, for assuring that a project is on track.

While Gantt charts have the advantage of simplicity, they can hide as much as they display. Indeed, the interrelationships between the various activities are not made explicit nor are the relationships between resources and the time to complete a task. Gantt charts can tell a manager if a program is *off* track, but they often cannot provide information about how to get it back *on* track.

---

3   Henry Gantt (1861–1919) was an American mechanical engineer and management consultant.

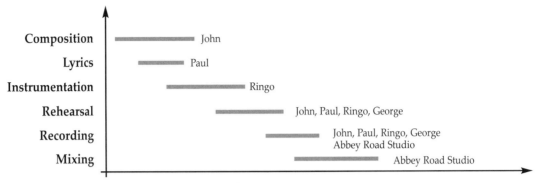

Figure 7.2

PERT/CPM

The most commonly used method for documenting the relationships between tasks and determining their relative importance to the project is the **Project Evaluation and Review Technique/Critical Path Method (PERT/CPM)**. PERT was developed in 1958 to help plan and schedule the US Navy Polaris submarine project. On the other hand, the DuPont Company and the Univac division of Remington Rand Corporation developed CPM to provide a method for controlling maintenance in the DuPont chemical plants. Later, it was noticed that these two methods shared many similarities and their approaches were combined in one method.

PERT/CPM graphs provide a general overview of a project. They consist of activities and events. Activities are operations in the project that consume resources and take time. Events occur at a point in time and represent the beginning, the end (or both) of an activity.

Table 7.2 shows the interdependencies among the various tasks shown in Figure 7.2 above.

N°	Activity	Resources	Estimate	Dependencies
1	Composition	John	5 weeks	0
2	Lyrics	Paul	3 weeks	0
3	Instrumentation	Ringo	6 weeks	1,2, 3
4	Rehearsal	John, Paul, Ringo, George	4 weeks	3
5	Recording	John, Paul, Ringo, George, Abbey Road Studios	4 weeks	4
6	Mixing	Abbey Road Studios	5 weeks	5

Table 7.2

The PERT/CPM graph looks like this (Figure 7.3).

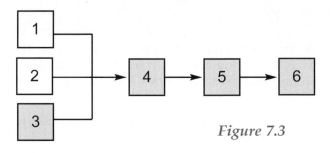

Figure 7.3

The most time-consuming path in the graph is called the critical path (this would be 3, 4, 5 and 6 in the example above). Each activity within this longest path is critical, as any delays in realising a critical activity will delay the entire project. The critical path can change during a project (as 'slippage' on a previously non-critical activity can extend the length of that path so that it becomes the longest).

Please note that the example above is extremely simplistic, for the sake of clarity. In real projects there can be hundreds – or thousands – of activities, and the diagrams are managed through a computer application, which instantly re-evaluates the critical path whenever something changes. In the EU institutions, it is mostly Microsoft Project that is used for this.

It is amongst the tasks of the project manager to constantly monitor the progress of the project and – if necessary – to reallocate resources and/or execute tasks in parallel in order to keep control of the critical path. There are some very nice tools on the market, which implement the above techniques and more. Probably the best known is Microsoft Project. So, if you are involved in project management you are strongly advised to get acquainted with these techniques.

Also in the EU administration there are many activities that can be considered as projects. To give some examples:

- The annual budget cycle (even if it is repetitive, every budget is unique)

- Organising a call for tender

- Organising a conference or public hearing

- Legislative procedures

You may have noticed that the above examples are projects that span multiple organisational entities (services, units, directorates, even institutions). This means that EU officials of all disciplines are being confronted with project work – even if they are not aware of it. The point is to understand how projects are managed and act accordingly in terms of prioritising and organising your contribution.

Symptoms of poor time management

The following list covers some of the most common symptoms of poor time management, regardless of the quantity of work you actually bring to a conclusion. If you recognise some of these symptoms in your own behaviour, there is likely some room for improvement.

- *Poorly defined goals* – Your goals help you to identify your priorities. They outline what you want to achieve, when you want to achieve it by, and why the task is important. If you do not have clearly defined goals, how are you supposed to know which tasks need to be done first?

- *Poor punctuality* – You are regularly late for your appointments or in completing your tasks. This may be due to you accepting too many tasks or your inability to assign the correct amount of time to your activities.

- *Rushing* – We all have to rush a little, from time to time, but if you find yourself constantly rushing from one appointment to another then you have an issue. You should allow sufficient time between appointments to cope with unforeseen events such as a previous meeting overrunning, or simply traffic jams.

- *Impatience* – Impatience is usually a sign of poor time management. You may accuse other people, or technology, of delaying you but the truth is that you have failed yourself by failing to manage your time properly.

- *Perfectionism* – You spend so much time trying to prepare and make sure that you perform your tasks perfectly that you either fail to start or go incredibly slowly. In reality, most of the time, 'good enough is best'.

- *Indecisiveness* – You are unable to choose an option and run with it. You spend excessive time going over the options without coming to a conclusion.

- *Saying 'Yes' to everything* – Constantly saying 'Yes' will leave you with an excessive workload. One of the quickest ways to improve your time management is to be assertive and learn to say 'No'.

- *Doing everything yourself* – It doesn't matter whether you are a Director, Head of Unit, Administrator or Assistant, there are always tasks which can be delegated, automated or outsourced. These tasks need to be identified and removed from your workload.

- *Procrastination* – Sometimes you know what needs to be done but you keep putting it off. Eventually, when you decide to complete the task, the deadline is usually approaching and you are under pressure to complete the task in time.

- *Lack of energy* – When you constantly have to work extra hard to catch up, your energy levels begin to drop and you lose motivation. It becomes harder to catch up and so you fall further behind which drains you of even more energy.

Poor time management impacts every area of your life, from work to relationships. Don't confuse being busy with being an accomplished time manager. Getting more

"I feel it's important to always have a plan to ignore."

work done does not automatically mean that you are managing your time effectively; if the extra tasks are unimportant, you are just filling your schedule. Focusing on getting the important tasks done is the key to effective time management.

Estimating time

It is important to realise that a time estimate for a task is not a single number, but a range of possibilities, a statistical entity. Everybody knows that if somebody wants to talk to you 'for a couple of minutes' it will most likely actually take 15 minutes, and if it is important it will be more like 45 minutes. On the other hand, there are no tasks with a negative duration, so the distribution of estimations is not symmetrical (Figure 7.4).

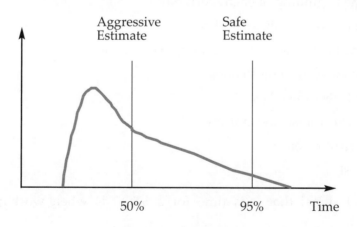

Figure 7.4

Most people have a tendency to give an estimate that they think they can make in 95% of the cases (they make a *safe* estimate). A safe estimate can easily represent twice the time of an aggressive estimate, one we think we can make in 50% of the cases.

In order to improve your own estimation of how long a given task will take it is a good idea to keep track of your own work and – based on your experience – use the actual (average) time you spent on similar tasks as the basis of your estimate. You can still decide if you want it to be safe or aggressive, depending on the importance, the urgency and circumstances you are in at that moment.

STOP

In his book 'The Inner Game of Work'[4] Tim Gallwey introduces the concept of *mobility*, which he defines as: 'the ability to move or adapt, change or be changed. It also means the ability to reach one's objectives in a fulfilling manner – to reach goals at the right time and in a way we feel good about. Therefore, mobility is not only change but fulfilment and harmony with one's progress.'

Not everything we do at work is mobility. The hard part is to remain conscious of what we are trying to achieve while busy working. The STOP tool is used to:

- **S**top
- **T**hink
- **O**rganise your thoughts, and
- **P**roceed

STOPs can be of any duration, maybe only for a few seconds. For example:

- STOP before you speak
- STOP at the beginning of each work day
- STOP at the end of each work day
- STOP at the beginning and end of any work project
- STOP to make a conscious change
- STOP to address mistakes
- STOP to correct miscommunication
- STOP to learn or coach
- STOP to rest

And a good signal that it is time for a STOP is when working just isn't fun anymore.

---

4   'The Inner Game of Work: Overcoming Mental Obstacles for Maximum Performance' (2000) by Timothy Gallwey.

Multitasking

'The first law of success is concentration – to bend all the energies to one point, and to go directly to that point, looking neither to the right or to the left.' – William Mathews, 19th century

Multitasking is doing multiple things – or performing multiple tasks – 'at the same time'.

Since the 1990s, psychologists have conducted experiments on the nature and limits of multitasking. The results of these experiments suggest that multitasking is not as efficient as work performed on a single task. Because the brain cannot fully focus when multitasking, people take longer to complete tasks and are predisposed to error.

When people attempt to complete many tasks at one time, or alternate rapidly between them, the error rate goes up and it takes far longer – often double the time or more – to get the jobs done than if they were done sequentially. This is largely because the brain is compelled to restart and refocus. Ultimately you want to shift important facts from your short-term memory to your long-term memory. Research shows that this process takes about 8 seconds of focused attention on a specific item. A study by David Meyer[5] and David Kieras[6] found that in the interim between each exchange, the brain makes no progress whatsoever. Therefore, multitasking people not only perform each task less well, but also lose time in the process.

In terms of your prioritising and organising competency this essentially means that you'd be better off planning to execute your tasks in a sequential way, keeping your focus on one task at a time.

Our limited multitasking capabilities are also severely challenged by modern technology. Office computers, Voice-over-IP telephones, smartphones and tablets are all designed to give us 24/7 accessibility. Besides the potentially devastating effect on our work-life balance this technology also impedes our prioritising and organising competency.

In his book 'The Shallows: What the Internet is doing to our Brains', one of my favourite authors, Nicholas Carr[7] states: 'Once I was a scuba diver in a sea of words. Now I zip along the surface like a guy on a Jet Ski'. Carr is finding it harder to concentrate and attend to long pieces of reading and writing. He also crystallises one of the most important debates of our time: as we enjoy the internet's bounties, are we sacrificing our ability to read and think deeply?

Even though I am (originally) an IT person myself, it is my opinion that information and communication technology has not lived up to its promise of improving our productivity, especially in the white-collar arena. One of the reasons for this is the introduction of too much multitasking amongst our workers, pushing them far too often into their panic zone.

One can conclude that having a good personal strategy for mastering technology is paramount for your prioritising and organising competency.

---

5   Professor David Meyer is the director of the University of Michigan's Brain, Cognition, and Action Laboratory.

6   David Kieras is a professor in the Electrical Engineering and Computer Science Department at the University of Michigan.

7   'The Shallows: What the Internet is doing to our Brains' (2011) by Nicholas Carr.

The art of delegation

No matter how efficient and masterful you are at your job, you have the same number of hours in the day as your colleagues. There are only so many tasks you can achieve within the same time frame, so to free yourself up and lighten the load: *delegate*.

The key to successful delegation is being absolutely clear about what you are expecting for the outcome. How much direction you provide to get from point A to B will depend on the level of expertise of the person doing the task.

You can read more about the art of delegation in Chapter 10 (Leadership).

Goal setting

'The greater danger for most of us is not that our aim is too high and we miss it, but that it is too low and we hit it.' – Michelangelo

Top-level athletes, successful business people and high achievers of all kinds use *goal setting*. Setting goals gives you long-term vision and short-term motivation. By setting sharp, clearly defined goals, you can measure and take pride in the achievement of those goals, and you can see progress in what might previously have seemed a long and pointless journey. You will also raise your self-confidence, as you recognise your own ability and competence in achieving the goals that you have set.

From Chapter 1 of this book you already know that 'SMART' stands for Specific, Measurable, Achievable, Realistic, and Time-bound. You will also have realised that it is important – both for your motivation and your development – to push the boundaries of your comfort zone by working in your learning zone. Now how can you achieve all this in your daily work at the office?

Edwin Locke[8] and Gary Latham spent many years researching the theory of goal setting. They identified five elements that need to be in place for us to achieve our goals: clarity, challenge, commitment, feedback, and task complexity.

Clarity – When your goals are clear, you know what you are trying to achieve. You can also measure the results accurately. That is why SMART is such a useful mnemonic. However, when a goal is vague it is not easy to measure, and it is not motivating. You may not even know you have achieved it. Write your goal down and be as detailed as possible. Then think about how you will measure your progress towards this goal.

Challenge – Is the goal outside your comfort zone? Consider how the goal makes you feel.

Commitment – Try to visualise in your mind how you will feel when the goal is achieved. Does it motivate you?

Feedback – Measure your own progress and ask for feedback from others. Schedule time to analyse your progress.

Task complexity – Is the behaviour to achieve your goal inside your learning zone? Is the task not too complex, thus pushing you into your panic zone? If so, break it into smaller, less complex sub-goals.

---

8   'A Theory of Goal Setting and Task Performance' (1990) by Edwin Locke et al.

Prioritising

I am sure you know the feeling of getting up for work in the morning with the sense of having so much to do that you don't know where to start. There are times when everything that you have to do seems like a priority, which makes it tough to figure out where to begin.

Don't worry; there are many techniques that can be used to prioritise the tasks you have to perform. Usually, these techniques are very simple and somewhat intuitive, but they work.

To-do list

By far the simplest technique is known as the to-do list. This is simply a list, in no particular order, of all the things you have to do, your tasks.

Don't keep your tasks on different post-it notes or in your head but at the beginning of each day or week, write on a sheet of paper what you want to get done and by when. Clearly, when making a new list you should not forget to transfer the tasks you have not finished from your previous list. You can refine this technique a bit by adding the amount of time you think it will take you (estimate) to perform every task and re-order the list in descending order (longest tasks first). You then work your way down the list assuming that the most important tasks are the ones that will take you the most time. Obviously, every time you complete a task you have to strike it from your list.

After completing your list with the associated time needed you may come to the conclusion that you won't be able to do everything in the time available. No problem! Maybe the remaining tasks are not that important after all, so you simply drop them. Maybe the remaining tasks are important but not urgent, so you simply move them to the next list. Tasks that are urgent *and* important are moved to the top of your list and you start working on these right away.

In many instances your to-do list related to the processes you participate in is 'generated' by the workflow system; the tasks will be in your 'inbox' and the deadline for execution will be clearly indicated. When you are part of a project team your project-related tasks will be given to you by the project manager, who is responsible for the overall timing and output of the project.

The 80/20 principle

Management thinker Joseph M. Juran first put the 80/20 principle into currency in the 1940s, dubbing it the *Pareto principle* (after the Italian economist Vilfredo Pareto, who in the 1890s observed that 80% of the land in Italy was owned by 20% of the population and that this distribution seemed to apply in many other cases too). The assumption is that most of the results in any situation are determined by a small number of causes.

This principle can also be applied to prioritising your tasks, based on the idea that most of the results (output) will be generated by a small proportion of your effort (input). When looking at your to-do list you simply pick those tasks that will generate the most (relevant) output and you take these as your priorities. The remaining tasks are executed when there is time left.

It is fair to say that this is true only up to a point and should not be taken as gospel in all cases. The principle cannot be applied to all kinds of work or tasks; it is not applicable across the board. For example, translators may spend time screening incoming work to find appropriate reference materials (before sending a job for freelance translation, so as to ensure a better final product), performing written or oral summaries of long texts with input from the party requesting the translation, or doing full-length translations. But they cannot say 'I'll do only summaries this week because the output will be greatest'. That is to ignore the crucial but very short one-and-a-half page letter waiting to be translated to a tight deadline.

The ABC method

The ABC method is a powerful priority setting technique that you can use every single day. This technique is so simple and effective that it can, all by itself, make you one of the most efficient and effective people in your team.

Once again, your to-do list is the starting point. Behind every item you put a letter A, B or C depending on the following criteria:

A –   Very important. This is something that you must do. This is a task for which there can be serious consequences if you fail to do it.

B –   A task that you should do, but it only has mild consequences. This means that someone may be unhappy or inconvenienced if you don't do it, but that's about it.

C –   A task that would be nice to do, but for which there are no consequences at all.

The Eisenhower matrix

Although it was Stephen Covey who made this method popular in his book 'First Things First'[9], the concept is originally credited to US President Dwight D. Eisenhower[10]

Whenever confronted with something that needed to be done, he would ask himself two questions: First, is the task important? Second, is it urgent?

Based on this, the task would end up in one of four categories: important and urgent, important but not urgent, not important but urgent, and neither important nor urgent.

Obviously the first priority should go to the tasks that are both important and urgent (quadrant No. 1 in the matrix in Figure 7.5). However, what is not so obvious is that tasks labelled important but not urgent get the next priority (No. 2). This is what Eisenhower's point was all about: 'What is important is seldom urgent and what is urgent is seldom important'. Tasks that are in quadrant No. 3 are typical candidates for delegation, and the ones in No. 4 can even be dropped because they are neither urgent nor important, so why bother?

9   'First Things First' (1996) by Stephen Covey.

10   Dwight D. Eisenhower (1890–1969) was the 34th President of the United States, from 1953 until 1961 and supreme allied commander in the 1944 D-day landings in Europe.

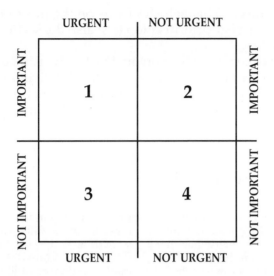

Figure 7.5

Tasks performed in the context of processes or projects are almost by definition important. Their urgency depends on the time constraints of the process or the timing of the project and whether the task is on the critical path or not. Doing your planning for the coming week is for sure important, but it probably is not urgent. Phone calls from outside are probably not important (unless you are waiting for one) and many text messages or emails are not important either.

There are tools that implement the Eisenhower matrix method on your personal computer or smartphone; you can even drag-and-drop to-do lists from other people in your team into your own matrix. For most people, however, a simple paper version will do.

Timeboxing

Timeboxing is used as a time management technique whereby the schedule is divided into a number of separate time periods – or *timeboxes*. Each timebox has its own deliverables, deadline and budget. It is also used for individual use to address personal tasks in a smaller time frame in order to improve the productivity of the user.

In project management, the three constraints are time, resources, and outcome. Changing one constraint will impact the rest. Without timeboxing, projects usually work with a predefined outcome. Under these circumstances, when some deliverables cannot be completed you will either have to adjust the time constraint, or add extra resources, or do both. With the timeboxing approach the time constraint is fixed, but the outcome may be reduced. This helps to focus on the most important deliverables, which requires of course a clear prioritisation (see also the section on expectation management in Chapter 5).

Individuals can use timeboxing for personal tasks. By using a reduced scale of time (e.g. one hour instead of a full week) and well-defined deliverables, personal timeboxing is said to help control perfectionist tendencies. Personal timeboxing also helps to overcome procrastination and many people find that the time pressure created boosts their creativity and focus.

Schedule for the unexpected

Most people have a tendency to fill their schedules to the edge with work and meetings, and then suddenly something unexpected comes up. An emergency that you have to focus on, even though you have other things to do; your boss who needs a last-minute answer, a stakeholder who suddenly demands your attention, or your kid that gets sick at school.

In those cases, you have to drop everything and deal with it. You put the other tasks off into the future, reschedule meetings, and rearrange tasks. Clearly, this can have a huge impact on your productivity.

Here's the secret: *schedule for the unex-* *pected*. Typically, I block out an hour a day, preferably late in the afternoon. No meetings, no phone calls. That way, when something comes up, I have an hour of flexibility to address it. Of course, you might need more or less than an hour. The important thing is to take the time you need to ensure that you are not always stressing everything out. By doing this, I have learned that while the unexpected always *seems* to come up, in reality it doesn't. In those cases, you get an extra hour to work on whatever needs doing — or head home early. It's an added bonus.

Planning tools

'In preparing for battle I have always found that plans are useless, but planning is indispensable.' – Dwight D. Eisenhower

Besides your to-do list it is a good idea to plan all your activities, whether they are process-related, project-related, related to your working conditions or your personal life.

In the old days most people had a 'personal organiser' – a small, usually leather-bound book – and they had it with them all the time. With the advent of the internet and smartphones these have been gradually replaced by a version 'in the cloud'. The iCalendar protocol is supported by most – if not all – platforms, which means that you can have one organiser for all your activities or tasks (both private and professional) and that you have access (read/write) from wherever you are (provided of course you have access to the internet). You can also share (parts of) your calendar with other people and even invite people for activities you plan to do. Some companies even offer 'cloud scheduling software' which makes scheduling activities with other participants even more convenient.

However, 'a fool with a tool is still a fool'.

If you use these tools you have to do it right. You have to put ALL your 'A' and 'B' (or '1' and '2') tasks or activities in there and respond accordingly when you receive the alert that the 'event' is about to start. You also have to schedule some time for the other activities and for the necessary breaks; in most situations it is sufficient to leave these time slots blank. Don't put every little activity in your calendar because otherwise you will have too much overhead or feel overwhelmed by all the things you are supposed to do (and be disturbed time and again by the alerts). It is also a good idea to work with larger blocks (with a minimum of say half an hour) so that you don't have to switch your focus too often.

Attention management

In their book 'The Attention Economy'[11], Thomas H. Davenport and J. C. Beck define the concept of attention as follows: 'Attention is focused mental engagement on a particular item of information. Items come into our awareness, we attend to a particular item, and then we decide whether to act.'

There are different kinds of attention. *Proactive attention* is the kind of sustained focus you need to draft an important memo, lead a team meeting or come up with creative solutions to a business problem. *Active attention* is necessary when you're making smaller day-to-day decisions, writing to-do lists or attending meetings. *Inactive attention* is more suited for tasks like deleting unnecessary emails or filing paperwork.

When an item of information has our attention we store it in our short-term memory, and the more focused our attention is, the more items of information we store.

Short-term (or working) memory acts as a kind of 'scratch-pad' for temporary recall of the information which is being processed at any point in time. It holds a small amount of information for a short period of time. The short-term memory has a limited capacity. Experiments by George Miller in 1956 suggest that the number of objects an average human can hold in working memory (known as 'memory span') is between 5 and 9 (7 ± 2, which is sometimes referred to as Miller's Law). However, memory span varies widely from person to person, and modern estimates of the average are typically lower, in order of just 4 or 5 items. Moreover, our memory span is not constant during the day and it depends to a large extent on our physical state and the environment we're in.

Based on this information, here is a way to organise your workday by managing your attention span. This technique is based on the work of Graham Allcott, author of 'How to Be a Productivity Ninja'[12] The goal is to help you become more efficient at the office by figuring out when during the day you are the most or least focused. Then you match those times with tasks that require the appropriate level of attention:

- Make a list of all the tasks (big and small) that you complete in a typical day.

- Next, decide whether each task requires proactive, active or inactive attention.

---

11 'The Attention Economy – Understanding the new Currency of Business' (2002) by Thomas H. Davenport and J.C. Beck.

12 'How to be a Productivity Ninja' (2015) by Graham Allcott.

- Think back over the last couple of weeks and ask yourself when you felt focused and productive. What time was that?

- With this information in mind, create a work schedule that matches the appropriate tasks to your attention level throughout the day.

Of course, you will have to make some exceptions. Even if you don't have as much flexibility as you would like, it is still useful to know what level of attention you need for a certain task. Just remember that attention management is about you dictating your time rather than having your tasks dictate to you. After all, only you know your brainpower best.

But beware! As a manager you can be faced with the underperformer who'll take solace from this and even exploit it. 'I'm not a morning person'; 'My biorhythms are at their highest at 6 pm – I do my best work then'; 'If you make me come in to work so early (9.30), you won't get anything out of me'. Try not to encourage this!

Procrastination

Procrastination is carrying out less urgent tasks in preference to more urgent ones, or doing more pleasurable things in place of less pleasurable ones, and thus putting off tasks to a later time, sometimes to the 'last minute' before the deadline. Procrastination is negative behaviour in the context of effective time management. Procrastination is wasting time.

A form of procrastination is also known as the *student syndrome*, the phenomenon whereby people will only start to fully apply themselves to a task just at the last possible moment before a deadline. The student syndrome usually includes more of a plan and sincerely good intentions. In project and task estimating, a time or resource buffer is applied to the task to allow for overrun or other scheduling problems. However, with student syndrome, because tasks are started at the last moment possible, the buffer for any given task is wasted beforehand, rather than kept in reserve. In this context it is also worth citing Parkinson's Law: 'work expands so as to fill the time available for its completion'[13] I would even add: 'and then some'.

If you are honest with yourself, you probably know when you are procrastinating, but how do you fight this bad habit?

The first step is *awareness*. When you find yourself doing low-priority tasks from your to-do list while higher priority tasks are put aside, or when you are waiting for the right mood or the right time to tackle an important task, or when you say yes to unimportant tasks that others ask you to do knowing that you have other work on your plate, you are probably procrastinating.

The next thing is to ask yourself the question *why* you are procrastinating. Is it because you don't like the task, you find it unpleasant? Is it because you are simply disorganised and can't distinguish priorities? Or is it because you are afraid of doing the task, or in other words the task will push you into your panic zone?

---

13   'Parkinson's Law: or the Pursuit of Progress' by C. Northcote Parkinson, first published in 1958.

Clear desk

Is your monitor framed with layers of post-it reminders? Is your workspace hidden under stacks of papers, or your guest chair buried under a pile of outerwear? A majority of people admit they judge co-workers by how messy they keep their work environment. Co-workers will associate a messy office with your organisational skills and assume their project or proposal will get lost in the landfill that is your desk.

Most people spend at least 30 minutes to an hour a day looking for things. In addition to saving time and money, a clear desk policy helps organisations reduce the risk of information theft, fraud, or security breaches caused by sensitive information being left unattended and exposed.

So, is a clear desk better for the workplace? As with many things in life, there is no clear-cut answer to this question. Proponents claim that people see measurable life improvements from becoming neat and tidy, and they can point to millions of euros in annual revenue as evidence of success. In contrast, many creative individuals with Nobel prizes and other prestigious awards prefer – and in fact cultivate – messy environments as an aid to their work.

"You didn't move something in my office did you? Because I can't find anything now."

Working at a clear desk seems to encourage people to do what is expected of them. But research also shows that a messy desk may confer its own benefits, promoting creative thinking and stimulating new ideas. Disorderly environments seem to inspire breaking free of tradition, which can produce fresh insights.

Once again the conclusion is that this is a matter of individual awareness and responsibility. If the clutter on your desk is too intimidating to tackle, you can set a regular reminder on your calendar to tidy up your workspace once a week. But if you feel comfortable in your mess and if you do not breach any official policy with that, then, by all means, stick to it.

Is doing overtime good or bad?

Now this is an interesting question worth some debate.

Let's first have a look at the regulations ruling this matter in the EU institutions – the Staff Regulations.

EU personnel – that is people who have a permanent or temporary employment governed by the Staff Regulations – have to work an average of 40 hours per week (this used to be 38, before the 2013 reform). In most places there is a 'flexitime' regime in place, meaning that individuals can arrive at work within given time ranges, they can have a flexible lunch break, and they can leave work in the evening at the time they choose. The only 'obligations' are an average of 40 hours per week and being present (in the office or at the workplace) during the 'core' time (usually 10AM-Noon and 2PM-4PM).

In many instances telework – or working from home – is allowed, within certain limits.

These arrangements have been designed to cope with cultural differences (Greeks and Finns, for example, tend to have rather different life styles) and to allow for staff to manage their personal work-life balance (people with children have very different needs in this respect from those without).

Whereas these rules are applicable to most statutory staff there are exceptions for certain categories (management, linguists, security staff, IT people, drivers ...) who are required to adapt their working hours to the circumstances. Also, these 'general' rules may be implemented differently in the individual institutions, directorates-general or even at unit level.

For external agents, the above rules do not apply. In Belgium it is forbidden by law to have a 'formal management' relationship between internal staff (representing the customer) and external staff (representing the supplier of services or goods). Imposing working hours would be an infringement in this respect. The working hours of external agents are governed by this person's employer (which is not the customer) and these will be fixed in the contract between the customer and the supplier.

What is overtime?

If – and when – EU statutory staff work more than the average of 40 hours (typically this is settled on a monthly basis) they can 'compensate' this time by taking extra time off (with the agreement of their superior and limited to one or two half-days per month).

Only time that exceeds these limits (after compensation) is considered to be overtime. Other than for some rare exceptions, this is not compensated (financially or with extra holidays), meaning that the employee is working for free during this overtime.

So – is doing overtime good or bad?

Allow me at this point to give a consultant's answer: 'it depends'.

There is nothing wrong with overtime as long as you are personally motivated for it. By this I mean that it is your own decision – based on your assessment of the situation – and it is not your boss who randomly imposes it on you. If imposed, there have to be good and compelling reasons for this and it has to be known and scheduled beforehand.

There is nothing wrong with overtime if you do it for the right reasons. Some people 'burn hours' by just being at the office, spending their time with daydreaming, surfing the internet, socialising all day long, or drinking coffee in the cafeteria. Doing overtime while not being productive but merely to build up a compensation time later on is not good, because you are actually 'stealing' time from your employer.

There is nothing wrong with overtime if it doesn't affect your productivity. But human beings are not machines that can go on and on without resting. Our attention span is limited in time and we can only be truly productive for a certain period of time, after which our output – or the quality of our work – decreases.

There is nothing wrong with overtime if it is necessary to deliver something urgent and important to schedule.

President Eisenhower once said: 'Usually, urgent things are not important, and most important things are not urgent.' These wise words have been converted by

cont....

Is doing overtime good or bad? – *continued*

management consultants like Steven Covey into personal productivity (or time-management) methods. The basic idea is to focus first on what is really important AND urgent, then on what is important but maybe not so urgent, and postpone – or even drop – the other tasks. Don't waste your time on things that are not important, and don't be inclined to opt for overtime to carry out work that may be 'urgent' but not important.

There is nothing wrong with overtime if you don't hurt yourself by doing it. By this I mean that you are taking serious risks of running into a burn-out – or a depression – when doing overtime is your only strategy for coping with high workloads or tight deadlines. This will at a minimum affect your motivation and productivity.

There is nothing wrong with overtime if you don't hurt your colleagues by doing it. Especially when you are in a managerial position and try to 'set a good example' by burning lots of time at the office, you may be putting pressure on your colleagues to do overtime against their will (see first argument above). Those people – your typical workaholics – who are doing overtime just to please the boss are hurting their colleagues by doing so.

Finally, there is nothing wrong with overtime if you keep control over your work-life balance. Work-life balance is a very individual thing and differs widely from person to person. It is even variable over time. Don't project your personal situation on that of your colleagues. Bear in mind that a good work-life balance is essential for your resilience.

Conclusion

There is no clear-cut, black-and-white answer to this question. An important point is not to confuse overtime with the consequences of procrastination. I once had a colleague who turned weekend working into a virtue: 'I worked overtime to finish this'. In fact, she was forced into spending the weekend doing it because she did not do the job during the week when she should have (and could have). It is important for colleagues and managers alike to distinguish true overtime from false.

Speed reading

A word here about *speed reading*, because it has a place among the 'best practices' of prioritising and organising, and will help you to manage your time better.

Speed reading, also known as *diagonal reading*, is about skimming through reading material to gather its general meaning and purpose. You browse through the documentation and read the titles, pull-out quotes and any diagrams or bullet lists. You then go back and read the table of contents and the summary, if applicable. This sets your mind up to better understand the purpose and terminology before you delve into the text. In fact, you already practise speed reading – most likely without being aware of it – whenever you flick through a newspaper or magazine, or browse the internet, in search of stories that you're really interested in.

Most diagonal readers give the content a first pass by reading a text 'passively' – just like one would browse a magazine, look at photographs, or watch television, i.e. they are not really paying attention to the small details, rather they are waiting for something to really pop out at them. The average person reads about 240 words per minute, whereas a diagonal reader 'scans' closer to 15 words per second or about 900 words per minute. So, there are at least three, and up to five important sections of an article that a diagonal reader will see in the approximately 10 seconds they will initially allocate to a text:

- The title or headline.
- The subtitles or subheadings within the text.
- Any bold, underlined, quoted, or otherwise highlighted text.
- Pictures, graphs, charts, or images of any nature.
- A summary of the article.

Effective speed reading takes a lot of practice to master – typically years – and it is not the purpose of this book to turn you into a proficient speed reader. There are, however, some ideas you can usefully apply when reading an everyday text:

- Don't read everything
- Don't read in order
- Don't try to understand everything

Let us now expand a bit further on these ideas.

There seems to be a strange idea (especially amongst translators, lawyers and engineers) that you have to read absolutely everything. This is just not true; you don't have to read everything! The idea behind this is that when you read, you should read with a purpose. Usually, this is the extraction of information from a piece of text. Once you have that information – you're done. There's no need to read any longer. In fact, I would say that most of the texts you will encounter are simply filler (or 'payload') – you don't need to read all of it, just the relevant parts. Also, well-written texts contain a lot of repetition. I have a rule: if I start reading a text and after a few sentences I still haven't found what I am looking for, I move on.

Another mistake is the idea that you have to read start-to-finish. There is absolutely no reason you can't start by reading the conclusion or summary, then go back to the introduction or jump around through different paragraphs or chapters. Sometimes it's worth picking what you're interested in from the table of contents or index and starting there. It's more than likely that you are reading this book in this way, so why not do it for all the documents you have to deal with?

The other common, but erroneous, idea is 'perfect' comprehension. There's no such thing. Of course, your comprehension will go down a bit when you speed read, but that is not really a problem. When you read, you should read for a purpose and for certain bits of information anyway – no one cares if you remember every single fact and figure from a text, or what the 7th word in the third sentence on page two was.

A corollary to this is that you don't need to understand absolutely everything in a piece of text. We mostly read to understand main concepts anyway. If you really must understand absolutely everything, you should be taking notes (or drawing a mind map), and you can always re-read certain sections to note down facts and figures.

A few other ideas that will help you with speed reading:

- *Summaries* are often as good as the whole text itself. If you are lucky, there will be a management summary or an introduction to the text you are reading. So, if there is, first have a look at this, as it may provide you with all the answers you need right away!

- *Eliminate distractions*. If you are surrounded by noise, even background noise like music, do everything you can to get rid of it. Isolate yourself with nothing but the text and a comfortable reading position. By eliminating potential distractions, your mind can better focus on absorbing the words on the sheets of paper or your screen.

- *Focus the right senses on reading*. Although many people are used to reading out loud or imagining a voice attached to the words, your mind may absorb the material faster by 'cutting out the middle men' and connecting them straight from the eye to the brain. Read without moving your lips. In fact, by using your finger or a pen as a guide, you can actually read and comprehend the material faster. Your finger can act as a pace-setter for your brain, going as fast as you can retain the information.

- *Read faster by using your peripheral vision* to focus on seeing the text as a whole before understanding the words individually. By using an imaginary line down the middle of the page, your mind can start to sort the text into blocks. You will start to read the pages in a diagonal fashion, rather than a linear way. This also allows you to focus on key words, rather than spending time on decorative phrases.

- *Take frequent breaks* by pacing yourself accordingly. By taking breaks, you give your mind a chance to rest and recoup since it is absorbing information much faster than it's used to. Read the text in installments, and take short breaks.

- *Don't speed read all the time*. The above speed reading tips should only be used when going through material produced by others. When you are revising your own texts, trying to make the meaning clearer, fashioning good arguments, or just weeding out spelling errors, you should NOT speed read. In that case you have to pay close attention to every word and idea to tidy up your text and make it is as good as you can.

Caveat: you need to differentiate between various reading tasks. For example, translators do speed read for scanning purposes or oral/written summarising, but they cannot translate a text they don't read in full detail. Translators do not have the luxury of deciding what parts of a text are important; that is for the desk-officer to decide.

Developing your prioritising and organising skills

Time management is not very difficult as a concept, but it's surprisingly hard to do it in practice. It requires the investment of a little time to prioritise and organise yourself. But once done, you will find that with some fine-tuning, your day, your week, and your month, fall into place in an orderly fashion, with time for everything you need to do. The distinction between urgent and important is the key to prioritising and organising your time and your workload.

Perhaps the most important thing is to stay calm and keep things in perspective. Remember that the world won't come to an end if you fail to finish your last task of the day; you can usually leave it until tomorrow, especially if you have prioritised judiciously.

Please refer to Chapter 1 (methodology) and Annex 5 for further development of this competency, have another look at the current chapter to find out about your options, and remember: YOU are responsible for your own development, not your manager, your colleagues, or your mentor.

The online toolkit that comes for free with this book can be used to follow-up on your development in this area. The toolkit can be found at:

https://www.johnharperpublishing.co.uk/the-ultimate-eu-career-development-toolkit/

Key points to remember

- Prioritising and organising is about making the best possible use of your time at work.
- Always use 'safe' estimates when estimating the time you will need to complete a task.
- Multitasking is detrimental to your overall performance.
- Use a to-do list to schedule your daily activities and provide for some slack.
- Delegate whenever possible.
- Don't work harder, but work smarter.
- Stay calm.

Your notes

8. Resilience

Competency definition: *'Remains effective under a heavy workload, handles organisational frustrations positively and adapts to a changing work environment.'*

'The difference between winners and losers is how they handle losing.' – Rosabeth Moss Kanter[1]

Resilience is the process of adapting well in the face of adversity, trauma, tragedy, threats or significant sources of stress. Resilience – the ability to effectively cope with losing, failing, and not getting what you want – is an important quality for anyone to cultivate in order to achieve success and well-being. To live and to work is to risk failure, and resilience helps people to bounce back from the inevitable adversities and obstructions that risk entails.

Resilience is ordinary, not extraordinary. Resilience is not a trait that people either have or do not have. It involves behaviours, thoughts and actions that can be learned and developed in anyone.

Resilience is sometimes confused with *perseverance*, but there is a difference. In short, perseverance keeps us going when we are convinced that we are on the right track, but we are just not getting enough traction to get to our destination. Resilience enables us to build a new track, fix the locomotive and start all over again when the wheels come off.

Another related concept is *grit*. Grit is a personal characteristic based on an individual's passion for a particular long-term objective, coupled with a powerful motivation to achieve that objective. This perseverance of effort promotes the overcoming of obstacles or challenges, and serves as a driving force in achievement realisation.

Developing resilience is a personal journey. People do not all react the same to traumatic and stressful events. An approach to building resilience that works for one person might not work for another.

Resilience

I frequently use the metaphor of a (coil) spring to illustrate the concept of resilience. Springs are constructional elements designed to retain and accumulate mechanical energy, working on the principle of flexible deformation of material.

First, imagine that you are compressing the spring and releasing it – gently – afterwards. The spring will come back to its original shape. The energy that was accumulated during compression will be released entirely, and the spring will not 'remember' anything of the event. That's what a spring is meant to do, that's what it is designed for.

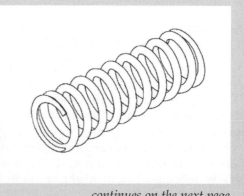

continues on the next page

---

1   Rosabeth Moss Kanter is a Harvard Business School professor.

continued

Now imagine that instead of compressing the spring you are extending it. Just a little bit. When released, the spring will come back to its original shape, just as it would after compressing it. However, when you extend it too much, the spring will not come back entirely – there will be a permanent deformation. One could say that the spring has 'learned' from the experience, because no matter how often you repeat the experiment (even compressing) the deformation will be permanent, and the spring will never return to its first original state again.

Finally, when you extend the spring too much, it will break. This is also a permanent state that can only be repaired by a serious intervention (soldering, welding or some mechanical fix).

I compare mental resilience with the behaviour of a spring. When subjected to 'normal' levels of stress (compression) we bounce back as if nothing happened. This is what we are meant to do, what we are 'designed' for. This is also what we are paid for at work. However, when subjected to 'abnormal' stress (either too high or in an unusual direction) we only have two options: learn from the experience and bounce back, or break. The mental equivalent of a spring breaking is known as 'burn out', and it will be very difficult to repair. The 'permanent deformation' obviously is the learning experience we get from adversity.

Change

'*There are only three certainties in life: death, taxes, and change.*' – Anonymous

The EPSO definition of resilience ends: '*… and adapts to a changing work environment.*' In fact, this definition is referring to *organisational change*.

Organisational change is any modification in the people, structure or technology of an organisation:

- *People*: changes in attitudes, expectations, perceptions and behaviours.
- *Structure*: changes in job, responsibilities, departments, management structure, organisational design.
- *Technology*: changes in work, processes, equipment, methods and software.

One can readily say that organisational change is constant, but it varies in degree and direction. Organisational change produces uncertainty, but it is not completely unpredictable, and organisational change creates both threats and opportunities.

Organisational change affects employees differently. While some will welcome it, others will become worried and stressed at the mere mention of change. They will fear that any reorganisation might challenge their standing and worry how they will fit into the new structure.

Clearly, the EU institutions are subject to organisational change, and that is why being able to adapt to a changing work environment is part of the core competencies of EU staff.

Stress

Stress is the body's response to change. Stress is defined in many different ways and the things that cause stress can vary from person to person. Stress affects our performance.

"You'll experience a certain amount
of stress in your new job, but don't
worry. We keep a defibrillator here
on my desk."

There are four types of stress:

- *Acute stress* is the type of stress we experience on a day-to-day basis – for example, the stress of getting our to-do list finished or the stress of unexpected obstacles.

- When a person rarely gets relief from stress, this is called *episodic acute stress*. This type of stress usually goes on for longer periods of time with little relief.

- *Chronic stress* is characterised as long-term stress, where there is little hope for relief. These are long-term situations where the person has given up trying to find a solution.

- Not all stress is bad; some stress can actually help us to perform better and challenge us. This type of stress is called *eustress*[2].

---

2 Not to be confused with EU stress ;-)

Dr Peter Nixon, a British cardiologist, developed a diagram called the Human Function Curve (Figure 8.2) that illustrates the balance of good and bad stress.

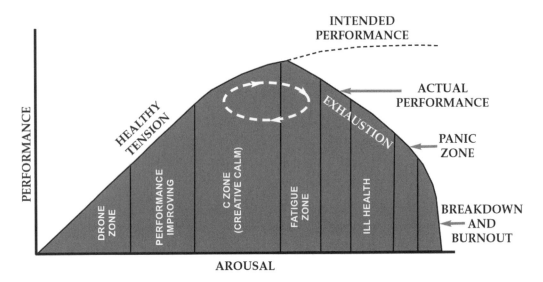

Figure 8.2

Nixon calls any state where we are awake and reacting to stimuli an *arousal state*, such as being at work. If we compare the amount of stress to our performance, our performance actually improves when we experience eustress. However, according to this model, there is a point where chronic stress can impede our performance. In Figure 8.2 you can see in the drone zone, for example, that our performance is low. We may be bored and not have enough positive stress for us to perform at a decent level. In the C zone, in contrast, we may experience eustress, which raises our performance. However, when we reach the fatigue zone, we could be experiencing chronic stress, which impedes our performance. As you can see, performance is actually improved with a certain amount of stress, but once that stress becomes episodic or chronic, our performance deteriorates.

'Boreout'

According to Peter Werder and Philippe Rothlin[3], it is the absence of meaningful tasks, rather than the presence of stress, that is the main problem for many workers. What they call 'boreout' consists of three elements: boredom, lack of challenge, and lack of interest. These authors disagree with the common perception that a demoti-vated employee is lazy; instead, they argue that the employee has lost interest in work tasks. Those suffering from boreout are 'dissatisfied with their professional situation'

3   'Boreout – Overcoming workplace demotivation' (2008) by Peter Werder and Philippe Rothlin.

because they are frustrated at being prevented – by institutional mechanisms or obstacles rather than their own lack of aptitude – from fulfilling their potential. Fulfilling their potential means using their skills, knowledge, and abilities to contribute to their organisation's development and/or receiving official recognition for their efforts. Such employees have given up and become resigned to their situation, experiencing boreout, which is effectively the opposite of burnout.

Here are some typical symptoms of boreout:

- Frequent private surfing on the internet combined with frequent usage of the 'Alt-Tab' shortcut.[4]

- Burning long hours at work: going as early as possible to the office and leaving as late as possible, without producing much.

- Procrastination: tasks are split up over more periods of time and are constantly interrupted or moved.

- Remaining work is taken home but not worked on.

- Emphasising to colleagues and supervisors continually how busy and overburdened you are.

- Feeling unsatisfied by your working situation and constantly feeling unchallenged and bored.

The dangerous effects of boreout should not be underestimated: dissatisfaction, apathy and the loss of appetite for life – not to mention the reduction of the organisation's efficiency resulting from bored employees spending hours of company time surfing the net.

"The secret to being interested in dull work? You're fired. See? Didn't it just become much more interesting?"

---

4   If you know what this means you may already have a problem.

Boreout has become widespread among employees around the world, although employers have only recently begun to recognise the problem. It is my personal feeling that in the EU institutions too this could be a major problem. Not because there's not enough interesting work to be done but because of the very political nature of the organisation. EU staff mainly have an administrative or – at best – a consultative role, and the real decisions are taken by politicians, based often on non-technical arguments. Also, due to the very competitive nature of the recruitment process, only the 'best' administrators and specialists are hired, only to find themselves in positions for which they are sometimes very much overqualified. For sure, this is a phenomenon to be considered by managers, leaders, and HR professionals alike.

Comfort zone

Your *comfort zone* is any type of behaviour that keeps you at a low anxiety level. Everyday activities that you are used to doing won't make you feel anxious and uneasy, so they are part of your comfort zone.

Brené Brown[5], a research professor at the University of Houston Graduate College of Social Work, has another definition of comfort zone: 'Where our uncertainty, scarcity and vulnerability are minimized – where we believe we'll have access to enough love, food, talent, time, admiration. Where we feel we have some control.'

Although people often refer to 'getting outside your comfort zone' in terms of trying new things, anything that raises your anxiety levels can be counted as being outside that zone. Anxiety is not something we are prone to go looking for, but a little bit can be surprisingly beneficial. We often need just a hint of anxiety to push us to get our work done, or to improve our performance.

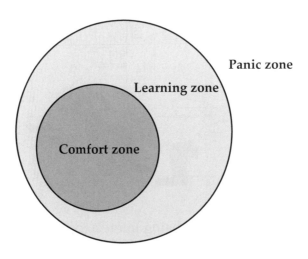

Figure 8.3

5   'The Gifts of Imperfection' (2010) by Brené Brown.

The comfort zone is often illustrated like the image in Figure 8.3, where the comfort zone extends into a learning zone, but eventually leads to a panic zone, where anxiety is too high.

How we deal with uncertainty

A lot of the anxiety that comes from leaving your comfort zone is due to uncomfortable levels of uncertainty. There is a reason that cooking dinner is no big deal when you do it all the time; you know what to expect. Driving a car for the first time, or skydiving, or starting a new job, are all activities that are full of uncertainty, and thus, anxiety. Uncertainty can make us respond more strongly to negative experiences. We are more likely to respond negatively to new things, even though we may come to like them over time.

Familiarity is comfortable and enjoyable, so it is no real surprise that new things get our guard up. From an evolutionary perspective, we see familiar things as more likely to be safe, and so we are more drawn to what we know. Trying new things also takes energy, so we are more likely to lean on old habits than take a new risk.

Breaking out of your comfort zone

So, should you try to break out of your comfort zone? Is it actually good for you to try? The answer is 'yes' – to some degree. 'We need a place of productive discomfort,' says Daniel H. Pink[6]. 'If you are too comfortable, you are not productive. And if you are too uncomfortable, you are not productive either. We can't be too hot or too cold.'

The objective is to reach that optimal level so that our skills increase and we become comfortable with that new level of anxiety — then we are in an expanded comfort zone. And ideally, we will get more used to those feelings of 'productive discomfort' and won't be so scared about trying new things in the future.

When mixed with a feeling of success, some anxiety and self-doubt can lead to personal growth. This is why outdoor adventures like rock climbing or skydiving can be so exhilarating: they induce anxiety and unease but when completed, they give us a huge feeling of accomplishment and increase our base levels of confidence.

From panic zone to comfort zone

A couple of years ago, I had the opportunity to help my daughter to learn how to drive a car. I am sure you can imagine that the first time she sat behind the steering wheel, not even knowing where to put her feet on the pedals, her 'level of anxiety' was very high; she was in – or very close to – her panic zone. So, I decided not to let her start the engine for that very first time, but just to explain a couple of general principles and show her where all the controls of the car could be found, and what these were used for. Giving her a bigger challenge would have been pointless, since the level of anxiety was too high.

The next step was to just let her start the engine and move forward for a couple of metres, giving her the feeling of how to play with the pedals to achieve this. Of course, we did this on a quiet parking lot in our neighbourhood, where no other vehicles or obstacles were in the way. Needless to say that the engine stalled numerous times and the first movements of the car

cont...

6   'Drive: The Surprising Truth about What Motivates Us' (2009) by Daniel H. Pink.

continued

were more like jumping than riding, but after a while (maybe 30 attempts or so) she had the initial 'feeling' of how the car responded to her actions. And that was it. She had accepted the first – small but achievable – challenge, moving into her learning zone.

Over subsequent lessons, each time with a couple of days in between, I gradually added challenges to her portfolio – driving around in circles (first gear), starting and stopping, emergency braking – until the time had come to use the clutch. The car, especially the gearbox, suffered a lot, but I considered that this was the price to be paid for her learning experience (it was my wife's car anyway).

Then came the day that we moved away from the parking lot and went for a drive on the road. We usually practised during the weekend and in an industrial area with little or no traffic around. She first had to get a better feeling of the vehicle, especially when driving at somewhat higher speeds. Initially, the trips we made were very short and always the same; the only purpose of this was to remove the anxiety that comes with driving in an unfamiliar environment, allowing her to concentrate on the driving.

Many weekends later we went out on real roads. I live in the countryside, so I could choose roads with very moderate traffic, just to let her gradually get used to the idea that she is not alone on the road, and that other drivers may make mistakes as well. In fact, she even had a little accident during that time. It was dark and rainy and she misjudged her braking distance to a car that stopped in front of us. There was some small damage to both cars (she was driving my own car this time) but nobody was hurt. I am sure that this was a great learning experience for her …

After a number of months of messing around on country roads we finally went to a (small) city to prepare her for the driver's exam.

In fact, she failed first time round. Not because of her driving skills, but because she had misinterpreted a rather complex traffic situation (I was sitting next to her and made the same mistake). Once again, tears were flowing, but once again this was a great learning experience. Anyway, the second time she got her driver's licence and since then has driven safely thousands of kilometres in very variable circumstances. I believe she is now inside her comfort zone.

Flow

'Flow' is a state of complete immersion in an activity, being completely involved in an activity for its own sake. Your whole being is involved, and you are using your skills to the utmost.

In his book 'Finding Flow', Mihaly Csíkszentmihályi[7] explains that flow is likely to occur when an individual is faced with a task that has clear goals that require specific responses. Flow also happens when a person's skills are fully involved in overcoming a challenge that is just about manageable, so it acts as a magnet for learning new skills and increasing challenges. If challenges are too low, one gets back to flow by increasing them. If challenges are too great, one can return to the flow state by learning new skills. Flow can occur when workers are engaged in tasks where they are able to focus entirely on the task at hand.

In addition to making activities more enjoyable, flow can lead to improved performance. Flow can also lead to further learning and skill development because the

7   'Finding Flow' (1998) by Mihaly Csíkszentmihályi.

individual must continually seek new challenges and information in order to maintain the state of flow.

Csíkszentmihályi produced a graphic (Figure 8.4) showing the relationship between the level of someone's skills and the level of challenge faced. As you can see, flow is most likely achieved when a high challenge level coincides with a high skills level.

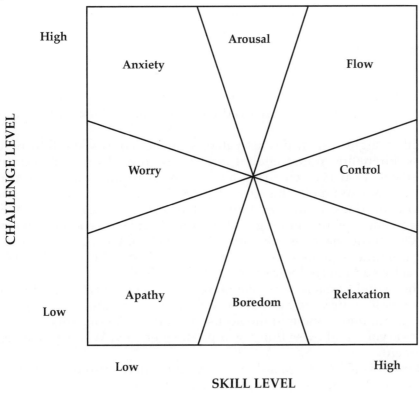

Figure 8.4

Owen Schaffer[8] proposed seven conditions for flow to occur:

- Knowing what to do
- Knowing how to do it
- Knowing how well you are doing
- Knowing where to go
- High perceived challenges

---

8   Owen Schaffer is lead usability analyst at Human Factors International, the world's largest company specialising in user experience design.

- High perceived skills

- Freedom from distractions

Schaffer also published a tool, the Flow Condition Questionnaire (FCQ), to measure each of these seven flow conditions for any given task or activity.

Fight or flight

The *fight or flight* response – also called the *acute stress response* – is a physiological reaction that occurs in response to a perceived harmful event, attack, or threat to survival.

When our fight or flight response is activated, sequences of nerve cell firing occur and chemicals like adrenaline, noradrenaline and cortisol are released into our bloodstream. These patterns of nerve cell firing and chemical release cause our body to undergo a series of very dramatic changes. Our respiratory rate increases. Blood is shunted away from our digestive tract and directed into our muscles and limbs, which require extra energy and fuel for running and fighting. Our pupils dilate. Our awareness intensifies. Our sight sharpens. Our impulses quicken. Our perception of pain diminishes. Our immune system mobilises with increased activation. We become prepared – physically and psychologically – for fight or flight.

When our fight or flight system is activated, we tend to perceive everything in our environment as a possible threat to our survival. By its very nature, the fight or flight system bypasses our rational mind and moves us into 'attack' mode. This state of alert causes us to see everyone and everything as a possible enemy. We may overreact to the slightest comment.

You can see how it is almost impossible to have a positive attitude to work when you are stuck in survival mode. The rational mind is disengaged. Making clear choices and recognising the consequences of those choices is not possible. We are focused on short-term survival, not the long-term consequences of our choices. When we are overwhelmed with excessive stress, our life becomes a series of short-term emergencies. We lose the ability to relax and enjoy the moment. We live from crisis to crisis, with no relief in sight. Burnout is inevitable.

General adaptation syndrome

The general adaptation syndrome (GAS) is a term used to describe the body's short-term and long-term reactions to stress; it was originally described by Hans Selye[9]. Stressors include such physical and environmental phenomena as starvation, being hit by a car, or dealing with severe weather. Additionally, people can suffer emotional or mental stressors such as the loss of a loved one, the inability to solve a problem, or having difficulties at work.

Holmes and Rahe (1967) developed a questionnaire called the Social Readjustment Rating Scale (SRRS) for identifying major stressful life events. They surveyed over

---

9   Hans Selye (1907–1982), an Austrian-born physician who emigrated to Canada in 1939.

5,000 medical patients and asked them to say whether they had experienced any of a series of 43 life events in the previous two years. Each event, called a life change unit (LCU), had a different 'weight' for stress. The more events the patient added up, the higher the score, and the more likely the patient was to become ill. You can try this questionnaire for yourself at:

http://www.mindtools.com/pages/article/newTCS_82.htm.

Selye thought that the general adaptation syndrome involved two major systems of the body, the nervous system and the endocrine (or hormonal) system. He then went on to outline what he considered as three distinctive stages in the syndrome's evolution. He called these stages the alarm reaction, the stage of resistance, and the stage of exhaustion.

The General Adaptation Syndrome

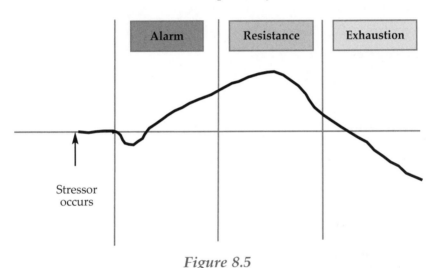

Figure 8.5

- *Alarm* – the first stage of the general adaptation syndrome, the alarm reaction, is the immediate reaction to a stressor. In the initial phase of stress, people exhibit a fight or flight response, which prepares the body for physical activity. However, this initial response can also decrease the effectiveness of the immune system, making people more susceptible to illness during this phase.

- *Resistance* – during this phase, if the stress continues, the body adapts to the stressors it is exposed to. Changes take place at many levels in order to reduce the effect of the stressor. For example, if the stressor is starvation, the person might experience a reduced desire for physical activity to conserve energy, and the absorption of nutrients from food might be maximised. Stage 2 is also named the stage of adaptation, instead of the stage of resistance.

- *Exhaustion* – in this stage, the stress has continued for some time. The body's resistance to the stress may gradually be reduced, or even collapse. Generally, this means the immune system, and the body's ability to resist disease, may be almost totally eliminated. People who experience long-term stress may succumb to heart attacks or severe infection due to their reduced immunity.

Burnout

Burnout is a state of physical, emotional or mental exhaustion combined with doubts about your competence and the value of your work. Burnout can result from various factors, including:

- Lack of control
- Lack of resources
- Unclear job expectations
- Dysfunctional workplace dynamics
- Mismatch in values
- Poor job fit
- Extremes of activity
- Lack of social support
- Work-life imbalance

The difference between stress and burnout is a matter of degree, which means that the earlier you recognise the signs, the better able you will be to avoid burnout. Here are some signals you have to pay attention to:

- *Chronic fatigue.* Lack of energy and feeling tired most days, or feeling a sense of anxiety about what lies ahead on any given day.
- *Insomnia.* Trouble falling asleep or staying asleep, or inability to sleep altogether.
- *Impaired concentration and attention.* Lack of focus and forgetfulness, or you can't get your work done and everything begins to pile up.
- *Physical symptoms.* Physical symptoms may include chest pain, heart palpitations, shortness of breath, gastrointestinal pain, dizziness, fainting, and/or headaches.
- *Increased illness.* Because your body is depleted, your immune system becomes weakened, making you more vulnerable to infections, colds, flu, and other immune-related medical problems.

- *Loss of appetite.* In the early stages, you may not feel hungry and may skip a few meals. In the latter stages, you may lose your appetite all together and begin to lose a significant amount of weight.

- *Anxiety.* Symptoms of tension, worry, and edginess. As you move closer to burnout, the anxiety may become so serious that it interferes with your ability to work productively and may cause problems in your personal life.

- *Anger.* Interpersonal tension and irritability. This may turn into angry outbursts and serious arguments at home and in the workplace.

- *Loss of enjoyment.* Not wanting to go to work or being eager to leave, or trying to avoid challenges and figure out ways to escape work all together.

- *Pessimism.* A general sense that nothing is going right or nothing matters, issues of trust with co-workers and family members and a feeling that you can't count on anyone.

- *Isolation.* In the early stages, this may seem like mild resistance to socialising; in the latter stages, you may become angry when someone speaks to you, or you may come into work early or leave late to avoid interactions with colleagues.

- *Detachment.* Removing yourself emotionally and physically from your job and other responsibilities; you may call in sick often, stop returning calls and emails, or regularly come in late.

- *Depression.* In the early stages, you may feel mildly sad, occasionally hopeless, and you may experience feelings of guilt and worthlessness as a result. At its worst, you may feel trapped, severely depressed, and think the world would be better off without you. (If your depression has reached this point, you should seek professional help immediately.)

You can read more about this topic in 'The Truth about Burnout'[10] or – on a lighter note – in 'Fried'[11]

Paradoxically enough, top performers are most likely to experience burnout, because they are given the toughest assignments with the biggest challenges. They are the most likely to struggle with overwork, and least likely to ask for help or set limits.

Burnout is not a simple result of hard work or long hours. The cynicism, depression and lethargy of burnout can occur when you're not in control of how you carry out your job, when you're working toward goals that don't resonate with you, and when you lack social support. If you don't tailor your responsibilities to match your true vocation, or at least take a break once in a while, you could face a mountain of mental and physical health problems. Beware!

---

10 'The Truth About Burnout – How Organisations Cause Personal Stress and What to Do About it' (2000) by Christina Maslach and Michael P. Leiter.

11 'Fried – Why you Burn Out and how to Revive' (2012) by Joan Borysenko.

Resilience factors

For sure, the origins of our stress are often outside of ourselves, and the way our body and mind react are largely physiological and thus beyond our immediate control. However, a combination of factors can contribute to our resilience. Many studies show that the most important factor is having caring and supportive relationships within and outside the family. Relationships that create love and trust, provide role models and offer encouragement and reassurance help reinforce a person's resilience.

Besides social support, several additional factors are associated with resilience, including:

- A healthy life style.

- A positive view of yourself and confidence in your strengths and abilities.

- The capacity to make realistic plans and taking steps to carry them out.

- Skills in communication and problem solving.

- The capacity to manage strong feelings and impulses.

All of these are factors that people can develop themselves. Some, or many of the ways to build resilience in the following pages may be appropriate to consider in developing your personal strategy.

Social support

Numerous studies indicate that social support is essential for maintaining physical and psychological health. Both the detrimental consequences of poor social support, and the protecting effects of good social support have been extensively documented. Social support has been described as 'support accessible to an individual through social bonds with other individuals, groups, and the larger community – a network of family, friends, neighbours, and community members.' One might add that the possibility of being able to call on the help of a mentor or a coach could also be counted as social support. Coaches like Ian McDermott[12] recommend the 'buddy system', especially for managers, in this respect.

With respect to exactly what social support means, perhaps the psychiatrist Sidney Cobb gave one of the best definitions. He proposed that social support was a subjective sensation in which the individual feels: 'That he is cared for and loved. That he is esteemed and valued; that he belongs to a network of communication and mutual obligation.'

Theoretical models of social support specify the following two important dimensions:

- A *structural dimension*, which includes network size and frequency of social interactions.

12   https://www.linkedin.com/in/ianemcdermott

- A *functional dimension* with emotional (such as receiving love and empathy) and instrumental (practical help such as gifts of money or assistance with child care) components.

Most research has found that the *quality* of relationships (the functional dimension) is a better predictor of good health than the *quantity* of relationships (the structural dimension), although both are important.

For EU staff, this may pose a particular problem, since the vast majority of those who work for the EU are expats. They have had to leave their homes, their relatives, colleagues and social networks behind, and may find it difficult to build a new network of social support from the ground up. I have seen brilliant people – highly skilled and motivated professionals – who could not cope with this. I remember one Spanish colleague who had left his girlfriend back home during the nine months of his probation period. He was so homesick and socially isolated that he decided to quit prematurely, giving up the prospect of life-long employment and an interesting job. I think this was probably the best decision he could make, because, if he had stayed, he was bound to run into serious trouble, deeply unhappy at work, and ultimately a burnout.

The EU institutions are well aware of this. That is why they are actively involved in the many leisure, sports and cultural clubs open to EU staff and their families, including athletics, dance, theatre, art and language exchange. I would also advise you to break out of the 'euro bubble' in and around Brussels, and join local organisations and (service) clubs. Belgians are known for their cordiality, and you will soon get genuine friends you can rely on.

The benefits of reading for pleasure

'*Reading is to the mind what exercise is to the body.*'[13] – Richard Steele

A recent study[14] conducted at the University of Liverpool explored the emotional, social and psychological benefits to adults of regular reading for pleasure.

Regular readers for pleasure reported fewer feelings of stress and depression than non-readers, and stronger feelings of relaxation from reading than from watching television or engaging with social media. Reading creates a parallel world in which personal anxieties can recede, while also helping people to realise that the problems they experience are not theirs alone. A fifth of respondents said reading helped them to feel less lonely.

Those who read for pleasure also have higher levels of self-esteem and a greater ability to cope with difficult situations. Readers have expanded models and repertoires of experience, which allow them to look with new perspectives and understanding on their own lives. Readers find it easier to make decisions, to plan and prioritise, and this may be because they are more able to recognise that difficulty and setbacks are unavoidable aspects of human life.

People who read regularly feel closer to their friends and their community than lapsed or non-readers. Reading not only produces greater understanding and empathy with others; it also gives a currency for sharing experience more meaningfully than is possible in ordinary social conversation. Readers also have a stronger and more engaged awareness of social issues and of cultural diversity than non-readers.

The conclusions of the study were that readers feel happier about themselves and their lives. Reading for just 30 minutes a week produces greater life satisfaction, enhances social connectedness and sense of community spirit, and helps protect against, and even prepare for life's difficulties.

13   Sir Richard Steele (1672–1729) was an Anglo-Irish writer and politician.
14   http://www.quickreads.org.uk/assets/downloads/docs/Galaxy-Quick-Reads-Report-FINAL%20.pdf

Mens sana in corpore sano

The expression *mens sana in corpore sano* – 'a sound mind in a sound body' – is widely used to express the idea that physical health is an important part of mental and psychological well being. Caring for your physical needs by eating healthy food, exercising, finding time to relax, and getting enough sleep can help you cope with stress:

- Eating healthily can help boost your brain's serotonin levels, which will combat higher cortisol associated with stress.

- Exercise and other physical activity produce endorphins – chemicals in the brain that act as natural painkillers.

- Stay well-hydrated – keeping the body hydrated helps the heart pump blood more easily through the blood vessels to the muscles and your brain.

- Sleep is a necessary human function – it allows our brains to recharge and our bodies to rest, which in turn reduces stress. Your brain needs downtime to stay sharp. If you don't get enough sleep, you'll tax your memory and start forgetting things. Stay rested so you can keep your mind alert.

- Limit your alcohol intake. Alcohol is a depressant, which means that it slows down the brain and the central nervous system's processes.

- Limit your caffeine intake. The effects of drinking coffee are long-lasting and exaggerate the stress response, both in terms of the body's physiological response as reflected in raised blood pressure and stress hormone levels, and also in terms of increasing a person's feeling of being stressed.

Stress and smoking

While I was still a smoker – I used to smoke cigars – I was convinced that smoking relieves stress. Studies have found, however, that in reality, smoking has the opposite effect: it causes long-term stress levels to rise, not fall.

In one study conducted at the London School of Medicine and Dentistry, researchers looked at 469 people who tried to quit smoking after being hospitalised for heart disease. At the start, the subjects had similar levels of stress and generally believed that smoking helped them to cope.

A year later, 41 per cent had managed to stay abstinent. After controlling for several factors, the scientists found that the abstainers had 'a significantly larger decrease in perceived stress,' roughly a 20 per cent drop, compared with the continuing smokers, who showed little change.

The scientists' hypothesis was that the continuing smokers were dealing with uncomfortable cravings between cigarettes multiple times a day, while the abstainers, after facing some initial withdrawal, had greater freedom from nicotine cravings and thus had eliminated a frequent and significant source of stress.

The bottom line: the calming effect of a cigarette is a myth, at least in the long term.

The brain is roughly 2% of one's body weight, but consumes about 20% of the oxygen. The ability to get more oxygen to the brain allows more of the brain to be accessed, and a healthy body can make this happen.

Positive thinking

'Optimism is a moral duty' – Immanuel Kant[15]

A study released in 2013 found that optimists have a better biological response to stress than pessimists. Researchers at Concordia University's Department of Psychology found that 'the stress hormone' cortisol tends to be more stable in people with a positive outlook.

Joelle Jobin[16] found that pessimists tend to have a higher stress baseline than optimists. Pessimists generally had trouble regulating their sympathetic nervous system when they go through stressful experiences. The inability to look on the bright side causes cortisol to stay constantly elevated.

Like most hormones in our bodies, 'the stress hormone' cortisol is complex with many functions. Although cortisol is linked to many health problems it is also our 'get up and do things hormone,' according to Jobin. Just like we have 'eustress' (good stress) and 'distress' (bad stress), we need cortisol to stimulate our sympathetic nervous system and kick-start our bodies into action.

Each of us has the free will to be an optimist or a pessimist. The daily choices of mindset and behaviour that we make create biological changes throughout our bodies that have long lasting ramifications.

Albert Ellis[17] discovered in 1955 that people's beliefs strongly affected their emotional functioning. In particular certain irrational beliefs made people feel depressed, anxious or angry and led to self-defeating behaviours. Ellis created the ABC model to help us understand the meaning of our reactions to adversity:

- A is the adversity – the situation or event.

- B is our belief – our explanation of why the situation happened.

- C is the consequence – the feelings and behaviours that our belief causes.

Adversity -> Beliefs -> Consequences

The word 'belief' means a conviction of the truth, actuality, or validity of something. So a belief is a thought with an emotional component (conviction) and a factual component (truth, actuality or validity). Beliefs can be either positive or negative. Having a negative belief is not necessarily a bad thing; however, when one believes in something that is false, a negative belief tends to become what Ellis called an 'irra-

---

15   Immanuel Kant (1724–1804) was a German philosopher, a central figure of modern philosophy.

16   https://www.linkedin.com/pub/joelle-jobin-concordia/44/223/52b

17   Albert Ellis (1913–2007) was an American psychologist.

tional' belief. Irrational beliefs are not friendly to happiness and contentment and are definitely unhelpful for getting one's basic desires for love and approval, comfort and achievement or success met.

Sometimes it's hard to identify our beliefs; we tend to be better at labelling our feelings. The B-C connections can be used in reverse to help us identify our beliefs. For example, feelings of guilt are often produced when we believe that we have violated another person's rights. B-C connections help us increase our self-awareness – an important first step to a resilient response to adversity.

In his Rational Emotive Behaviour Theory (REBT) Ellis argues that:

- Unconditional self-acceptance, other-acceptance and life-acceptance are of prime importance in achieving mental wellness.

- People and the world are fallible and people are better off accepting themselves and others, life's hassles and unfairness, as they are.

- People should consider themselves valuable just as a result of being alive and kicking, because all humans do both good and bad deeds and have both (not either/or) good and bad attributes and traits.

Clearly, all this should certainly not be an excuse to just 'cop out', i.e. take the easy way out of a sticky situation; you are responsible for your own behaviour and development after all.

Lastly, for reading matter, I would strongly recommend the UK psychologist/author Gill Hasson, who has written an excellent and very easy to read guide to Mindfulness and another one on Emotional Intelligence. They are really well worth recommending as background reading.

Planning

'To achieve great things, two things are needed: a plan and not quite enough time.' – Leonard Bernstein[18]

We all come across periods of very high workload and tight deadlines, but some people simply don't know how to handle this. They freak out, and start running around like headless chickens. Not sufficient progress is made and, obviously, the deadlines are not met. This creates even greater stress.

Before I start with our individual behaviour during these periods of high stress, let me mention what the bestselling author on change and motivation, John Kotter, says about urgency. In his book 'A Sense of Urgency'[19] Kotter identifies the single biggest factor to successful change: creating a true sense of urgency. Urgency he says, is 'a compulsive determination to move, and win, now.'

---

18   US composer and conductor (1918–1990)
19   'A Sense of Urgency' (2008) by John P. Kotter.

Resilient behaviour in these situations is to keep your cool, step back a bit, and make a plan. The key to managing your stress under these circumstances is to kill the negative emotions and stay in control.

One of my coachees (a Spanish banker) gave me a great metaphor for this. He told me that the worst thing you can do when facing a dangerous snake is to freeze, because the snake will eventually kill you. Instead back away from the snake, analyse the situation, and work out how to kill the snake yourself.

Planning does not mean working longer hours, dropping holidays, or taking work home during the weekends. Now I am not saying that – from time to time – you cannot do this, but it has to fit into your plan; if burning long hours at work is your only strategy to cope with workload stress you are bound to run into a burnout.

Planning means *staying in control*, and not being controlled by your negative emotions. Planning means cutting the big problem into smaller chunks, allocating time and resources, deciding on the priorities, outsourcing, delegating or asking for help, and possibly even renegotiating the expected outcome or deadlines. Breaks and time to relax should also be part of your plan.

Create a to-do list every day with no more than 10 items numbered in order of priority. Tackle your most challenging to-do items first thing in the day when your brain is most refreshed. Review your list at the end of every day.

Learn to say 'No' – sometimes. It may be pressures from family and/or work that lead to too much stress, and sometimes it may be expectations that you have of yourself that might not be completely realistic. *If you don't set priorities for your own life, someone else will.*

Don't allow a heavy workload to frustrate you. When the pressures are coming from something over which you have no control, rather than fight against it, accept it and move on, like a true professional.

Dealing with variations in workload

Variations in workload occur in virtually every work environment; periods of heavy workload are followed by relatively calmer periods. This can be due to the inherently periodic nature of the organisation's activities (e.g. meeting agendas, budget cycle, etc.) or simply because of holiday periods.

We have already seen how good planning can help you cope with the periods of heavy workload, but effective management of your agenda can be very useful during the calmer periods as well. Here are some things you can schedule for the calmer periods at work:

- *Taking care of your backlog.* Activities that were postponed during the 'busy' period because they were not urgent – and not so important – can usefully be performed during a calmer period. Typically, dealing with unanswered emails is one of these activities.

- *Cleaning up.* Reorganising your desktop, filing documents, inventory, etc.

- *Anticipating future work.* Preparing forms, questionnaires, checklists, contact lists, etc.

- *Planning.* It is often possible to plan ahead, even when not all the necessary details are available yet.

- *Professional and personal development.* Training, workshops, seminars and conferences.

- *Networking.* Calmer periods are great opportunities to take care of your operational, personal, and strategic networks (see Chapter 9 to find out the difference).

- *Recharging your batteries.* Clear your brain by taking holidays, spending more time on the things you enjoy, etc.

Communicating and problem solving

Mental noise is the constant chatter of the mind that never stops. It is the inner conversation that goes on constantly in the mind. This mental noise is like a background noise that never ceases, from the moment of waking up to the moment of falling asleep. It is a sort of inner voice that constantly analyses everything about what you are doing, what is going on around you, and the people you meet.

The mind also repeats the same thoughts over and over again, like in a loop, like a record that got stuck. If these are positive thoughts, that's fine. However, too often, they are negative thoughts that intensify stress, worry, anger or frustration.

Clearly, thinking is a vital activity required for solving problems, analysing, comparing, studying, planning, etc. – but too often, the mind wanders where it will, occupying your attention with trivial matters and unimportant, useless thinking that wastes your time and energy.

The mind is a tool therefore that needs to be kept under control. The *mental noise theory* states that clear communication happens only when we overcome a certain degree of mental distraction. It further suggests that when people are stressed, they have greater difficulty hearing, understanding and remembering information.

Here are some important things to keep in mind when communicating under stress in the workplace:

- *Listen first.* The higher the level of stress, the more important it is to show that you are listening. People are more willing to listen to what you have to say when they believe you are listening to them in turn. In the words of Stephen Covey: 'Seek first to understand, then to be understood'.

- *Clarity, brevity and repetition.* Remember, the greater the stress, the greater the need for clarity, brevity, and repetition. To help people understand your message, provide information in small portions that are easily absorbed. Use familiar words and simple sentences, and repeat important points, to be sure that you are understood.

- *Make it personal.* Use face-to-face communication, not email, to help get your message across during times of high stress. When interacting in person, pay particular attention to body language, as this is directly linked to people's emotions.

Another human trait that often blocks communication is our tendency to focus on the negative. This is called *negative dominance theory* or negativity bias. Because of this bias, people generally attach more weight to negative statements – and remember them longer – and this tendency of concentrating on what is perceived to be negative becomes even stronger when we are stressed out. So it is important to considerably increase the ratio of positive to negative statements in times of high stress.

The more stressful our environment, the more we need to connect and communicate. In times of crisis and anxiety people need to feel listened to, and feel that they belong to the group. In these circumstances, more than ever, our communication must demonstrate compassion, conviction, truthfulness and credibility. Our presentations, conversations and documents must be brief, clear and repeat key messages. Remember that the characteristics of good communication don't change under stress; they just become more important.

Self-control

'You have power over your mind – not outside events. Realise this, and you will find strength.' – Marcus Aurelius[20]

Self-control separates us from our primitive ancestors and from the animals, thanks to our large prefrontal cortices. Rather than responding to immediate impulses, we can plan, we can evaluate alternative actions, and we can refrain from doing things we may eventually regret.

For most people, stress or boredom makes them instinctively reach for something to allay it, and this often takes the instant-gratification form of sugar, alcohol, nicotine or distractions like social media.

Train yourself to be mindful enough to know when you are entering your danger zone (i.e. feeling stressed out, tired, bored, etc.). Becoming more conscious of your mood and the likelihood of lapsing will help you to act with intention instead of habit. But it is not enough to simply try to break a bad habit; the process is much more effective when actively replacing it with a good habit. If you're addicted to nicotine, try chewing gum to address the oral fixation, but avoid substituting food for the cigarette. Remember, this isn't just a habit you're trying to kick; it's a lifestyle adjustment. Cultivate a new way of being.

Anger management involves spotting the triggers for anger as early as possible and expressing these feelings and frustrations in a cool, calm and composed way. Anger management is about unlearning ineffective coping mechanisms and re-learning more effective ways to deal with the problems and frustrations associated with anger. There are many anger management techniques that you can learn and practise by yourself. However if you experience a lot of regular anger then seeking help, usually in the form of a counsellor, can be more effective.

---

20   Military leader, philosopher and Roman emperor from 161 to 180.

Dealing with change

In the workplace, change is inevitable, and dealing with change requires some mental adjustments:

- Approach change as a process; processes take time.
- Embrace change; choose to give positive meaning to changes.
- Be prepared to move with changes because they are going to happen anyway.

If you are aware of an upcoming change, such as a move or a new job, you can help to alleviate stress about the event in multiple ways:

- *Create an action plan.* By setting (SMART) goals and creating a series of steps to get from one intermediate objective to another, you will feel more in control of the situation, which should help minimise your stress.
- *One change at a time.* If you have a big change coming up, it's important that you create consistency in the rest of your life as much as possible. For example, if you're going to be changing jobs soon it may be best not to attempt to change personal habits (stop smoking for example) at the same time.
- *Rely on your social support network.*

Sometimes, change occurs without warning. Here too, there are a number of steps you can take to help you cope and adapt:

- *Relax.* Try to take time to relax every day, even if it's only for a few minutes. You can also use relaxation techniques like meditation or deep breathing as a tool for coping with stress.
- *Laugh.* Laughter can help decrease the effects of stress.
- *Seek professional support.* If stress management techniques do not work for you, then seek care from a qualified professional such as a life coach, a therapist, or social worker.

Working with your manager

'The single biggest problem in communication is the illusion that it has taken place.' – G.B. Shaw[21]

Like most large administrations, the EU institutions are *hierarchical organisations.* A hierarchical organisation is a structure where every entity, except one, is subservient

---

21   Anglo-Irish playwright, 1856-1950.

to a single other entity. Members of hierarchical organisations mainly communicate with their immediate superior and with their immediate subordinates. Structuring organisations in this way is useful because it can reduce the communication overhead by limiting information flow. However, this is also its major limitation.

Communication builds relationships, including the working relationships that allow people within an organisation to coordinate their efforts for the common good. Communication flows up, down and across the levels of an organisation. Communication flowing up the chain of command gives management valuable information about the state of affairs. Feedback, reports, suggestions and work needs all flow from subordinate to manager. Communications that flow down from one level to the next range from operational to strategic matters. Operational matters include directives, feedback, training and appraisals. Starting at the top, though, management must also provide leadership by communicating broader concerns — guiding principles, such as the organisation's vision, mission and strategic goals.

The problem is that communication is never perfect. This is because all organisations are built with people, and people aren't perfect. Our hierarchical superiors are normal human beings too, with their inherent imperfections. Perfect leaders or perfect managers do not exist; even the most highly esteemed, world-class leaders have their personal weaknesses and blind spots. Your superior may be inexperienced in their new job; they may have been promoted to their 'level of incompetence' (the Peter Principle, discussed earlier); or – at worst – they may have a hidden agenda. In any case, your interaction with management will never be without stress and anxiety.

Having worked with numerous not-so-inspiring managers in my own career, I learned that they provided me with unique opportunities for developing my own leadership skills, and learning 'what not to do' when managing people myself. However bad your manager may be, you can always develop ways to handle your relationship with him or her in a better way. Rather than think of your line manager as your 'boss', think of them as a difficult 'client' – one you have to figure out how to work with if you want to get ahead, even if you'd rather not be in that situation.

**"I have a few complaints about
how you're doing your job
as my boss."**

In any event, it's better for you to work with the management rather than against it; here are some strategies to help you on your way:

- *Know their 'why'.* The better you understand what your manager does, and more importantly, why they do it, the better positioned you are to deliver results, manage expectations, and avoid lose-lose situations. When you know what drives your manager, you can structure your views and communicate in ways that line up with their core values, concerns and priorities.

- *Adapt your communication style.* If you have ever done a personality assessment like the MBTI (see Chapter 2), try to find out what your manager's preferences are, and how these may be different from yours. It can help you adapt your communication style and save a lot of tension.

- *Work around their weaknesses.* Exposing your manager's incompetence will only reinforce your misery and may even damage your own reputation. By doing what you can to help your manager succeed, you lay a solid foundation for more success for yourself.

- *Keep your mind focused on top performance.* Never let your manager's bad behaviour be an excuse for your own. As Gandhi wrote: 'Be the change you want to see in the world.' In this case, act like the leader you wish your manager was.

- *Have the courage to speak up.* Instead of saying nothing, suffering in silence, or complaining privately to colleagues, speak up; you at least owe your manager the opportunity to respond.

If things really don't work out, there still is the Staff Committee to complain to. The Staff Committee is a statutory committee that represents the interests of your institution's staff vis-à-vis management and assures continuous contact between management and staff.

And don't forget: nothing lasts forever. On average, we only work for the same manager for a couple of years; natural staff mobility will take care of that. In the EU institutions staff mobility is even actively encouraged, so if you are finally moving away from a bad manager, nobody will blame you for that.

Personality type and stress

Everybody has a different reaction to stress. One of the main differentiators is our personality. Table 8.1 lists some possible tactics you can apply, depending on your MBTI preferences:

Your Preferences	Your Stressors	Possible Tactics
Extraversion	• Working alone • Having to communicate mainly in writing • Lengthy work periods without interruptions • Having to reflect before taking action • Having to focus in depth on one thing • Getting feedback in writing only	• Networking with others outside your team • Asking others to voice their ideas • Paying attention to written communication • Allowing others to think about your ideas before they provide feedback
Introversion	• Working with others • Having to communicate mainly by talking • Interacting with others frequently • Having to act quickly, without reflection • Too many concurrent tasks and demands • Getting frequent and verbal feedback	• Arriving at work early, taking advantage of the quiet time • Intentionally seeking private/reflective time, taking a walk over lunchtime or the long way home • Planning private breaks to collect your thoughts • In meetings, voicing even partially thought-through perspectives
Intuition	• Having to attend to realities • Having to do things the proven way • Having to attend to details • Checking the accuracy of facts • Needing to focus on past experience • Being required to be practical	• Practise presenting information in a step-by-step manner • Providing specific examples of vital information • Honouring organisational values surrounding experience and tradition • Reading the fine print and getting the facts straight
Sensing	• Attending to own and others' insights • Having to do old things in a new way • Having to give an overview without details • Looking for the meaning of facts • Focusing on possibilities • Too many complexities	• Getting involved in projects that require long-range or future thinking • Practise brainstorming • Preparing yourself to look for patterns • Going beyond specifics, trying to discover meaning and themes
Thinking	• Using personal experience to assess situations • Adjusting to individual differences and needs • Noticing and appreciating what is positive • Focusing on processes and people • Using empathy and personal values to make decisions • Having others react to questioning as divisive	• Working on projects in which alternative causes and solutions are evaluated in personal terms • Reminding yourself that factoring in people is logical even if people aren't • Softening critical remarks, finding the positive too • Asking for others' opinions and concerns; looking for points of agreement before discussing issues

continued overleaf...

continued

Your Preferences	Your Stressors	Possible Tactics
Feeling	• Analysing situations objectively • Setting criteria and standards • Critiquing and focusing on flaws • Being expected to use logic alone to make decisions • Asking questions that feel divisive	• Practise laying out an argument by saying 'if…then', or by considering the causes and effects • Understanding that critical feedback is often given in the spirit of improving your professionalism • Paying attention to stakeholders' concern regarding project/work • Using brief and concise language to express your wants and needs
Judging	• Waiting for structures to emerge from process • Too much flexibility around time frames and deadlines • Having to marshal energy at the last minute • Staying open to re-evaluation of tasks • Dealing with surprises	• Seeking out projects that have definite planning and milestones • Trying to wait on a decision for a few days, continuing to gather more information and paying attention to ideas that may come up • Understand that work is progressing despite differences in work styles • Making your own milestones and deadlines
Perceiving	• Having to organise their and others' plans • Working with time frames and deadlines • Others' distrust of last minute energy • Having to finish and move on • Developing contingency plans • Being required to plan ahead	• Recognising that deadlines set by the organisation may not be negotiable • Using a past decision you believe others rushed to demonstrate the advantages of slowing down to gather more information • Becoming active in projects where the process is just as important as the outcome • Keeping surprises to a minimum and reducing your options

The upside of stress

'The Upside of Stress'[22] is a book that brings together research on the relationship between resilience and mindset. Author Kelly McGonigal[23] works together science, stories, and exercises with the idea of showing you:

• How to cultivate a mindset to embrace stress.

• How stress can provide focus and energy.

• How stress can help people connect and strengthen close relationships.

22 'The Upside of Stress – Why Stress is good for You, and how to get Good at It' (2015) by Kelly McGonigal.
23 Kelly McGonigal (1977) is a health psychologist who is known for her work in the field of 'science help'

- Why your brain is built to learn from stress, and how to increase its ability to learn from challenging experiences.

McGonigal's TED talk[24] on the same subject has had more than 7 million views.

Developing your resilience

Resilience is ordinary, not extraordinary. Resilience is not a trait that people either have or do not have. It involves behaviours, thoughts and actions that can be learned and developed in anyone.

Please refer to Chapter 1 (methodology) and Annex 6 for further development of this competency, have another look at the current chapter to find out about your options, and remember: YOU are responsible for your own development, not your manager, your colleagues, or your mentor.

The online toolkit that comes for free with this book can be used to follow-up on your development in this area. This toolkit can be found at:

https://www.johnharperpublishing.co.uk/the-ultimate-eu-career-development-toolkit/

Key points to remember

- Stress is the body's response to change.

- Stress is defined in many different ways and stress and the types of things that cause stress can vary from person to person.

- Your social network is by far the most important tool to become resilient.

- You can control stress and stay in control by carefully anticipating and planning work and life.

- Stress can be turned into positive energy and stressful situations are – in fact – learning opportunities.

24   http://kellymcgonigal.com/2014/11/15/watch-my-ted-talk-how-to-make-stress-your-friend/

Your notes

9. Working with others

Competency definition: 'Work co-operatively with others in teams and across organisational boundaries and respect differences between people.'

'It takes two flints to make a fire' – Louisa May Alcott[1]

Some things are easy to achieve by working on your own, but there will inevitably be many times when you have to work with other people to get a job done.

Working with others is the ability to effectively interact, cooperate, collaborate and manage conflicts with other people in order to complete tasks and achieve shared goals. This includes working with just one other individual, either in person or at a distance, or working in small or large groups of people, for example co-workers, managers, stakeholders, and contractors.

Wherever people work together, groups will be formed. People will belong to one or more groups, with each group having a different goal and purpose. These groups may be formal or informal. Formal groups are created to complete defined tasks, whilst informal groups are created voluntarily and are made up of individuals with common interests or roles. Informal groups are not usually recognised by the organisation but they can have significant impact upon the work of others.

Effectively working with others involves understanding and working within the group's culture, rules and values; joint planning and decision-making; negotiating and compromising; expressing one's opinions and ideas and respecting those of others, including people of differing backgrounds; and being flexible in terms of roles, including knowing when to take a leadership role and knowing when to seek a team approach.

Groups versus teams

'The nice thing about teamwork is that you always have others on your side.' – Margaret Carty

In English, the words 'group' and 'team' can sometimes be used interchangeably, but in other situations there are clear differences in meaning between them. For example, we have a football team, not a football group – or we have a special interest group, not a special interest team. While the differences may be subtle, they are indeed different, and we need to understand what those differences are.

In the business world – and by extension in public administration – there are *work groups* and *work teams*. A work group is two or more individuals who are either dependent or independent in their activities and may or may not work in the same department. A work team has members who work interdependently on a specific, common goal to produce an end result for their organisation.

1   Louisa May Alcott (1832–1888), American writer, most famously of 'Little Women'.

In work teams, the leader acts as a facilitator; the members actively participate in the discussions and influence the outcome. It is the team members who decide on the distribution of work assignments. In contrast, in work groups it is the leader who dominates and controls the group; it is very clear who is in charge, and the leader will conduct the meetings and assign work to the group members.

Usually, work teams meet more often than work groups. Work groups may meet periodically, based on the manager's style, primarily to listen to and share information. Teams, in contrast, do much more than communicate when they meet. Team meetings are opportunities for planning work, solving problems, making decisions about work, and reviewing progress. In short, meetings are vital to a team's existence.

Dependent-level work groups are the traditional work unit or department-level groups, with a supervisor who plays a strong role as the superior. Each person in a dependent-level work group has their own job and works under the close guidance of the manager. In fact, most problem solving, work assignments, and other decisions affecting the group come from the manager.

Independent-level work groups are the most common form of work groups on the business scene. Like a dependent-level work group, each person is responsible for their own main area. But unlike the dependent level, the manager tends not to function like a controlling boss. Instead, staff members work on their own assignments with just general direction and minimal supervision. Sales representatives, research scientists, accountants, lawyers, police officers, and teachers are among the professionals who tend to work in this fashion. People in those professions come together in one department because they serve a common overall function, but almost everyone in the group works fairly independently.

Members of an *interdependent-level* entity rely on each other to get the work done. Sometimes members have their own roles and at other times they share responsibilities. However, in either case, they coordinate with one another to produce an overall product or set of outcomes. When this interdependence exists, you have a team.

As you can see from the above, the situation in the European Commission – and the other EU institutions for that matter – offers a very mixed picture in terms of groups and teams, and it is not always clear from the organogram whether Sector ABC or Unit XYZ is a group or a team. Also, some entities work at a dependent level, while others are either independent or interdependent. Many groups or teams do not even show up on the organogram, and we talk of 'task forces' (i.e. teams) or – sometimes, interinstitutional – 'work groups' or 'committees' that are set up on a more or less ad hoc basis to serve a certain purpose. Clearly, it is up to the participants to find their way in this labyrinth, and interact with the other participants accordingly.

Group dynamics

One of the main sources of stress in the workplace has to do with work relationships. *Group dynamics* is a system of behaviours and psychological processes occurring within a group, or between groups. The study of group dynamics can be useful in dealing with conflicts and stress, but also in understanding decision-making behaviour.

In 1965 Bruce Tuckman[2] identified four stages of group development, adding a fifth stage in his later writings ten years later.

Stage 1: Forming

In the Forming stage, personal relations are characterised by dependence. Group members rely on safe, patterned behaviour and look to the group leader for guidance and direction. Group members have a desire for acceptance by the group and a need to know that the group is safe. Serious topics and feelings are avoided. During this stage, group members are assessing one another and the scope of the task and how to approach the task.

Stage 2: Storming

The next stage, Storming, is characterised by competition and conflict in the personal-relations dimension and organisation in the task-functions dimension. As the group members attempt to organise for the task, conflict inevitably affects personal relations. Individuals have to adjust their feelings, ideas, attitudes, and beliefs to suit the group organisation. These reflect conflicts over leadership, structure, power, and authority. Some group members will like the fact that real issues are starting to surface while others will feel uncomfortable.

Stage 3: Norming

In the Norming stage, interpersonal relations are characterised by cohesion. Group members are engaged in active recognition of all members' contributions, community building and maintenance, and solving of group issues. It is during this stage of development (assuming the group gets this far) that people begin to experience a sense of group belonging and a feeling of relief as a result of resolving interpersonal conflicts. Group members are now listening to each other better and identify themselves as part of a group. In some groups, the fact so much work was invested in reaching this stage may mean group members become reluctant to change anything.

Stage 4: Performing

Not all groups do reach the Performing stage. If group members are able to evolve to stage four, their capacity, range, and depth of personal relations expand to true interdependence. In this stage, people can work independently, in subgroups, or as a total unit with equal facility. There is support for experimentation in solving problems and an emphasis on achievement. The overall goal is productivity through problem solving and work.

Stage 5: Adjourning

Tuckman's final stage, Adjourning, involves the termination of task behaviours and disengagement from relationships. In some texts this stage is also referred to as Mourning.

Tuckman's original work simply described the way he had observed groups, whether they were conscious of it or not. Later work recognised that the real value is in identifying where a group is in the process, and helping it to move to the Performing stage. In the real world, groups are often forming and changing, and each time that happens, they can move to a different stage. A group might be happily

---

2   Bruce Tuckman (1938) is Professor Emeritus at Ohio State University; he carried out research in the theory of group dynamics.

Norming or Performing, but a new member might force them back into Storming. Leaders will be ready for this, and will help the group get back to Performing as quickly as possible.

There are many other models of group development, to name a few: Tubb's Systems model, Fisher's theory of decision emergence in groups, Poole's multiple sequences model, McGrath's Time, Interaction, and Performance (TIP) theory, etc.

Esprit de corps

'Esprit de corps' is a French expression (also used in English) that refers to a collective group spirit and solidarity. Esprit de corps is one of Henri Fayol's[3] 14 administrative principles. The principle states that an organisation must make every effort to maintain group cohesion. It notes that dividing your competition is a clever tactic, but dividing your own team is a serious error.

Being ex-military myself you will not be surprised that I will use an example from a military context – where people rely on each other for their own survival – to illustrate the notion of esprit de corps. In the military this notion can take extreme proportions, up to the level of being immoral or illegal. Check the following fragment of dialogue from 'A Few Good Men', a fantastic movie with Jack Nicholson as Colonel Jessep – the Commanding Officer – and Tom Cruise as a junior military lawyer, Lt. Daniel Kaffee, who defends two Marines accused of murder; they contend they were acting under orders.

Col. Jessep: You want answers?

Kaffee: I think I'm entitled to.

Col. Jessep: You want answers?

Kaffee: I want the truth!

Col. Jessep: You can't handle the truth!

[pauses]

Col. Jessep: Son, we live in a world that has walls, and those walls have to be guarded by men with guns. Who's gonna do it? You? You, Lt. Weinburg? I have a greater responsibility than you could possibly fathom. You weep for Santiago, and you curse the Marines. You have that luxury. You have the luxury of not knowing what I know. That Santiago's death, while tragic, probably saved lives. And my existence, while grotesque and incomprehensible to you, saves lives. You don't want the truth because deep down in places you don't talk about at parties, you want me on that wall, you need me on that wall. We use words like honor, code, loyalty. We use these words as the backbone of a life spent defending something. You use them as a punchline. I have neither the time nor the inclination to explain myself to a man who rises and sleeps under the blanket of the very freedom that I provide, and then questions the manner in which I provide it. I would rather you just said thank you, and went on your way, Otherwise, I suggest you pick up a weapon, and stand a post. Either way, I don't give a damn what you think you are entitled to.

Kaffee: Did you order the Code Red?[4]

Col. Jessep: I did the job I...

Kaffee: Did you order the Code Red?

Col. Jessep: You're Goddamn right I did!

Please note that I have mentioned the notion of esprit de corps in the background part of this chapter, and not in the context of 'best practice', and I did this for a good reason. Esprit de corps is a two-edged sword and there are times when esprit de corps in a small group sense can be very much against esprit de corps in a broader sense, the broader public interest or the interest of an organisation as a whole. A recent example from another field would be the rigging of markets by small groups of traders working closely together in large banks – their esprit de corps was tremendous, but they did huge damage to their organisation's reputation or even solvency.

---

3   Henri Fayol (1841–1925) was a French mining engineer who developed a general theory of business administration known as Fayolism.

4   'Code Red' was an illegal punishment ordered by a commanding officer but executed by someone in the unit.

Group structure

A group's structure is the internal framework that defines members' relations to one another over time. As discussed above, groups come together for many different reasons and in many different ways. However, to ensure that individuals can work together effectively, it is important that everyone should recognise and understand the roles and responsibilities of others, and how they can contribute to getting things done efficiently and well.

Roles can be defined as a tendency to behave, contribute and interrelate with others in a particular way. Roles may be assigned formally, but more often are defined through the process of role differentiation. Role differentiation is the degree to which different group members have specialised functions.

In many professional or administrative meetings there is the role of *moderator*. The moderator takes on the role of a formal or informal chair, and has to show awareness of the expected outcome (the mandate) and manage the sequence of events during the meeting by actively guiding the discussions and making sure that everyone gets a chance to contribute. Thus it is a high profile role in steering the group and achieving a successful outcome. The essential element is to periodically summarise what has been said by others thus far, and also to try to advance the discussions by closing as many open points as possible and then proposing the next step or the way forward.

A second role is that of *timekeeper*. A timekeeper monitors the process from a scheduling point of view. He or she keeps an eye on the clock and warns the group when there is a risk of time overrun. The timekeeper is not a standalone role and anyone, at any point, can remind the group of the time left and where you are in the discussion.

In many professional meetings, there is a *secretarial function* for taking notes, and drafting the minutes.

Status differentials are the relative differences in status among group members. When a group is first formed the members may all be on an equal level, but over time certain members may acquire status and authority within the group; this can create what is known as a *pecking order* within a group.

What is an optimal team size?

'*Too many cooks spoil the broth*' – an expression meaning that a team turns out to be inefficient if too many people take part in it, as it becomes more difficult to coordinate, communicate with all members and maintain the necessary discipline. The reason lies in the mathematics of networks. To understand the magnitude of this effect, let's look at the number of connections in a team, which is $N(N-1)/2$ (Figure 9.1):

Notice that after the low-digit numbers the equation tends towards $N^2/2$, with N representing the number of team members. The number of connections within the network grows much faster than the number of team members does. And that creates an obvious problem: human beings can only handle, or maintain, much smaller numbers of connections. In fact, the optimal size of small teams is the same as the effective range of short-term memory in our brains. Our minds seem to work best in the zone of seven, plus or minus two. On top of that, the connections are not perfect, because of the imperfection of human communication mechanisms.

Thus the ideal size of a team is around three to four people. When more people are needed, the overall efficiency of the team will decrease rapidly.

This simple observation also has far-reaching implications for the so-called *span of control* of managers and leaders. The commonly accepted definition of 'span of control' is as follows: 'the number of subordinates directly reporting to a leader or a manager.'

- 2 members = 1 connection

- 3 members = 3 connections

- 4 members = 6 connections

- 5 members = 10 connections

- 6 members = 15 connections

- ...

- 16 members = 120 connections

- ...

- 50 members = 1225 connections

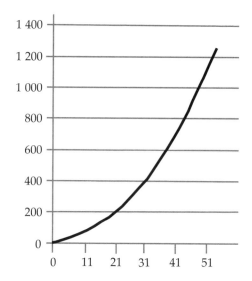

Figure 9.1

In hierarchical organisations of the past it was not uncommon to see average spans of 4 or even less, and the relationship was basically top-down – the manager simply telling the subordinate what to do. In fact, there were even fewer (N) connections, since the subordinates were not even supposed to communicate with each other.

In 1916, Henri Fayol[5] proposed that subordinate employees should be allowed to communicate directly with each other, but only when their superiors had agreed upon this procedure. This principle became known under the name of 'Fayol's bridge'. This can be considered as a first attempt to create a horizontal integration of related activities under a certain level of self-management.

As information technology has advanced, many organisational structures have 'flattened' and average spans have moved closer to 10, resulting in fewer middle managers having to manage more subordinates (sometimes for less money). The idea behind this is that a considerable amount of decision making can be delegated to staff at lower organisational levels. This is the application of Fayol's bridge combined with the principle of employee initiative that he also proposed. In this model, supervision of staff is reduced from constant direct control to 'exception handling'; simply having access to a supervising manager is considered sufficient to satisfy the need for control in standard situations. Peter Drucker[6] referred to this principle as the *span of managerial responsibility* and underpinned the importance of self-directed, cross-functional teams.

5   See footnote 3.

6   Peter Drucker (1909–2005) was an Austrian-born American management consultant, educator, and author.

This trend has inevitably strengthened the case for development of 'core competencies' for all staff at all levels. For a 'flatter' organisation to thrive, everybody needs to be aware and responsible – and that takes more than just professional competence in the specific technicalities of one's own tasks.

How rituals deliver performance

All organisations have rituals – ranging from regular routines like coffee breaks, weekly team meetings and unit meetings, to major, less frequent events like annual meetings and retirement parties. It is important to understand that rituals like these are levers for improving the organisation's performance, because:

- Rituals create a shared identity

- Rituals stimulate the emotions and reduce anxiety

- Rituals reinforce desired behaviours

- Rituals bring team members' external networks into the family

Hence, as an individual, it is important to participate in your organisation's rituals, and not belittle them as a waste of time.

Groupware

Whereas personal productivity tools like word processing and spreadsheets most certainly have improved each individual's information processing capabilities, they do not necessarily result in improvement in the productivity of teams as a whole. Staff can end up spending more and more time in looking for relevant information and less and less using it in a significant and productive manner.

	Asynchronous[7]	Synchronous
Collocated[8]	• Resource sharing (printers, shared folders, DropBox) • Document Management systems	• Voting systems • Decision support
Non-collocated	• Email • News groups • Mailing lists • Web content management • Group calendars • Workflow systems • Knowledge management systems • Social media	• Chat rooms • Voice conferencing • Videoconferencing • Shared whiteboards

Table 9.1

7   Not occurring at the same time; the opposite of synchronous.

8   Meaning grouped together in a system or order; used in logistics.

Groupware systems typically reside on a network (private intranet or public internet). They can be typically categorised along two dimensions: time and space (Table 9.1)

Obviously, these systems have a tremendous effect on how people work together, but care has to be taken to make sure that the right tools are used for the right purpose: as we said before, 'a fool with a tool is still a fool'. Moreover, they typically impose constraints in terms of privacy and data protection, and add some significant overhead cost to streamlining the communication processes.

Personality types

The notion of personality type was introduced in Chapter 2. You will remember that – for MBTI – there are 16 possible personality types, resulting from four dichotomies of preferred behaviour. Even though these 16 type-indicators are not evenly spread across the population one can easily understand that the chances of having to work with people who have a different personality type than yours are huge. For example, in a group of six people, with each person potentially having one out of 16 personality types, the number of possible combinations is 16^6, which is over 16 million!

In practical terms this means that *every group of people you ever work with will be different* in respect of the mix of personality types around the table. The bad news is that there is not much you can do about this; you have to work with the people who happen to be in the same group as you are. The good news, however, is that you can adapt your own behaviour in order to cope with the differences, by taking the (presumed) personality traits of the other participants into account.

Working with other cultures

In Chapter 2, we looked at how Geert Hofstede uses the analogy of our cultural background with the way computers are programmed. He calls such patterns of thinking, feeling, and acting *mental programs*, or, *software of the mind*.

Culture is, in essence, a set of shared values that a group of people holds. Every culture has rules that its members take for granted. Few of us are aware of our own biases because cultural imprinting is begun at a very early age.

Of course, we are all individuals, and no two people belonging to the same culture are guaranteed to respond in exactly the same way. However, most caricatures tend to have a substantial slice of truth in them, and generalisations are valid to the extent that they provide indications as to what you will most likely encounter – and how those differences might impact communication.

High-context or low-context cultures

In some cultures, personal bonds and informal agreements are considered far more binding than any formal contract. In others, the meticulous wording of legal documents is viewed as vital.

High-context cultures like the Mediterranean, Latin American, African, Arab, and Asian leave much of the message undetermined – to be implied through context, non-verbal cues, and between-the-lines interpretation of what is actually said. These cultures are looking for meaning and understanding in what is *not* said – in body language, in silences and pauses, and in relationships and empathy. In contrast, *low-context cultures* (most of the Germanic and English-speaking countries) expect messages to be unambiguous and detailed. These cultures place emphasis on sending and receiving accurate messages directly, and on being precise with spoken or written words.

Sequential or synchronic cultures

In *sequential cultures* like English, German, Swedish, and Dutch, people think of time sequentially – as a linear commodity to 'spend,' 'save,' or 'waste'; people give their full attention to one agenda item after another. This can lead to a preoccupation with timelines that plays right into the hands of shrewd negotiators from other cultures; all they need to do is find out about your schedule and wait until right before your deadline to present an offer. (Think of what happened in the recent Greek crisis.)

In *synchronic cultures* (including southern Europe and Asia) the flow of time is viewed as a sort of circle – with the past, present, and future all inter-related. Time is a constant flow to be experienced moment by moment, and as a force that cannot be contained or controlled. This influences how people in those cultures approach deadlines, strategic thinking, investments, developing talent from within, and the concept of 'long-term' planning.

Affective or neutral cultures

Reason and emotion both play a role in communication. Which of these dominates depends upon whether we are *affective* (readily showing emotions) or emotionally *neutral* in our approach. Members of neutral cultures (Scandinavians, Dutch, and Japanese for example) do not announce their feelings, but keep them carefully controlled and restrained. In affective cultures – such as Italian and French – people will show their feelings openly by laughing, smiling, grimacing – and sometimes crying, shouting, or walking out of the room.

This does not mean that people in neutral cultures are cold or unfeeling. But in the course of normal business activities, people from neutral cultures are more careful to monitor the amount of emotion they display.

Once again, I need to caveat these broad generalisations because individuals vary greatly, and I invite you to judge these statements based on your own experience.

In conclusion: there is no single best approach to communicating with one another. The key to cross-cultural success is to develop an understanding of, and a deep respect for, the differences.

Active listening

'Two monologues do not make a dialogue.' – Jeff Daly

A way to become a better listener is to practise *active listening*. This is where you make a conscious effort not only to hear the words that another person is saying but, more importantly, try to understand the complete message that is being sent. In order to do this you must pay attention to the other person very carefully.

There are five key elements of active listening. They all help you ensure that you hear the other person, and that the other person *knows* you are hearing what is said.

Pay attention – Give the speaker your undivided attention, and acknowledge the message by:

- Looking at the speaker directly, keeping eye contact.
- Putting aside distracting thoughts.
- Not mentally preparing a rebuttal.
- Avoiding distractions like side conversations.
- Observing the speaker's body language.

Show that you are listening – Use your own body language to convey your attention by:

- Nodding occasionally.
- Smiling and using other facial expressions (avoiding a 'poker face').
- Noting your posture and making sure it is open and inviting.
- Encouraging the speaker to continue with small verbal comments like 'yes', and 'hmm'.

"Sorry. I was filtering out
your conversation spam.
What were you saying?"

Provide feedback – Our personal filters, assumptions, judgements, and beliefs can distort what we hear. As a listener, your role is to understand what is being said. This may require you to reflect what is being said by:

- Paraphrasing: 'What I'm hearing is …' and 'Sounds like you are saying …'
- Asking questions to clarify certain points: 'What do you mean when you say …?'
- Summarising the speaker's comments periodically.

Defer judgement – Interrupting is a waste of time. It frustrates the speaker and limits full understanding of the message:

- Allow the speaker to finish each point before asking questions.
- Don't interrupt with counter arguments.

Respond appropriately – Active listening is a model for respect and understanding. You are gaining information and perspective. You add nothing by attacking the speaker or otherwise putting him or her down:

- Be candid, open, and honest in your response.
- Assert your opinions respectfully.
- Treat the other person in a way that you think he or she would want to be treated.

It is a luxury to be really listened to, to be truly heard. Active listening will support your colleagues both personally and professionally, and you will improve your own productivity.

Empathy and sympathy

Empathy is the experience of understanding another person's condition from their perspective. You place yourself in their shoes and feel what they are feeling. The word 'empathy' was brought into use in 1909 by British psychologist Edward B. Titchener. While the word's spelling borrows from an ancient Greek word, *empátheia*, which meant 'passion,' Titchener used 'empathy' for the purpose of translating a German word (*einfühlungsvermögen*) and its concept of shared feeling.

Empathy is not to be confused with *sympathy*. When you sympathise with someone, you have compassion for that person, but you don't necessarily share their feelings. Sympathy has broader applications that don't necessarily have to do with one person's feelings for another. You can sympathise with a cause, for instance, or with a point of view that resonates with you. The word 'sympathy' comes from the ancient Greek *sunpathos*, meaning 'with/together' and 'suffering.'

The capacity to sympathise and empathise is considered vital for a sense of humanity – the ability to understand one's fellow humans and their problems. People who lack this capacity are often classified as narcissistic, sociopathic, or in extreme cases, psychopathic. However, these terms are only applicable if a person consistently lacks the capacity to sympathise or empathise with others.

In general, there are many cases where people may not feel sympathetic or empathetic due to lack of knowledge or because their experiences are different; this does not imply abnormal behaviour. On the other hand, some people are overly empathetic and can eventually be overwhelmed by the negative feelings they take on from their relationships and encounters with other people.

To start using empathy – and sympathy – more effectively when working with others consider the following:

- *Examine your own attitude.* Are you more concerned with getting your way, winning, or being right? Or, is your priority to find a solution, build relationships, and accept others as they are?

- *Try to see things from the other person's point of view.* You will probably realise that they are not in fact stupid, evil, unkind, stubborn, or unreasonable; they are most likely just reacting based on the knowledge and understanding they have.

- *Acknowledge the other person's perspective.* Acknowledgement does not always equal agreement. You can 'agree to disagree'.

- *Practise active listening.*

I would also advise you to have a look at the TED talk[9] on empathy given by Daniel Goleman[10].

Preparing for a meeting

'Knowing is not enough; we must apply. Willing is not enough; we must do.' – Goethe

Meetings are critical for team development and task management. However, meetings can easily fail without adequate preparation and leadership. A large part of what makes a meeting successful occurs in the preparation phase. Although it may vary by committee, department or unit, there are seven key responsibilities expected of chairs or moderators before a meeting takes place:

- *Clarify purpose and aims.* The purpose of a meeting should be stated at the top of the meeting agenda. A weekly or monthly staff meeting may not require meeting aims beyond the agenda items.

- *Create an agenda.* An agenda is a structure that guides and supports the meeting. An agenda helps focus the group's work on achieving desired outcomes. Good agenda items provide focus and structure for a meeting.

- *Schedule the meeting properly.* Scheduling a meeting involves much more than just making a list of attendees. It requires identifying key people who ideally

9   http://www.ted.com/talks/daniel_goleman_on_compassion?language=en
10   Daniel Goleman (1946) is an author, psychologist, and science journalist specialising in emotional intelligence.

must attend and either finding times that work for them or at the very least notifying them as far in advance as possible of when the meeting will take place. Once an optimal date and time are decided on, a meeting location can be selected. Sometimes, of course, the choice of meeting location dictates the time of the meeting and how long it can go on for – and you certainly don't want to find you have to leave a meeting room before your business is finished just because someone else has booked it.

- *Post and send out the agenda.* An agenda should be sent to participants ahead of time to help them prepare to participate. Don't leave this to the last minute or you will simply irritate people.

- *Circulate supporting information.* You should always circulate supporting documentation to participants in advance of the meeting. However, deciding how much documentation to send out can present a problem. Some people won't want to look at anything prior to the meeting and some will conscientiously read everything they receive. Focus therefore on the documentation that it is *essential* people study in advance, and make it clear that that is what you are sending them.

- *Make room arrangements.* Ensure that the meeting room is set up properly. Apparently trivial details (are there enough chairs? Are there drinks, and if so enough cups/glasses?) can certainly influence people's perceptions of how professionally run a meeting is and hence of your authority in steering it. Most importantly, make sure that all participants are going to be able to see and hear each other properly.

- *Arrange for a secretary.* The secretary of the meeting takes notes on paper, laptop or on flip charts. Meeting notes should be distributed as soon after the meeting as possible. The longer the delay, the less confidence the members will have that their contribution will result in action. For groups that meet regularly, the secretary is responsible for keeping previous meeting notes and agendas in one place where they can be referenced later such as from a notebook or shared network drive, etc.

Group negotiation

Virtually all groups work under some type of constraint. The constraint may be time, it may be resources, it may be regulatory/compliance factors, or it may be technical limitations. These constraints lead to the necessity to balance conflicting demands. This then leads to the need for effective negotiations between the group members in order to optimise the project and group performance (Figure 9.2).

The **Thomas-Kilmann Conflict Mode Instrument**[11] (TKI) provides a suggested negotiation strategy for different conflict contexts. Based upon the desire to retain the relationship between team members and need to achieve a solution, different negotiation strategies are suggested.

---

11 http://www.kilmanndiagnostics.com/overview-thomas-kilmann-conflict-mode-instrument-tki

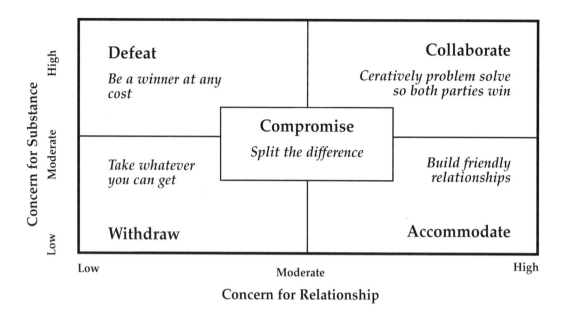

Figure 9.2

Obviously, collaborative approaches are often desired but, unfortunately, some of those you have to deal with may see themselves as opponents and will attempt to 'win' at all costs. It is therefore a good idea to be aware of the following negotiating strategies, so you understand what is really going on:

- *Fait accompli strategy.* One side does whatever it wants and expects the other side to accept the terms and the outcome without further ado.

- *Standard practice strategy.* The claim is that what is being suggested is acceptable because it is 'standard practice'. If you are negotiating in an area that is unfamiliar to you, make sure you research any 'standard practice' claims before agreeing to them.

- *Deadline strategy.* If the other side knows your deadline, they may delay giving you a draft (and possibly throw in a few very late changes) until the last minute to gain the advantage. The closer you are to your deadline the more concessions you're likely to make.

- *Decoy strategy.* This strategy involves inflating the importance of a minor issue to mask the importance of a larger issue or a hidden agenda. If the other side concedes what they have made you believe is a major issue, but what is for them a minor one, they will then expect you to concede on one of your truly important issues.

- *Faking withdrawal strategy.* Faking an intention to withdraw from a prospective deal is another strategy to be wary of. Its purpose is to gain a concession, usually a significant one, by pretending to be unconcerned about whether the deal happens or not.

- *Limited authority strategy.* This strategy involves the other side trying to avoid making concessions by claiming they don't have the authority to make concessions on their own.

- *Salami strategy.* The salami technique is used to gain concessions piece by piece. The basic premise is this: instead of trying to grab the whole salami, cut off thin slices over time.

Conflict resolution

I think it is time to introduce at this point the **Goals, Roles, Processes** and **Interpersonal Relationships** (GRPI) model that was first presented by Richard Beckhard[12] in 1972. Goals, Roles, Processes and Interpersonal Relationships are four critical and interrelated aspects of teamwork. The GRPI is a four-step project-planning tool to help team leaders ensure productivity, efficiency and quality:

G – Goals: the goals of the project are agreed to by the team.

R – Roles: the roles and responsibilities of each team member are determined.

P – Processes: the actual project processes or activities are defined, estimated, and planned.

I – Interpersonal: as the project unfolds, everyone begins to work together and the interpersonal relationships are established and strengthened.

For *conflict resolution*, this model can be used in reverse order. If conflict arises in the team, you should first see if there is any interpersonal issue involved and, if there is, work on resolving that. However, you should always check the next higher level to see if the problem goes deeper into the project. Moving up a level, you need to see if there is a difference of opinion as to what the team should be doing, and how it should be done. If that is the problem, then resolve that issue and usually the interpersonal relationships will be re-established.

If there are *process* problems look further up to see if there are problems with the assignment of roles and responsibilities. Once those are resolved, the responsible person can then make decisions about the processes, and the interpersonal relationships will be re-established. If there are problems with the roles, check to ensure that the team is aligned to the project goals. If there is misalignment on goals, that must be resolved before you can even begin to create and execute a viable plan. Often if the issue is goal alignment, the stakeholders must be brought in to align the team members on the project objectives.

---

12 Richard Beckhard (1928–1999) was an American academic and pioneer in the field of organisation development.

Assertiveness

Assertiveness is an attitude and a way of relating to the outside world, backed up by a set of abilities. You need to see yourself as being valuable, and this goes hand in hand with you valuing others equally, respecting their right to an opinion. Many people find it difficult to communicate honestly, directly and openly with other people. It is sometimes said about assertive behaviour that it involves being aggressive. It doesn't! Assertiveness involves clear, calm thinking and respectful negotiation where each person is entitled to their opinion. Assertiveness, properly understood and applied, ensures that you – and other people – are not hurt, used or abused.

There are only two alternatives to being assertive: being passive or being aggressive. Passive modes of communication are in reality an attempt to punish or undermine the other person: playing games, being sarcastic, or remaining silent all together. Aggression involves bottling up feelings that eventually explode, leaving no room for communication.

Assertiveness includes:

- Being clear about what you feel, what you need and how it can be achieved.

- Being able to communicate calmly without attacking another person.

- Being able to say 'no', rather than agreeing to do something just to please someone else.

- Being happy to defend your position, even if it provokes conflict.

- Being confident about handling conflict if it occurs.

- Understanding how to negotiate if two people want different outcomes.

- Being able to talk openly about yourself and being able to listen to others.

- Having confident, open body language.

- Being able to give and receive positive and negative feedback.

- Having a positive, optimistic outlook.

The nice guy syndrome

'Nice Guys have a difficult time comprehending that in general, people are not drawn to perfection in others. People are drawn to shared interests, shared problems, and an individual's life energy.' – Robert Glover

The 'nice guy syndrome' refers to a behavioural pattern of being overly nice to others. A leading authority on this topic is Dr Robert Glover, a therapist who specialises in working with men with the nice guy syndrome, and author of the best-selling self-help book for men 'No More Mr Nice Guy'[13]. According to Dr Glover, all nice guys operate on the same basic paradigm: 'If I can hide my flaws and become what I

---

13   'No More Mr Nice Guy' (2003) by Robert Glover.

think others want me to be then I will be loved, get my needs met, and have a problem-free life.'

A nice guy's primary goal is to make other people happy. Nice guys are dependent on external validation and avoid conflict at any cost. According to Glover, nice guys are guided by the following three 'covert contracts':

- If I am a good guy, then everyone will love me and like me (and people I desire will desire me).

- If I meet other people's needs without them having to ask, then they will meet my needs without me having to ask.

- If I do everything right, then I will have a smooth, problem-free life.

These covert contracts operate at an unconscious level. They don't work for a number of reasons, but nice guys are convinced they should.

As a result of this syndrome, nice guys have mediocre careers compared with how skilled they are, no matter how hard they work, and they sabotage almost every aspect of their lives:

- They appear needy and insecure.

- They are generic and predictable.

- They end up ignoring their own needs and not taking care of themselves.

- They end up not being there for the people who really matter, because they try to please everybody.

- They are full of repressed rage and they tend to detonate at the most inappropriate times.

- They lie, hide and they try to get what they want in indirect, manipulative ways.

In conclusion: being a 'nice guy' is not a healthy or productive way of being; the concept is flawed.

Even after you realise that being a nice guy does not work, your automatic thinking will still be influenced and disempower you. You will need to consciously change your thinking and change your behaviour. Specific actions may include:

- Express yourself more, even when you may upset someone.

- Ask for what you really want and say 'no' to others.

- Take more time for yourself and take care of your own needs.

- End toxic relationships that go nowhere.

The earlier you start, the faster you will enjoy the benefits of no longer being too much of a 'nice guy'!

Parliamentary procedure

'Robert's Rules of Order'[14] is the short title of a book, originally written by United States Brig. Gen. Henry Martyn Robert in the 1870s and revised at intervals ever since, containing rules of order intended to be adopted for use by a deliberative assembly. The procedures prescribed by the book were loosely modelled on those used in the United States House of Representatives, with such adaptations as Robert saw fit for use in other assemblies.

According to Robert's Rules of Order, *parliamentary procedure* is based on the consideration of the rights of the majority, of the minority (especially a large minority greater than one-third), of individual members, of absentee members, or all of these groups taken together. It provides common rules and procedures for deliberation and debate in order to place the whole membership on the same footing and speaking the same language. The book states:

> 'The application of parliamentary law is the best method yet devised to enable assemblies of any size, with due regard for every member's opinion, to arrive at the general will on the maximum number of questions of varying complexity in a minimum amount of time and under all kinds of internal climate ranging from total harmony to hardened or impassioned division of opinion.' (*Robert's Rules of Order Newly Revised*, 11th edition: Introduction, p. liii)

In the EU, obviously, parliamentary procedure – or variants – is used throughout all the 'official' meetings that take place in the various institutions and agencies, but it is also applied in many 'internal' meetings across the board. So, if you haven't yet done so at this point in your career, it's a good idea to get acquainted with the ideas and rules governing this kind of meeting.

Brainstorming

Brainstorming is a group creativity technique by which efforts are made to achieve a solution to a specific problem by gathering a list of ideas spontaneously contributed by its members. Alex F. Osborn popularised the term in his book 'Applied Imagination'[15].

Brainstorming provides a free and open environment that encourages everyone to participate. Original ideas are welcomed and built upon, and all participants are encouraged to contribute fully, helping them develop a rich collection of creative solutions.

When used during problem solving, brainstorming brings team members' diverse experience and backgrounds into play. It increases the richness of ideas investigated, which means that you can often find better solutions to the problems that you face. It can also help you get buy-in from team members for the solution chosen – after all, they are likely to be more enthusiastic about an approach if they were involved in developing it. What's more, because brainstorming is amusing, it helps team members bond, as they solve problems in a positive, rewarding environment.

---

14   http://www.robertsrules.com/
15   'Applied Imagination: Principles and Procedures Creative Problem Solving' (1953) by Alex F. Osborn.

"Before we start this round of wide-open brainstorming, I'd just like to remind you that all ideas that are not mine must be rejected."

Brainstorming is popular for two reasons, one good and one bad. The good reason is that a typical brainstorming session brings people together in the creative process, and increases the social nature of the project. If the meeting is run properly, everybody feels as though they are contributing to what they will be working on in the future. More importantly, it gets people thinking and communicating with each other about topics relevant to their work.

The bad reason that brainstorming is popular is that it is an easy way for bad managers to pretend that the team is involved in the direction of the project. A team leader can be convinced that he or she knows how to cultivate and work with ideas that are not their own simply by holding a meeting.

The most important thing about a brainstorming session is what happens after it ends, because some good ideas will surface, no matter how poorly you run a brainstorming meeting. But depending on what happens after the session, those ideas may or may not impact anything.

While brainstorming can be effective, it's important to approach it with an open mind and a non-judgmental attitude. If you don't do this, people are likely to clam up and the number and quality of ideas, and morale, will suffer as a consequence.

Gamestorming

Humans are hardwired to play games. We play them for fun. We play them in our social interactions. We also play them at work, but that last one is tricky; playing games and work don't seem like a natural pairing.

The authors of 'Gamestorming'[16] have a different perspective. They contend that embracing and understanding game mechanics can generate multiple benefits in many

16 'Gamestorming: A Playbook for Innovators, Rulebreakers, and Changemakers' (2010) by Dave Gray, Sunny Brown and James Macanufo.

work environments, particularly those where old hierarchical models are no longer applicable, like the creatively driven knowledge work of today's cutting edge industries.

- Overcome conflict and increase engagement with team-oriented games.
- Improve collaboration and communication in cross-disciplinary teams with visual-thinking techniques.
- Improve understanding by role-playing customer and user experiences.
- Generate better ideas and more of them, faster than ever before.
- Shorten meetings and make them more productive.
- Simulate and explore complex systems, interactions, and dynamics.
- Identify a problem's root cause, and find the paths that point toward a solution.

Visual meetings

When people work visually they have better ideas, make better decisions, and are more committed to producing results. Author David Sibbet in his book 'Visual Meetings'[17] provides many ideas to unlock creativity, collaboration, and breakthrough thinking:

- Use graphic recording, visual planning, storyboarding, idea mapping, and similar techniques.
- Give better presentations without resorting to PowerPoint.
- Consult and sell ideas with graphics and visualisation tools.
- Get beyond paper and whiteboards to tablets, iPads, and other new media platforms.
- Make all meetings more interesting and productive.
- Improve both face-to-face and virtual group work.

Six Thinking Hats

'Six Thinking Hats'[18] is a bestselling book by Edward de Bono[19] that provides a tool for group discussion and individual thinking involving six coloured hats.

Team members learn how to separate thinking into six clear functions and roles. Each thinking role is identified with a symbolic 'thinking hat' and team members can adopt in turn the roles and thought patterns associated with each hat.

- The 'White Hat' calls for information known or needed: 'the facts, just the facts.'

---

17   'Visual meetings: How Graphics, Sticky Notes & idea mapping can transform group productivity' (2010) by David Sibbet.
18   'Six Thinking Hats' (1985) by Edward de Bono.
19   Edward de Bono (1933) is a Maltese physician, psychologist, author, inventor and consultant.

- The 'Yellow Hat' symbolises brightness and optimism. Under this hat you explore the positives and probe for value and benefit.

- The 'Black Hat' is judgement – the devil's advocate, or why something may not work.

- The 'Red Hat' signifies feelings, hunches and intuition. When using this hat you can express emotions and feelings and share likes, dislikes, loves, and hates.

- The 'Green Hat' focuses on creativity: the possibilities, alternatives, and new ideas.

- The 'Blue Hat' is used to manage the thinking process. It is the control mechanism that ensures the Six Thinking Hats guidelines are observed.

Networking

Networking is about making connections and building enduring, mutually beneficial relationships. The word 'work' is part of networking, and it is not easy work, because it involves reaching outside the borders of your comfort zone.

Figure 9.3

There are basically three forms of networking: *operational, personal* and *strategic*.

The purpose of *operational networking* is getting work done efficiently, or – in other words – building and maintaining the capacities and functions required of the groups you are part of. Your contacts are mostly internal and orientated towards your current activities. Key contacts are prescribed mostly by your tasks and the organisational structure, so it is relatively clear who is relevant. Operational networks include not only direct reports and superiors but also peers within an operational unit, other internal players with the power to block or support a project, and key outsiders such as suppliers and clients. Operational networking focuses on depth: building strong relationships.

As you move into a leadership role, your network must reorient itself externally and toward the future. In *personal networking*, enhancing personal and professional development is key; providing referrals to useful information and contacts. Contacts are mostly external and orientated towards current interests and future potential interests; this means that it is not always clear who is relevant. According to the famous *six degrees of separation principle*[20], our personal contacts are valuable to the extent that they help us reach, in as few connections as possible, the distant person who has the information we need. Personal networking focuses on breadth: reaching out to contacts that can make referrals.

Finally, for *strategic networking* the purpose is figuring out future priorities and challenges. Contacts are both internal and external and orientated towards the future. Having lateral and vertical relationships with other people outside your immediate control becomes a lifeline for figuring out how your own contributions fit into the big picture. What distinguishes a leader from a manager is the ability to figure out where to go and to enlist the people and groups necessary to get there. As they step up to the leadership transition, some managers accept their growing dependence on others and seek to transform it into mutual influence. Others dismiss such work as 'political' and, as a result, undermine their ability to advance their goals.

Building a network is less a matter of skill than of will. When first efforts do not bring quick rewards, some may simply conclude that networking isn't among their talents. But networking is not a talent; nor does it require an expansive, extroverted personality. It is a skill, one that takes practice.

'Wikinomics'

'Throughout history corporations have organised themselves according to strict hierarchical lines of authority. Everyone was a subordinate to someone else— employees versus managers, marketers versus customers, producers versus supply chain subcontractors, companies versus the community.

There was always someone or some company in charge, controlling things, at the 'top' of the food chain. While hierarchies are not vanishing, profound changes in the nature of technology, demographics, and the global economy are giving rise to powerful new models of production based on community, collaboration, and self-organisation rather than on management and control ....

Smart companies are encouraging, rather than fighting, the heaving growth of massive online communities—many of which emerged from the fringes of the Web to attract tens of millions of participants overnight. Even ardent competitors are collaborating on path-breaking science initiatives that accelerate discovery in their industries. Indeed, as a growing number of firms see the benefits of mass collaboration, this new of way organising will eventually displace the traditional corporate structures as the economy's primary engine of wealth creation.'

(From: 'Wikinomics – How Mass Collaboration Changes Everything.'[21])

---

20   'Six degrees of separation' is the theory that everyone and everything is six or fewer steps away, from any other

21   'Wikinomics: How Mass Collaboration Changes Everything' (2010) by Don Tapscott and Anthony D. Williams. person in the world.

Developing your working with others skills

Making others feel important requires that you appreciate the people around you and remind them of their positive qualities. It embodies the idea that you notice their talents and abilities and that in doing so you boost their self-esteem and increase their sense of self-worth.

When people feel appreciated, they are more likely to be happier and more productive. This creates a pleasant environment that is more conductive to relationships where people enjoy working with each other and are more positive. People inherently want to know that they are valued. If you work on making them feel appreciated you will be validating your relationship with them.

Please refer to Chapter 1 (methodology) and Annex 7 for further development of this competency, have another look at the current chapter to find out about your options, and remember: YOU are responsible for your own development, not your manager, your colleagues, or your mentor.

The online toolkit that comes for free with this book can be used to follow-up on your development in this area. This toolkit can be found at:

https://www.johnharperpublishing.co.uk/the-ultimate-eu-career-development-toolkit/

Key points to remember

- Focus your energy on being interested, not interesting.
- Working with others increases your energy, efficiency and creativity.
- Diversity makes the most of a range of skills and knowledge.
- It improves understanding, communication and a sense of shared purpose.
- Without collaboration, nothing is possible.

Your notes

10. Leadership

Competency definition: 'Manage, develop and motivate people to achieve results.'

'A leader is a dealer in hope.' – Napoleon Bonaparte

The EPSO definition of leadership indicates that the EU institutions seek two – distinct but concurrent – capacities: people who are both potentially good 'managers' and also potentially good 'leaders'. Management consists of controlling a group or a set of entities to accomplish a goal. Leadership refers to an individual's ability to influence, motivate, and enable others to contribute toward organisational success. Influence and inspiration distinguish leaders from managers, not power and control. I will expand on this distinction further on in this chapter.

In EPSO competitions the leadership competency is only assessed in the case of candidates in Administrator-level (AD) competitions; Assistant-level (AST) candidates are not assessed on this competency.

How can the assessment of leadership be considered relevant to AD competitions across-the-board, given the fact that for some of the biggest competitions no previous (management) experience of any kind is required? The reason is that EPSO selects candidates to be eligible for life-long employment at the EU. Even inexperienced recruits will eventually be promoted to a position where they will have to apply their leadership competency, so it is important that people have at least a basic understanding and the proper attitude towards leadership and management, as they will need it throughout their career. ASTs subsequently seeking to become ADs will have to go through 'certification' training, during which their leadership competency will be further developed.

Established administrators who are called for the duties of Head of Unit have to take the Management Training Program[1] (MTP) in the European School of Administration (EUSA), where their leadership competency will be sharpened. External applicants for middle management positions in the EU are extensively assessed by EPSO in this particular competency.

Note: a major review of middle management recruitment and functions at the Commission was taking place as this book went to press. A draft proposal is that internal candidates for management posts will in future also be assessed in an Assessment Centre, similar to what happens for potential recruits via EPSO.

Leadership versus management

'I have a dream.' – Martin Luther King Jr.

Leaders lead people. Managers manage tasks. There is a difference.

Managers have subordinates; they have a position of authority vested in them by the organisation. Management is transactional; it operates within the framework of a

---

1   EUSA's objective is to provide a range of learning and development opportunities that contribute to an improvement in the performance of staff who exercise or who may exercise management responsibilities, thereby helping them and their institution achieve greater effectiveness.

fixed set of rules. The manager tells the subordinate what to do, and the subordinate does this because they have been promised a reward (a salary, a promotion…) for doing so.

Managers are paid to get things done (they are subordinates too), often within tight constraints of time, resources and results. Managers are relatively risk-averse and they will seek to avoid conflict wherever possible.

Management is 'Motivation 2.0' (see page 41).

Leaders have followers, not just subordinates. Many leaders do also have subordinates, but only because they are also managers. However, when they want to lead they have to give up their formal authority because following (or being led) is a voluntary activity. This does not mean that leaders do not pay attention to tasks – in fact they are often very achievement-focused. What they do realise, however, is the importance of inspiring others to work towards their vision, or the vision of the institution.

Leaders are also relatively risk-seeking. They consider it natural to encounter problems and hurdles that must be overcome along the way. They are thus comfortable with risk and will seek routes that others avoid, seeing them as opening up potential opportunities for advantage, and will happily break rules in order to get things done. (Up to a point! Leaders have to set a good example as well, and sometimes that means very visibly obeying certain rules – such as presence during core time, seeking or passing on information correctly and at the appropriate time, etc. Some rules can be happily broken – others come at a cost).

Leadership is 'Motivation 3.0' (see page 41).

	MANAGER	LEADER
Role	Transactional	Transformational
Vision	Short-term	Long-term
Values	Results	Achievements
Approach	Plans around constraints	Sets direction
Concerns	Do things right	Do the right things
Appeals	The Head	The Heart
Decisions	Makes	Facilitates
Control	Formal	Informal
Culture	Endorses	Shapes
Actions	Directs	Inspires
Risks	Minimises	Embraces
Rules	Makes	Breaks
Direction	Status quo	Challenges
Focus	Managing work	Leading people
Collaborators	Subordinates	Followers

Table 10.1: Managers and leaders compared

John and Pierre: a manager and a leader

Imagine that John is the manager of a McDonalds franchise and Pierre is the chef of a fine, French cuisine restaurant. John has to make sure that his restaurant is properly operated and complies with all McDonalds' standards, policies and strategies. John cannot choose the style of the decoration, the way food is prepared, the ingredients or even the way he hires and manages staff as everything is dictated by McDonalds. McDonalds wants to give the same experience to all its customers, worldwide. *John is a manager.*

Pierre, on the other hand, has a dream. Pierre wants to create a unique and superb customer experience. He wants to distinguish his restaurant from the crowd. His dream is to gain a Michelin Star – or even two – and he does whatever it takes to obtain this award, and to keep it for years thereafter. Besides being an excellent cook and manager Pierre has to inspire his co-workers to follow his dream. *Pierre is a leader.*

According to John Kotter[2] management is a set of practices: planning, budgeting, staffing, controlling, problem-solving. Management makes a system function the way it was designed to function while leadership is about creating a vision and motivating people to buy into it.

Contrasting the qualities of leaders 'versus' managers of course involves something of a paradox, given that many people have to be both. Managers still can have the responsibility for leading their team into new challenges while making sure systems and procedures operate properly. Likewise even the most out-front leaders must make sure that the systems and procedures are in place to deliver on their vision – a general who leads his troops from the front is ill-advised to forget his supply lines.

In his book 'Too Many Bosses, Too Few Leaders'[3] Rajeev Peshawaria presents the underlying dynamics of what it takes to be a great leader; it is less a 'how to' and more a 'why' exploration of what leadership is about. Leadership is a special talent that goes far beyond just being a boss, and he shows that deciding to develop that talent is a critical choice. According to Peshawaria, it is clear that *trust* is one of the keys to organisational or group performance; he therefore calls trust *the currency of leadership*.

The competency of leadership is, in fact, the combination of all the other core competencies, and then some (Figure 10.1).

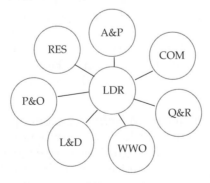

Figure 10.1

2   John Kotter (1947), best-selling US author and management consultant who taught at the Harvard Business School.

3   'Too Many Bosses, Too Few Leaders' (2012) by Rajeev Peshawaria.

An effective leader combines all the other competencies in such a way that result is greater than the sum of the constituting parts.

Leadership styles

There are as many ways to lead people, as there are leaders.

Leaders typically have a dominant style, one they use in a wide variety of situations. However, there is no one 'best' style – leaders must adapt their style to the people being led and to the situation at hand. This is a key point. As a leader, you sometimes have to be autocratic (with some people) while 'laissez-faire' with others. Much depends on the level of independence of the individual concerned – some need a lot more hand-holding than others. It's a delicate balancing act, and one that we don't always get right. The important thing is that you shouldn't beat yourself up about getting it wrong occasionally, but just learn from the mistake.

Fortunately, a number of useful frameworks that describe the main ways that people lead have been developed. When you understand these frameworks, you can develop your own approach to leadership, and become a more effective leader as a result.

Lewin's leadership styles

Psychologist Kurt Lewin[4] developed his 'leadership styles' framework in the 1930s, and it provided the foundation of many of the approaches that followed afterwards. He argued that there are three major leadership styles:

- *Autocratic* – Also known as *authoritarian* leadership style. These leaders provide clear expectations for what needs to be done, when it should be done, and how it should be done. This style of leadership is strongly focused on both command by the leader and control of the followers. There is also a clear division between the leader and the followers. Autocratic leaders make decisions independently, with little or no input from the rest of the group. This can be appropriate when you need to make decisions quickly, when there's no need for team input, and when team agreement isn't necessary for a successful outcome. However, this style can be demoralising, and it can lead to high levels of absenteeism and staff turnover.

- *Democratic* – Also known as *participative* leadership style. These leaders make the final decisions, but include team members in the decision-making process. Democratic leaders offer guidance to group members, but they also participate in the group and allow input from other group members. As a result, team members tend to have high job satisfaction and high

---

4 Kurt Zadek Lewin (1890–1947) was a German-American psychologist, known as one of the modern pioneers of social, organisational, and applied psychology in the United States.

productivity. This is not always an effective style to use, though, when you need to make a quick decision.

- *Laissez-faire* – Also known as *delegative* leadership. Leaders give their team members a lot of freedom in how they do their work, and how they set their deadlines. They provide support with resources and advice if needed, but otherwise they don't get involved. This autonomy can lead to high job satisfaction, but it can be detrimental if team members don't manage their time well, or if they don't have the knowledge, skills, or self-motivation to do their work effectively.

The Blake-Mouton managerial grid

A popular framework for thinking about leadership was developed by Robert Blake and Jane Mouton[5]. They look at a leader or manager in two dimensions:

- *Concern for people* – This is the degree to which a leader considers the needs of team members, their interests, and areas of personal development when deciding how best to accomplish a task.

- *Concern for production* – This is the degree to which a leader emphasises concrete objectives, organisational efficiency and high productivity when deciding how best to accomplish a task.

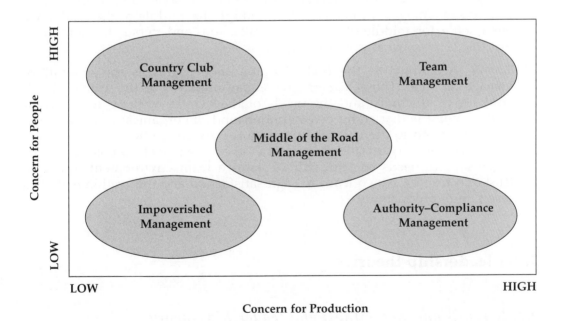

Figure 10.2

---

5 'The Managerial Grid III: The Key to Leadership Excellence' (1985) by Robert Blake and Jane Mouton.

Blake and Mouton defined the following five leadership or management styles, as in Figure 10.2.

- *Country Club* – This style of manager is most concerned about the needs and feelings of the members of their team. They operate on the assumption that as long as team members are happy and secure then they will work hard. What tends to result is a work environment that is very relaxed and fun but where productivity suffers due to lack of direction and control.

- *Authority-Compliance* – Managers in this category believe that employees are simply a means to an end. Employee needs are always secondary to the need for efficient workplaces delivering maximum output. This type of manager is very autocratic, has strict work rules, policies, and procedures, and views punishment as the most effective means to motivate staff.

- *Impoverished* – This type of manager is mostly ineffective, failing to lead or manage at all. They have neither a high regard for creating systems for getting the job done, nor for creating a work environment that is satisfying and motivating. The result is a place of disorganisation, dissatisfaction and disharmony.

- *Middle-of-the-Road* – This style sits somewhere between the 'country club' and the 'authority-compliance' types. It may at first sight appear to be an ideal compromise. However, when you compromise, you can easily end up losing the more positive aspects of the other two styles and keeping only their disadvantages. Managers who adopt the middle-of-the-road style often settle for middle-of-the road results, too, and persuade themselves that this is the most anyone can expect.

- *Team* – According to the Blake-Mouton model, this is the summit of managerial style. These leaders give equal emphasis to the organisation's need for productivity and the needs of the people working for it. Their starting point is that staff need to understand the organisation's goals and what they need to deliver. When employees are committed to, and have a stake in the organisation's success, their personal needs and the organisation's needs coincide. This creates a team environment based on trust and respect, which leads to high satisfaction and motivation and, as a result, high productivity.

Other leadership theories

The Hersey-Blanchard 'situational leadership' theory

The Hersey-Blanchard[6] 'situational leadership' theory, or model, says that you need to use different leadership styles depending on the maturity of your team members, and defines a range of leadership styles and maturity levels. The model argues that

---

6   'The Management of Organizational Behavior' by Paul Hersey and Ken Blanchard was first published in 1969.

with relatively immature individuals, you need a more directing approach, while with more mature people, you need a more participative or delegating leadership style. It has been developed in line with research over the decades since first put forward.

"From now on, my bad decisions will be called leadership experiments."

Six emotional leadership styles

Goleman, Boyatzis and McKee detailed their 'six emotional leadership styles' theory in their 2002 book, 'Primal Leadership.'[7] The theory explains the strengths and weaknesses of six leadership styles that you can use – Visionary, Coaching, Affiliative, Democratic, Pacesetting, and Commanding. It also shows how each style can affect the emotions of your team members.

The pacesetter

Once, one of the worst members of my team was a 'pacesetter'. She had extremely high performance standards for others (which, rather ironically, she didn't achieve herself and had a blind spot about it when that was pointed out). She bad-mouthed those she considered poor performers without having access to the overall picture (which I did) and, as a result, she 'poisoned the atmosphere' as a colleague put it. I had to step in – not very successfully, unfortunately. She reacted very badly and really could not understand why I was unhappy with her behaviour. It was always everyone else's fault ...

---

7   'Primal Leadership' (revised edition published 2013) by Daniel Goleman et al.

Flamholtz and Randle's leadership style matrix

Flamholtz and Randle's 'leadership style matrix' aims to show the best leadership style to use, based on how capable people are of working autonomously, and how creative or 'programmable' the task is.

The matrix is divided into four quadrants – each quadrant identifies two possible leadership styles that will be effective for a given situation, ranging from 'autocratic/benevolent autocratic' to 'consensus/laissez-faire.' For instance, a person with a high level of education, skill, motivation and independence is likely to want autonomy. Someone with low motivation and skill will need – and may want – more feedback and interaction, so that he or she can complete the task successfully.

You will always find some people in the 'wrong job' who may be highly educated and skilled but are demotivated by doing a job they don't want to do or that is way below their competence levels. This, unfortunately, has become more common in the EU institutions as a result of a European Court of Justice (CoJ) ruling requiring competitions to be opened up to individuals who are vastly overqualified for the jobs involved. Many AST staff are perfect examples of this, with jobs being held by PhD holders who are more qualified than even their Directors. The result has been highly counterproductive in my view. It has also meant there are fewer job opportunities for those who need them most – the less skilled and those with just a secondary education. The CoJ judgment may have been (on the surface) an attempt at fairness in that it sought equality of input and of treatment, but it significantly failed to consider equality of outcome.

Personality type and leadership

The concepts of personality type and the Myers-Briggs Personality Type Indicator (MBTI) were introduced in Chapter 2. The MBTI is based on the idea that there are basic human differences in ways of perceiving and processing information. These differences inevitably show up in the working environment.

These differences in personality type can be the root cause of many interpersonal conflicts.

People who are extravert may find that introverts are hard to read, and may even go so far as to judge them as indifferent, hard-hearted, and even arrogant. Introverts may unfairly judge extraverts as being superficial, unreliable, and dishonest.

Referring back to the MBTI classification shown in Figure 2.1 in Chapter 2, a person who values data and focuses on what is actually present (S = Sensing) will often seem too analytical and detail-oriented to a person who focuses on the big picture and uses intuition (N = Intuition).

'Thinking' (T) people can view 'Feeling' (F) people as too emotional, while 'F's' can find that 'T's' are too task-oriented and uncaring.

One of the biggest sources of conflict, however, shows up in differences between J (Judging) and P (Perceiving). A person whose style is a 'J' will be an early starter, will organise their work with attention to deadlines, and may find it offensive when others are late or indecisive. On the other hand, P-style people prefer to keep their options open, and wait until the last minute before completing or deciding. The two different personalities can drive each other crazy in a work environment.

Understanding and accepting fundamental differences in human behaviour is essential for managers and leaders alike, and self-awareness is the cornerstone for developing emotional intelligence.

The question 'What personality type makes the best leader?' often comes up. This question does not have a simple answer because all types can be effective as well as ineffective. Studies of thousands of leaders and managers worldwide have shown some profile types to be more predominant, however. This does not imply that these types make better managers, only that they are more predominant in leadership positions. There is a majority of 'Thinking' and 'Judging' preferences among leaders and managers. This is not unexpected, since the structure and values of most organisations favour logical and decisive behaviour. It may even be that 'Thinking' and 'Judging' behaviour has become the accepted description of what it means to lead and people with these preferences are seen as 'leadership material'.

Bear in mind that the most important element in the MBTI – or in any assessment tool – is the improved ability to understand oneself and those one works with[8].

Leadership in a multicultural environment

'United in Diversity' is the motto of the European Union. It signifies how Europeans have come together, to work for peace and prosperity, while at the same time being enriched by the continent's many different cultures, traditions and languages. This idea is indeed reflected in the composition of the staff of the EU institutions, as most EU employees are expats who have decided to live and work abroad – in Brussels, Luxembourg, or any of the many other locations worldwide where the EU has its activities.

In their book 'Leadership in a Diverse and Multicultural Environment'[9] authors Mary Connerly and Paul Pedersen make the case that, no matter how highly skilled, well trained, or intelligent you are, if you make the wrong or culturally inappropriate assumptions, you will not be accurate in your assessment, meaningful in your understanding, or suitable in your interactions as a leader.

It is difficult to know the cultures of others until, and unless, you have an awareness of your own culturally learned assumptions, as these control your life.

A leader has only two choices: to ignore the influence of culture or to attend to it. In either case, however, culture will continue to influence the behaviour of others, with or without the leader's intentional awareness.

Multicultural awareness provides a safe and accurate approach to managing differences across groups in our multicultural populations.

The working culture in the Commission and the other EU institutions is characterised by its diversity. Many studies have underlined the diversity of cultural, linguistic, professional, and even ideological backgrounds. This needs to be considered by all members of staff, especially by those in a leadership role. That said, the Commission has also developed its own 'in-house' culture that is a further layer to master.

---

8   'Leadership Development: Maturity and Power' (1994) by L & N Barr.
9   'Leadership in a Diverse and Multicultural Environment' (2005) by Mary Connerly and Paul Pedersen.

Communication

'The art of communication is the language of leadership.' — James Humes[10]

There's no mystery here. Regardless of whether we are talking about politics, business, the military, or sports, the best leaders are top-class communicators. Their values are clear and concrete, and what they say supports those values. It is simply impossible to become a great leader without being a great communicator.

The best communicators are great listeners and intelligent in their observations. Great communicators are skilled at sensing the moods, dynamics, attitudes, values and concerns of their audience. Not only do they read their audience well, they also possess the ability to adapt their message to the audience without missing a beat. The message is not about the messenger; it is about meeting the needs and the expectations of those you're communicating with.

'Real Leaders Don't Do PowerPoint'[11] highlights a number of very interesting ideas on how to become a more confident, commanding and compelling communicator. The author explains how real leaders speak to make a difference, to promote a vision, to change the way people think and feel and act.

Motivating others

'Control leads to compliance; autonomy leads to engagement.' – Daniel H. Pink

Being able to motivate others is the most important trait of both managers and leaders. Managers may be more inclined to use the extrinsic motivators (carrot-and-stick), while leaders will motivate their followers with the three elements of intrinsic motivation – *autonomy, mastery,* and *purpose* – in mind.

Autonomy is the extent to which an employee can use their own judgement in making decisions and carrying out their work. Autonomy is strongly related to 'psychological ownership', which is defined as the extent to which an employee feels as though the organisation or the job is 'theirs' – to the point that the organisation and their role in it becomes an important part of an employee's self-identity. Many studies have shown how important the feeling of ownership is for employees.

Managers and leaders can increase the autonomy of staff and co-workers and thus their motivation by:

- Involving people in making decisions that influence their work.

- Encouraging people to apply their own judgement when solving problems.

- Avoiding directive styles of management, excessive monitoring, or unnecessary approval procedures.

Mastery has everything to do with keeping people in their learning zone, by setting realistic challenges – and allowing them to make mistakes. We all want to get better at

---

10   James C. Humes is an author and former presidential speechwriter.
11   'Real Leaders Don't Do Powerpoint – How to Speak so People Listen' (2009) by Christopher Witt.

doing things. It is why learning a language or an instrument can be so frustrating at first. If you feel like you're not getting anywhere, you lose interest and you may even give up. A sense of progress, not just in our work, but in our capabilities, contributes to our inner drive.

Managers need to calibrate their expectations of what staff *ought* to do by looking realistically at what they *can* do. If the must-do tasks are too difficult, people will become worried and feel out of their depth. If the must-do tasks are too easy, they will get bored. The objective should be to give people tasks, with the necessary space and support, which stretch them in a way that fosters increasing mastery and personal growth. This requires paying more attention to how staff are approaching and feeling about their tasks, in order to avoid them losing heart in trying to cope with tasks that don't match their capabilities.

Finally, *purpose* is also related to psychological ownership through the concept of 'task identity', the extent to which a job allows someone to be involved from the beginning to the end of a project.

Managers and leaders can increase 'purpose' by:

- Communicating how employees' activities contribute to the final product so they can see the results of their work and how it fits into the 'bigger picture'.

- Involving employees in more aspects of work by having them participate in the planning, reporting, and evaluation of projects rather than mere execution.

- Providing employees with the opportunity to completely finish any work they start.

- Explaining their decisions and how they have come to them.

I absolutely encourage you to read Daniel Pink's book 'Drive: The Surprising Truth About What Motivates Us'[12]. As a manager – or leader – of people you have to factor this into your own behaviour.

Leadership vs. management revisited

I experienced perhaps one of the more extreme examples of the difference between leadership and management in my own career when working with outsourced staff, also known as 'body shopping'.

Body shopping is the practice of sub-contracting, where one organisation buys in the technical expertise of another organisation's employees. It enables organisations to access skilled individuals or a team of professionals to work remotely or on their premises, in conjunction with its existing teams. Body shopping can help an organisation deal with the pressures of staff shortages on a short or longer-term basis, or to plug critical technology skills gaps within its own staff. For IT staff, body shopping is widely used by public administrations, especially for developing software.

In my activities as a software development manager at both the Flemish Community and the EU administration I had to deal with more than half of my staff being body shoppers; staff who were hired from external companies for the sole purpose of developing software systems.

cont...

12   'Drive: The Surprising Truth about What Motivates Us' (2011) by Daniel H. Pink.

> ### Leadership vs. management revisited – *continued*
>
> Under Belgian law it is illegal to have a 'hierarchical' relationship with external staff; there can only be a contractual relationship between the customer and the supplier – who is the real 'employer' of these resources. In practice this meant that I had the *responsibility* for the results, but not the formal *authority* over those doing the work; I had to be their *leader*, but could not be their *manager*. The 'stick-and-carrot' approach was not applicable in this context, and other – softer – motivation techniques had to be applied.

Starting with 'why?'

> *'Every organisation in the world knows WHAT they do, some organisations know HOW they do it, but very few organisations know WHY they do what they do.'*

This is the main idea behind Simon Sinek's book 'Start with Why – How Great Leaders Inspire Everyone to take Action'[13]. In studying the leaders who have had the greatest influence in the world, Simon Sinek discovered that they all think, act, and communicate in the exact same way – and it's the complete opposite of what everyone else does. People like Martin Luther King Jr., Steve Jobs, and the Wright Brothers might have little obvious in common, but they all started with the question *'why?'*

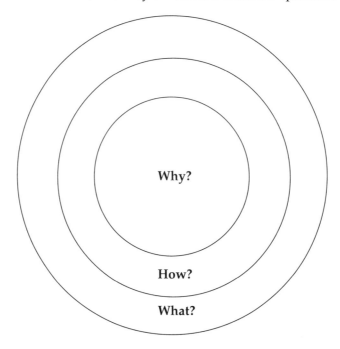

Figure 10.3

---

13   Start with Why – How Great Leaders Inspire Everyone to take Action' (2009) by Simon Sinek.

Sinek claims that there is actually a biological explanation for this; when we are communicating from the inside out we're talking directly to the limbic system. The limbic system supports a variety of functions including emotion, behaviour, motivation, and long-term memory. In fact we are addressing the person through their heart, not their mind. Allow me to suggest that you have a look at Sinek's TED talk[14] where he explains in more detail his simple but powerful model for inspirational leadership.

Coaching and mentoring

'Treat someone as he wants to be and he will become that person.' – Goethe

George Matthew Adams[15] observed that there are high spots in all of our lives and most of them have come about through support and encouragement from someone else. Whether the encouragement came informally or through a deliberate, formal program, helping us personally or professionally, we can all easily identify people who influenced and shaped our future; those were or are our coaches and mentors.

For managers and leaders it is important to realise that our subordinates and co-workers need our support and encouragement as well. In fact, the degree to which we coach, or mentor, others defines to a large extent how good – or bad – we are as managers or leaders.

It is easy to get confused about the differences between coaching and mentoring. The purpose and expected outcome of each is distinctly different although, at times, some overlap exists.

Mentoring is a pairing of a more skilled or experienced person, usually in the same field of knowledge, with a less experienced person. Ideally mentors have no line management relationship to the mentee. Mentors will often provide direction and advice and should open organisational doors for mentees. Mentors should provide a neutral sounding board, assure total confidentiality, and have no agenda other than assisting their mentees in their development and in reaching their goals. Mentoring involves helping people to develop their career, skills and expertise, drawing upon the experience of the mentor. Mentoring focuses on the 'horizontal' development (learning) of the mentee.

Coaching. While 'master-pupil' relationships have existed throughout human history, coaching as a discipline – and profession – is relatively new[16]. Its first application in a business context was pioneered in the 1980s by Sir John Whitmore[17] and Timothy Gallwey[18], author of 'The Inner Game of Work', who challenged traditional ideas by claiming that a coach's role was to remove or reduce the internal obstacles to a person's performance, without the need for much technical input from the coach. They defined coaching as: *'Unlocking a person's potential to maximise their performance.'*

14 http://www.ted.com/talks/simon_sinek_how_great_leaders_inspire_action
15 George Matthew Adams (1878–1962) was an American newspaper columnist.
16 https://www.youtube.com/watch?v=6fld90L6Hkw
17 Sir John Whitmore is chairman of Performance Consultants International, the foremost provider of coaching, leadership development and performance improvement in the workplace globally.
18 'The Inner Game of Work: Focus, Learning, Pleasure and Mobility in the Workplace' by Timothy Gallwey.

In their opinion, coaching is about helping people to learn rather than teaching them. Coaches need not have first-hand experience of the coachee's line of work. Leaders and managers can use coaching techniques successfully in the management and development of team members. Coaches will ask 'powerful' questions and not offer or give advice; it is up to the coachee to find the answers. Coaching focuses on the 'vertical' development of the coachee.

Another interesting book is 'Coaching for Performance'[19], by John Whitmore. Over 500.000 copies sold! I had the pleasure of attending a three-day classroom training at Whitmore's institute, Performance Consultants International (PCI). If you ever have the opportunity, I can only recommend it.

There are many models for coaching, depending of the type of coaching, but for performance coaching the widest used model is the GROW model, which is used throughout this book as well.

Leading by example

We have all experienced situations where the boss tells everyone to stay late, and then leaves early to pick up the kids from school. We probably know supervisors who criticise people for spending time on the internet and have their Facebook open all day long …

There is hardly anything worse for the troops' morale than leaders who practise the 'Do as I say, not as I do' philosophy. No matter what the situation is, double standards always feel like betrayals. They can be very destructive. Being a poor role model is the easiest way to undermine your own authority.

Don't underestimate the fact that as a leader you are carefully watched by others. This can be for negative reasons, such as envy of your position or, more positively, because people want to follow your example – so make sure that example is a good one!

"Tell everyone who's been following
my example that they're fired."

---

19   'Coaching for Performance – GROWing human potential and Purpose' (2009) by John Whitmore.

'Leaders eat last'

In his travels around the world since the publication of his bestseller 'Start with Why', Simon Sinek noticed that some teams were able to trust each other so deeply that they would literally put their lives on the line for each other. Other teams, no matter what incentives were offered, were doomed to infighting, fragmentation and failure. Why?

The answer became clear during a conversation with a Marine Corps general.

'Officers eat last', he said.

Sinek watched as the most junior Marines ate first while the most senior Marines took their place at the back of the line. What's symbolic in the chow hall is deadly serious on the battlefield: great leaders sacrifice their own comfort – even their own survival – for the good of those in their care.

This principle has been true since the earliest tribes of hunters and gatherers. It's not a management theory; it's biology. Our brains and bodies evolved to help us find food, shelter, mates and especially safety. We've always lived in a dangerous world, facing predators and enemies at every turn. We thrived only when we felt safe among our group.

Our biology hasn't changed in fifty thousand years, but our environment certainly has. Today's workplaces tend to be full of cynicism, paranoia and self-interest. But the best organisations foster trust and cooperation because their leaders build what Sinek calls a Circle of Safety that separates the security inside the team from the challenges outside.

The Circle of Safety leads to stable, adaptive, confident teams, where everyone feels they belong and all energies are devoted to facing the common enemy and seizing big opportunities.

As he did in 'Start with Why', Sinek illustrates his ideas with fascinating true stories from a wide range of examples, from the military to manufacturing, from government to investment banking in another book called 'Leaders Eat Last'[20].

The biology is clear: when it matters most, leaders who are willing to eat last are rewarded with deeply loyal colleagues who will stop at nothing to advance their leader's vision and their organisation's interests. It's amazing how well it works.

Team building

When I was thinking about where to cover the subject of team building, my first idea was to put it in Chapter 9 (working with others); but then I realised that it would be better to address the *organiser* of any team building initiative – the leader or manager of the team.

Research has shown that the effectiveness of team building differs substantially from one organisation to another. The most effective team building efforts occur when members of the team are highly interdependent, highly knowledgeable, and when organisational leadership actively establishes and supports the team. Effective team building must also incorporate a link to the ultimate objective of the organisation.

These conditions imply that team building only works for real teams, and not for 'groups' of loosely associated people who happen to work for the same boss. I have heard of 'away days' for groups of 300 people (an entire Directorate) and, frankly, I don't believe in their effectiveness. The cost and effort needed to organise such an event will

20   'Leaders eat Last: Why some teams pull together and others don't' (2014) by Simon Sinek.

never be compensated by higher productivity of the group as a whole. At such large events people will stick together in small groups of 4 to 6 and spend their entire day like that, without any deeper contact with the other participants.

In addition, the level of interdependence is not high enough, and the 'ultimate objective' is too high-level and unclear to most participants. At best, people will enjoy themselves together with a few of their close colleagues during this extra day off, and they will be happy to take advantage of the free food and drink. But their productivity at work will not go up as a result. When this activity is not mandatory, but on a voluntary basis, many people will find an excuse for not participating (too much work to do, have to collect the children from school, not feeling well, etc.) simply because they don't see the point of it.

Leaders and managers should be aware of these limitations, and organise team-building events only for volunteers, not during office hours, and possibly only partially cover the expenses. Do not use team-building events to boost your own popularity, because people won't buy it.

Much appreciated – by 1 in 5

For a number of years my wife and I have participated in an annual activity that is organised by a dedicated and enthusiastic team of teachers at the school where my wife works. It is always a pleasant surprise to find what exactly is going to happen that day: it could be a short trip including a visit to a museum or an interesting venue; a walk in the woods; or driving around the countryside with old-timers, with a quiz thrown in. In any case, it is a full-day event with catering and transport included. These events always take place at the weekend, and the participants have to cover their own expenses.

Despite the fact that there are over 100 teachers and administrative staff, the number of participants (including husbands and wives) rarely exceeds 40. This means that only around 20 per cent – or one out of five – colleagues and partners take part in the event, and strangely – or not strangely – enough it's always the same people who do so. Moreover, during the day, people tend to stick together in smaller groups: maths and science teachers, language teachers, and administrative staff …

Feedback

'I praise loudly, I blame softly.' – Catherine the Great

Catherine the Great was the most renowned and the longest-ruling female leader of Russia, reigning from 1762 until her death in 1796 at the age of 67. She came to power following the assassination of her husband, Peter III, at the end of the Seven Years' War. During her reign, Russia was revitalised, growing larger and stronger than ever before and becoming recognised as one of the great powers of Europe.

Catherine understood that even absolute despots cannot hold power without the support of others, and if a ruler is able to maintain a position, without leadership skills, people will be led nowhere. You can occupy a throne and accomplish nothing.

Catherine's philosophy of leadership is one of the most vital skills any influencer can develop:

Praise, when given, should be generous and whole-hearted. When it is public, specific, clear, and generous, loyalty is won. Those who are praised will follow their leader practically anywhere. Others will follow as well, in hopes of earning such praise.

However, choose the target for your praise wisely. Some people love the attention – others shy away from it. I've known someone perform *less* well after public praise because they so hated being praised in public; they did their utmost to prevent it happening again – by lowering their performance. You need to know who will bask in the glow and who'd prefer not to make a big deal of things. In the latter case I talk to them in private and explain that I haven't put the spotlight on them precisely because I know they don't like it. They appreciate that better because they feel I am attuned to their needs and receptive to their feelings, including shyness. That said, I do still mention them at meetings but not in an over the top way – just a word of thanks.

Blaming softly has to be clear, direct, and specific – but private. The aim is to keep the circle of criticism as small as possible and make corrections quickly, gently, and graciously. The leader who blames softly knows that no loyalty is earned through humiliation, and that a person who can save face can develop into a valuable leader as well. We must not destroy people in the process of making them better.

Catherine the Great had a point. If we make a big deal of praise and handle criticism frankly and discreetly, we will develop the kind of leadership that can help us reach for the sky.

It is important to remember that the goal of feedback is not to tell people what to do or how to do it. That is mistaking the process for the goal. The actual goal of feedback – even negative feedback – is to improve the behaviour of the other person.

How to give feedback

Praising good performance is easy, but what about those times when someone on your team needs a kick in the butt more than a pat on the back?

Here are some ideas to work with:

Make negative feedback uncommon. When a work environment becomes filled with criticism and complaint, people stop caring, because they feel that they will get criticised whatever they do. Also, when managers stockpile problems, waiting for the 'right moment', employees can become overwhelmed. Changes in behaviour are more easily achieved when negative feedback is administered in small doses and in real time, immediately after the fact.

It is better to give negative feedback orally. People who avoid confrontation are often tempted to use email to give negative feedback. Email is more easily misunderstood than oral feedback and it can look like you are 'building a case' against the person you are giving feedback to, by systematically documenting your (negative) feedback in writing. On the other hand, *positive feedback is best given in writing* because something put in writing usually has longer lasting impact than something dropped into a conversation.

I am, I should emphasise, talking here about one-off feedback unlikely to lead to disciplinary action (i.e. where you are expecting performance to improve). Nowadays, HR will not entertain a negative appraisal report without documentary evidence over the year to back it up – including emails. Our human resources units have actually insisted on occasion that particular individuals who performed badly should be given 'satisfactory' because of the lack of a paper trail indicating dissatisfaction. Of course in those cases

cont...

How to give feedback – *continued*

the poor performer needs to know that a case is being built.

Ask powerful questions. Most of the time, people know when they are having problems and may even have good ideas about how to improve which need to be drawn out of them. Asking questions such as 'How could you have done better?' and 'What do you think you could do with improving?' involves the other person in building a shared plan. You can give better feedback if you understand how the other person perceives the situation. Asking powerful questions such as, 'Why do you approach this situation in this way?' or better 'What was your thought process?' can lead other people to discover their own solutions and their own insights.

Listen before you speak. Effective feedback begins with active listening, paying attention, stepping into the other person's shoes, appreciating his or her experience, and helping to move that person into a learning mode.

Be willing to accept feedback yourself. In fact, few things are more valuable to managers than honest feedback from their staff. Feedback from your subordinates is to be treasured rather than discouraged or ignored; after all, nobody is perfect and not even the best manager has nothing to learn.

Management coaches sometimes advise the 'sandwich approach'. In this approach you insert the negative feedback between two pieces of positive feedback. It's a common method, but the sandwich approach may have the effect of undermining both your feedback and your relationships with your direct reports. Effective leaders are transparent about the strategies they use when working with others. The sandwich approach is designed to influence others without telling them what you are doing – in other words manipulate them. People don't like to be manipulated.

And a final tip: *Be careful in the way you give feedback.* Some cultures have a very open and accepting approach to feedback, but others don't. You can cause incredible damage if you offer personal feedback to someone who is not used to it, so be delicate, and start gradually.

Appraisal

Appraisal is formalised feedback. The appraisal system as provided for by Article 43 of the Staff Regulations is an important opportunity to look back at the past year, and reflect on the future, both for the staff member and the so-called reporting officer.

From my own experience as a Head of Unit, and thus reporting officer for the staff under my supervision, I know that appraisal is often looked upon as a tedious, time-consuming and highly bureaucratic burden. However, you should see this as a real exercise in leadership. Through its formalised nature, and the (at least theoretical) decoupling from the yearly promotion exercise, both the staff member and the supervisor get the opportunity to have an open and honest conversation, for which otherwise over the course of the year time or courage may be lacking on both sides.

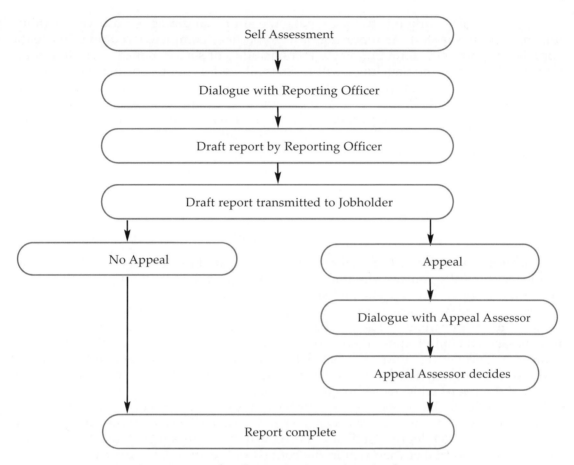

Figure 10.4: the Commission appraisal system

In the Commission's appraisal system (see Figure 10.4)[21], the self-assessment is the first and mandatory step in the yearly process. In fact, the self-assessment is structured into exactly the categories of the appraisal report: Efficiency, Abilities, Conduct in the service, Languages, Responsibilities, Learning, and General comment, and there is a clear mapping with the eight 'core competencies' as discussed in Chapter 1.

The self-assessment is a golden opportunity to take stock of important events during the past year. The staff member is not being asked to say if he or she is good or bad at their job, but rather to highlight their achievements and their ambitions for the future.

The qualitative appraisal report brings together the information relating to the individual staff member's performance during the past year. The report should cover the main aspects of the year, including any work that may have been done outside their own unit or DG.

If the staff member thinks that their report is not a fair reflection of the dialogue, they can appeal. The appeal will be dealt with by the hierarchical superior of the reporting officer.

---

21   https://myintracomm.ec.europa.eu/hr_admin/en/appraisal_promotion/

As a manager your job is to try to make the appraisal dialogue positive, meaningful, and helpful for staff. As reporting officer you have complete freedom to write the appraisal report, but promotion is the responsibility of senior management in a separate exercise. Senior management will discuss all staff in the DG or institution, grade by grade, to arrive at a proposal for who should be promoted, within the budget available. The goal is that all good performers should be promoted at the rates laid down in the Staff Regulation. The proposal of senior management will then be discussed with staff representatives and considered by the Joint Promotion Committee, finalised and published.

360-degree feedback

The term *360-degree feedback* refers to an appraisal and feedback system in which an employee (typically someone in a managerial or supervisory position) is evaluated by one or more supervisors, peers, and subordinates.

One of the great advantages of undergoing a 360-degree feedback evaluation is that it increases self-awareness. The feedback allows the individual to discover strengths, weaknesses and blind spots (behaviours and actions that they exhibit but are not aware of). Uncovering blind spots is key for continuous improvement and enables the employee to focus on developing skills in overlooked areas. It is – in effect – the application of the Johari window technique (see Chapter 2).

There used to be a 360-degree feedback system, for senior staff only, in the Commission, but that system has been suspended. Experience over the past years has shown that the 360-degree feedback mechanism is more suitably used as a career development tool rather than within the context of the appraisal exercise.

The European School for Administration (EUSA) uses the 360-degree mechanism for participants in training courses. This tool takes the form of a self-assessment of their competencies and feedback from colleagues that they have chosen to be consulted. A feedback report is produced automatically. The tool aims to help participants recognise, understand and manage their interpersonal behaviour and emotions effectively.

Committing to the target of 40% women in management, DG CONNECT's HR Committee on 11 May 2015 decided to give priority to a group of women, with the aim of increasing the likelihood of successful application to middle management positions. To achieve these objectives a 360-degree feedback assessment tool – an online questionnaire – has been selected. This tool helps participants to identify their strengths and areas of development. Each woman participating in the project receives feedback from different raters: their line manager, their selected peers and their team members.

The online toolkit that comes with this book gives you the opportunity to ask for 360-degree feedback, anonymously. Please do use it!

Delegation

A leader or a manager cannot – and should not – do everything by themselves; if they try, they will not be successful. Moreover, trying to do everything by yourself is a symptom of poor time management (see also the prioritising and organising chapter). Learning how to *delegate* is an indispensable skill for a leader or a manager in any organisation.

Worst is the 'control freak' type of manager who won't delegate and has staff afraid to take the smallest of decisions independently – and who then leaves the office for days or weeks at a time, leaving everything just blocked until their return.

Delegation involves giving others the authority to act on your behalf, accompanied with (a degree of) accountability for results. Effective delegation distributes the workload more evenly, helps an organisation to run more smoothly and efficiently and allows more people to become actively involved and motivated.

You *can* delegate:

- Tasks that are urgent but not important (priority 3 in the Eisenhower matrix).

- When there is a lot of work.

- When someone else has a particular skill or qualification which would suit a specific task.

- When someone expresses an interest in a task.

- When someone might benefit from the responsibility for his own development.

On the other hand *don't delegate:*

- Things you simply don't like doing.

- Your own important tasks (priority 1 and 2 in the Eisenhower matrix).

- Things that are usually your specified responsibilities.

- A task to someone who may not possess the skills necessary to do the task successfully.

I would personally not delegate the non-important/non-urgent tasks (i.e. priority 4 in the Eisenhower matrix) because this can convey the message that you don't value the person, which may cause demotivation.

Many people have difficulty delegating. Most often they would prefer to do the task themselves to make sure the 'job gets done right'. While this method can be more convenient, it can also result in the loss of followers. Sharing your authority with others can be the greatest single motivator in retaining followers and strengthening the organisation.

Managers often achieve their positions after being technical specialists themselves. They will have an opinion or view on how to 'fix' situations or problems. They believe that it's faster to tell someone what to do – or do it themselves – rather than give their subordinates an opportunity to figure it out. By always providing the answers, managers take away the opportunity for those they manage to learn and come up with alternative, and potentially better, ways of doing things.

The secret to great delegation is to empower your people to make decisions when you are not around. That way, they won't rely on you to keep the wheels turning. If a manager doesn't let things get through the gate without personally reviewing them, that holds up the entire organisation.

However, you should bear this important caveat in mind. *You can delegate work and authority, but not ultimate responsibility.* In the case of something going wrong, the blame is all yours if that failure occurs because you delegated a task to someone lacking the necessary skills. It is your fault since you delegated to the wrong person.

Unfortunately, the opposite scenario can also apply: a manager, such as the head of a department, can have responsibility but not authority. He or she might be held responsible for making something happen, but lacks the actual authority to enforce any directives or incentives. This is one of the major stressors that middle managers face. This is particularly an issue in the case of underperformance by a member of staff, where managers have very little in the way of tools (other than feedback) to effect a change of behaviour. Some staff take full advantage of this lack of authority (i.e. they happily chomp on every carrot they are given, knowing there is no real stick).

Give and take

'*Give, and it will be given to you.*' – Luke 6:38

According to organisational psychologist Adam Grant[22] there are three types of people in this world: *givers* (those who prioritise helping others), *takers* (those who help themselves) and *matchers* (those who seek equal benefit for themselves and others). After investigating years of psychological studies as well as conducting his own research, Grant concluded that givers are the most successful. He says:

'Givers bring out the best in others. One big part of that is seeing more potential in people than they see in themselves. Givers are often looking at the people around them as diamonds in the rough, investing in such a way that they're able to allow these people to achieve greater potential than they thought possible.'

Givers also become role models and change behaviour norms for the group, Grant argues, making others more likely to help each other and share knowledge – which can ultimately contribute to an environment of greater creativity and innovation. You can read more in his book 'Give and Take – Why Helping others Drives our Success'[23].

Prioritising and organising for managers

You can't give the benefit of your advice to other people if you don't allow time to plan and do this, so you need to spend more time on priorities, preparation, and follow-up – and less time in meetings.

Reducing the time you spend in meetings will give you more time to think strategically.

First, reduce the number of meeting invitations you accept.

cont...

---

22   Adam Grant (1981) is an author and professor at the Wharton School of the University of Pennsylvania.

23   'Give and Take – Why Helping others Drives our Success' (2014) by Adam Grant.

Prioritising and organising for managers – *continued*

- Ask the organiser of the meeting for the agenda so you can pass on your comments beforehand (this may on occasion force the organiser to actually produce an agenda!).
- Send someone else from your team to convey your position (this will help that person to see 'the bigger picture').
- If the meeting is only tangentially relevant to your work, excuse yourself from the meeting but request a copy of the minutes.

Second, reduce the number of meetings you schedule yourself — and reduce their length.

Opt for the least 'costly' investment of time that will still achieve your goal. Don't schedule a meeting for something that you can resolve in a phone call, and don't make a phone call for something that can be communicated in an email. If you really must schedule a meeting, challenge yourself to keep it as short as possible.

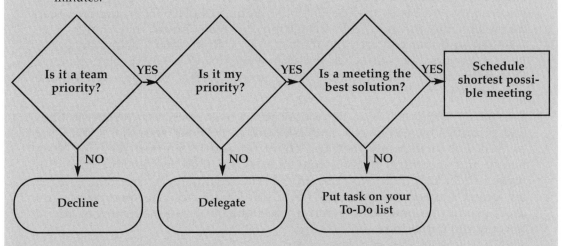

Third, start the meeting on time and aim to finish promptly to schedule.

Be on time yourself ('*l'exactitude est la politesse des rois*'[24]) and don't wait for late-comers before starting. Remember that you are burning the precious time of all those attending, so don't punish those who are on time by rewarding those who aren't.

Figure 10.5: do I need a meeting about it?

Leading your former peers

Becoming the manager of your former peers is a particular challenge; you need to establish your authority and credibility, without acting like the promotion has gone to your head.

Much as for any other upcoming change, you have to prepare this transition carefully. So, rather than waiting for a promotion to be announced, think first about what

---

24 'Punctuality is the politeness of kings'.

management style you'd like to apply, then challenge yourself to demonstrate those skills while you are still working side-by-side with your peers. That way, when you *are* promoted, there will be no surprises: people will already know what to expect, based on their past experience of your planning, decision-making, communication, and collaboration skills.

Here are some tips on what to do when the promotion has become a fact:

- *Address the elephant in the room.* Schedule a meeting to sit down with your new team. This doesn't necessarily have to be in a formal setting; invite them for lunch or a coffee. Even if your promotion hasn't been announced officially yet, you can bet on it that the grapevine has done its job already. Announcing the transition in a friendly atmosphere will remove the uncertainty and break the ice. Establish your authority from day one. Step decisively into the new role by letting the team know that things have changed, and that you are now their manager. Right after this first meeting, have a conversation with each individual regarding how expectations have changed; don't underestimate the power of a simple, one-on-one conversation.

- *Renegotiate your friendships.* Be honest about how your own responsibilities and priorities have changed, and ask how your friend sees theirs changing as well. Let them know they can count on you to support them in being happy and successful in their role and ask for their loyalty in return, but make it clear that there won't be any special treatment. Accept that you can no longer have close, personal friendships with your former peers. You don't need to become remote and unreachable, but you may want to attend fewer social gatherings.

- *Tread lightly at first.* You probably have loads of ideas about how to lead the team. But don't introduce any major revamps right away. You need to demonstrate your new authority without stepping on toes or damaging relationships. You can identify a few smaller decisions you can make fairly quickly, but postpone bigger ones until you've been in the role longer and have time to gather feedback.

- *Make use of your advantages.* You are more likely to find someone you trust to give you feedback than would a complete stranger to the team. After all, you know your former colleagues very well and know who is trustworthy and who is not. Leverage this knowledge to ask for honest feedback.

- *Look beyond your team.* During this type of transition, it's easy to become overly focused on your former peers. Ask yourself how you can build credibility with new counterparts and how you can build a connection with your own new boss.

Taking up the reins

I once had a rather striking experience of myself becoming the leader of my peers. One of my younger colleagues was actually the son of our boss, and everybody more or less expected that he was 'earmarked' as his father's successor. It came as a surprise when one day the boss called me into his office and announced he was going to retire. This was rather unexpected, because he was still relatively young (57); however, we all knew that he was suffering from bad health (he actually died a year later). My surprise was even greater when he told me that the board of directors had decided (on his recommendation) that I was to be his successor.

Needless to say, I expected problems with the son, but that didn't happen. He was wise enough to understand that he was too young and inexperienced to take on this role. In fact, he was even relieved, because becoming the boss would have prevented him from doing what he was really good at – being a brilliant system administrator.

With the other team members I had no problems either, because I was by far the oldest and most experienced member of the team, so I didn't face a challenge in trying to establish my credibility and authority; I already had it.

I remember this period, which lasted over four years, as one of the happiest in my entire career, and when I left to explore different horizons I happily recommended the son as my successor. I believe he is still holding this position many years later, and doing a perfect job.

Integrity

'You are what you do, not what you say you'll do.' – C.G. Jung

Integrity means that we do not behave in ways that go against our essence; that we behave with honesty, reliability, and caring – with ourselves and with others. Doing what you say you will do is a matter of integrity.

I don't trust people who don't keep their word. Decades ago I had a boss who had clearly reached his 'level of incompetence'[25]. He said different things to different people, trying to save face with the person he was actually talking to. To his boss, the general manager, he promised one thing, while he was instructing the external consultants to do something different. The financial manager then got yet another version of his story, and as for his immediate colleagues, well, they didn't know what to think about all of this. I remember this episode as one of the most unhappy of my entire career, because I didn't trust my boss, I felt unsafe.

I lose respect for people whose word doesn't mean anything to them. If you want to feel respected by others, then you need to say 'yes' when you mean 'yes' and 'no' when you mean 'no', and not allow your fear of rejection to get in the way of being a trustworthy person.

---

25   According to the Peter Principle (see Chapter 1) 'managers rise to the level of their incompetence'.

We cannot feel worthy when we let others down. People who default on their word do not value themselves enough to act with integrity. Self-worth is the result of treating others with caring and respect.

When people have the sense that a leader is worthy of their trust they will invest time and take risks in ways they never would if their leader had a reputation built upon lack of integrity. Keep in mind that people will forgive many things where trust exists, but will rarely forgive anything where trust is absent.

Authentic leadership

'To thy own self be true.' – Polonius, in Shakespeare's 'Hamlet'

In 2003, following a series of corporate scandals in the US, Bill George[26] made the case that we needed new leaders, not just new laws, to get us out of the corporate crisis in his book 'Authentic Leadership'[27].

According to George, authentic leaders are 'self-actualized'[28] individuals who are aware of their strengths, their limitations, and their own emotions. They also show who they really are to their followers. They do not act one way in private and another in public; they don't hide their mistakes or weaknesses out of fear of looking weak. Authentic leaders lead with their hearts, not just their minds. They are not afraid to show their emotions, their vulnerability, and to connect with their employees. This does not mean that authentic leaders are 'soft.' Being open about yourself helps to break down hierarchical barriers. It is only when your staff know the person behind the façade that you start building the foundations of good leadership: trust and respect.

Besides being open and honest with their followers, authentic leaders always put the mission and the goals of the organisation ahead of their own self-interest. They do the job in pursuit of results for the organisation, not for their own power, money or ego. Authentic leaders focus on the long-term stakeholder's value. They realise that to nurture individuals and an organisation requires hard work and patience, but the approach pays large dividends over time.

A man for all seasons

My wife and I were recently binge watching the 'The Tudors' on Netflix. The series is based upon the reign of King Henry VIII of England. One of the key players, Sir Thomas More, refused to endorse King Henry VIII's desire to divorce his first wife, Catherine of Aragon, because she could not bear him a son. Henry VIII wanted to marry Anne Boleyn, the sister of his former mistress. I was so impressed by More, whose sense of principle was such that he chose to die rather than lose his integrity. Sir Thomas More was a man of significant personal power, deeply loved by his family and the people. I realised that it was his authenticity that gave him the strength to die rather than compromise his integrity in order to live. In his eyes, his life would not be worth living if he were not true to himself. He was, in the words of the title of a play about him 'a man for all seasons'.

---

26   William W. George is Professor of Management Practice at Harvard Business School.
27   'Authentic Leadership – Rediscovering the Secrets of Creating Lasting Value' (2003) by Bill George.
28   'The full realization of one's potential, and of one's true self' (Abraham Maslow).

Followership: the other side of leadership

'I must follow the people. Am I not their leader?' – Benjamin Disraeli[29]

The other side of leadership is *'followership'*. It seems reasonable that if leadership is important to performance, followership must have something to do with it too. But strangely, followership gets only a small fraction of the exposure that leadership does.

Followership is a straightforward concept. It is the ability to take direction well, to get in line behind a program, to be part of a team and to deliver on what is expected of you. One could say that it is closely related to 'delivering quality and results' as described earlier in this book. However, being a good follower is sometimes looked down on. This is a pity because the practical reality is that one does not progressively reach more responsible leadership positions without demonstrating an ability to follow and function effectively as part of a group. The fact is that in organisations everybody is *both* a leader *and* a follower depending on the circumstances. How well the followers follow is probably just as important to an organisation's success as how well the leaders lead.

Quite a number of interesting studies have been conducted on the topic of followership. To name a few which you can check out if you are interested:

- Zaleznik's follower typology: based on control and activity.

- Kelley's follower typology: five different types.

- Kellerman's follower typology: five different types.

- Chaleff's follower typology: based on type of support.

Followership will always be in the shadow of leadership. Nonetheless, while it is true that an organisation is only as good as its leaders, it is also only as good as its followers. *There are no leaders without followers.*

Developing your leadership competency

Leadership skills play a large role in your career development. Often, your technical skills can only take you so far. To help you move forward in your career, you need soft skills such as the ability to be a good leader. Few people are born to be leaders. Most of us need to practise being a good leader, and that is why leadership development is so important.

Please refer to Chapter 1 (methodology) and Annex 8 for further development of this competency, have another look at the current chapter to find out about your options, and remember: YOU are responsible for your own development, not your manager, your colleagues, or your mentor.

---

29   19th century British Prime Minister.

The online toolkit that comes for free with this book can be used to follow-up on your development in this area. The toolkit can be found at:

https://www.johnharperpublishing.co.uk/the-ultimate-eu-career-development-toolkit/

Key points to remember

- Managers and leaders should realise that they can be a cause of sub-optimal performance of their staff.
- Motivation is an on-going, everyday aspect of leadership.
- Ask people what motivates them: create opportunities; adapt objectives.
- Trust is the currency of leadership; be yourself.
- Lead by example.
- Shut up and listen.
- Replace ego with empathy.
- Communicate, communicate, and communicate.

Your notes

Annex 1.   Self-assessment worksheet for analysis and problem solving

Please refer to 'How to use the self-assessment worksheets' on page 21.

Anchors

1.   Analyses and prioritises situations to identify and solve problems.

2.   Solutions increase efficiency and improve quality.

3.   Involves others in solving problems and making decisions.

4.   Factors organisational goals into decisions.

5.   Makes clear, transparent, and timely decisions.

6.   Dealing with complexity.

7.   Identifying the relevant aspects from a mass of information.

8.   Proposing useful and practical solutions.

9.   Gathering information from various sources and critically evaluating it.

10.   Using judgement and analysis to find solutions to problems.

Indicators

	UNSATISFACTORY	IMPROVEMENT NEEDED	MEETS EXPECTA-TIONS	EXCEEDS EXPECTA-TIONS	EXCEPTIONAL	
anchor	1 - Extremely Weak 2 - Very Weak	3 - Weak 4 - Fair	5 - Satisfactory 6 - Good	7 - Strong 8 - Very Strong	9 - Excellent 10 - Outstanding	Score
1.	Has difficulty distinguishing between critical and noncritical issues. Loses focus when resolving larger issues. Misunderstands or misinterprets key elements of information.	Needs help with analysing and prioritising problems. Tends to focus on simple operational issues.	Solves urgent, high impact problems first.	Analyses and prioritises critical problems. Stays focused on critical problems until they are successfully resolved.	Analyses and prioritises critical problems accurately and quickly. Maintains a sense of urgency in solving even complex problems.	

cont...

	UNSATISFACTORY	IMPROVEMENT NEEDED	MEETS EXPECTA-TIONS	EXCEEDS EXPECTA-TIONS	EXCEPTIONAL	
anchor	1 - Extremely Weak 2 - Very Weak	3 - Weak 4 - Fair	5 - Satisfactory 6 - Good	7 - Strong 8 - Very Strong	9 - Excellent 10 - Outstanding	Score
2.	Rarely proposes innovative solutions. Produces 'quick fixes' that do not yield lasting or quality results.	Proposes solutions that are usually short-term. Is rarely transformative in terms of greater efficiency and/or improved quality.	Finds solutions that effectively address issues and are easily sustainable.	Finds solutions that change the workplace both in terms of increasing efficiency and enhancing the quality of products and services. Makes processes more efficient.	Finds solutions that consistently transform the workplace. Delivers products and services that improve quality significantly.	
3.	Rarely collaborates with peers and stakeholders. Doesn't look for more efficient ways to do things.	Collaborates with others only when asked to. Prefers to solve problems independently.	Collaborates effectively with others to solve problems and make decisions.	Is highly collaborative in terms of seeking input to solve problems and make decisions.	Consistently and effectively seeks input from all peers and stakeholders. Is agile and decisive.	
4.	Makes decisions that have minimal or no impact in terms of improving the quality of products and services, or in aligning with department goals.	Makes decisions that focus on immediate, short-term issues, losing sight of larger departmental goals and initiatives.	Keeps organisational and departmental goals in mind when solving problems and making decisions.	Makes decisions and takes actions that align with organisational and departmental goals and initiatives.	Always has 'big picture' in mind and helps others see it. Consistently aligns decisions and actions with organisational and department goals and initiatives.	
5.	Has difficulty articulating rationale for decisions. Often defers decision-making to others.	Makes decisions that are sometimes not clear. Tends to put off decisions on more complex issues.	Makes sound decisions based on facts and experience.	Makes decisions that consistently support and facilitate desired outcomes.	Consistently makes clear, transparent, and timely decisions. Makes decisions that consistently align with organisational and departmental goals.	

	UNSATISFACTORY	IMPROVEMENT NEEDED	MEETS EXPECTATIONS	EXCEEDS EXPECTATIONS	EXCEPTIONAL	
anchor	1 - Extremely Weak 2 - Very Weak	3 - Weak 4 - Fair	5 - Satisfactory 6 - Good	7 - Strong 8 - Very Strong	9 - Excellent 10 - Outstanding	**Score**
6.	Does not gather a sufficiently clear picture of the problems in their full complexity. Omits important facts and details from analysis.	Captures the global picture but misses a number of important details.	Understands and summarises the main issues involved.	Understands the problem and links up the elements. Takes on board all the available information and fits everything together.	Analyses and interprets the available data correctly and completely. Gives a concise and systematic overview of the situation.	
7.	Is overwhelmed by high volumes of information and gets lost. Focuses more on the superfluous than the essential.	Misses logical links between items of information. Is distracted by side issues.	Tackles main problems and is not distracted by secondary issues. Distinguishes between relevant and less relevant information.	Simplifies the complex without neglecting key issues or details that matter.	Differentiates clearly between the relative importance of the different issues.	
8.	Proposes solutions that do not tackle main issues to be addressed. Proposes solutions that contain elements used as justification for rejecting alternative options.	Proposes solutions that are impractical because of their implications. Proposes solutions that do not take all the factors into account.	Proposes reasonable but not particularly visionary solutions. Proposes workable solutions.	Proposes solutions that deal effectively with all aspects of the problem. Proposes solutions that exceed the expectations of the stakeholders.	Consistently proposes solutions that reflect a balanced analysis and sound judgment.	
9.	Does not identify inconsistencies or contradictions in available information. Bases analysis on information from only a few of the available sources.	Is more descriptive than analytical in their approach.	Takes into account different sources of information available. Compares and contrasts information drawn from different sources.	Analyses problems by comparing and contrasting information drawn from all available sources.	Refers to the available sources and assesses the relative significance of each one. Identifies and resolves inconsistencies or contradictions in available information.	

	UNSATISFACTORY	IMPROVEMENT NEEDED	MEETS EXPECTATIONS	EXCEEDS EXPECTATIONS	EXCEPTIONAL	
anchor	1 - Extremely Weak 2 - Very Weak	3 - Weak 4 - Fair	5 - Satisfactory 6 - Good	7 - Strong 8 - Very Strong	9 - Excellent 10 - Outstanding	**Score**
10.	Relies more on intuition than on analysis. Ignores options that should be explored.	Makes proposals without thinking through their implications. Does not make a convincing case for their recommendations.	Explores different options in search for solutions. Considers the implications of their proposals.	Tests different options to determine which provides the optimum solution. Weights up options and anticipates possible objections to preferred choices.	Considers all the options before deciding on the best way forward. Reacts to developments as the implementation unfolds.	

Total Score

An online version of this questionnaire can be found at:

https://www.johnharperpublishing.co.uk/the-ultimate-eu-career-development-toolkit/

Annex 2. Self-assessment worksheet for communicating

Please refer to 'How to use the self-assessment worksheets' on page 21.

Anchors

1. Demonstrates effective written communication skills.

2. Adapts written communication to the level of the audience.

3. Writes clearly, in a visually appealing manner.

4. Explains ideas clearly, simplifies the complex.

5. Is methodical, structured and precise in speech.

6. Adapts verbal communication to the level of the audience.

7. Communicates clearly and knowledgeably.

8. Shares information with others.

9. Seeks input from others.

10. Protects private and confidential information.

Indicators

	UNSATISFACTORY	IMPROVEMENT NEEDED	MEETS EXPECTA-TIONS	EXCEEDS EXPECTA-TIONS	EXCEPTIONAL	
anchor	1 - Extremely Weak 2 - Very Weak	3 - Weak 4 - Fair	5 - Satisfactory 6 - Good	7 - Strong 8 - Very Strong	9 - Excellent 10 - Outstanding	**Score**
1.	Creates documents that are poorly written, unstructured, grammatically incorrect, or contain too many spelling errors. Uses incomplete sentences or bad punctuation.	Creates documents that are disorganised or contain many grammar or spelling errors. Uses too long sentences, too verbose, or overly complex.	Keeps sentences and paragraphs short and concise. Leaves out words that do not contribute to the main focus of the communication. Writes documents that are syntactically and semantically correct.	Creates documents that are consistently clear and persuasive.	Writes documents that are always complete, concise, clear, concrete, correct, considerate and courteous.	

	UNSATISFACTORY	IMPROVEMENT NEEDED	MEETS EXPECTATIONS	EXCEEDS EXPECTATIONS	EXCEPTIONAL	
anchor	1 - Extremely Weak 2 - Very Weak	3 - Weak 4 - Fair	5 - Satisfactory 6 - Good	7 - Strong 8 - Very Strong	9 - Excellent 10 - Outstanding	**Score**
2.	Creates documents that are either overly simplistic or too complex and therefore not adapted to the audience.	Creates documents that are somewhat disorganised and/or not appropriate for the audience. Uses slang, jargon, acronyms, or unexplained concepts or ideas.	Focuses on the needs of the audience. Uses simple language, without over-using clichés, jargon, and expressions or trying to impress with difficult words.	Creates documents that are concise and comprehensive and convey all the ideas that need to be addressed.	Writes documents that consistently address all the needs of specific individuals and groups within the audience.	
3.	Creates visually unappealing documents; large blocks of continuous text without punctuations or whitespace.	Makes inappropriate use of colour coding, text formatting, capitalisations, etc. Uses no illustrations or visual elements.	Creates visually appealing documents with appropriate use of whitespace, indentations and graphical elements.	Makes appropriate use of colour coding, text formatting, capitalisations enhancing the underlying structure and ideas.	Writes visually engaging documents, illustrated with tables and graphs enhancing the messages to be conveyed.	
4.	Does not finish sentences or stops mid-sentence and expects the audience to second-guess and draw conclusions. Gets blocked and has difficulty in finding the right words to express himself. Speaks too fast and is difficult to follow. Has bad articulation or truncates his/her words.	Does not always clearly structure his/her ideas; has difficulty in articulating his/her thoughts. Is hesitant and transmits uncertainty with body language or tone of voice. Does not engage spontaneously with his/her audience.	Speaks clearly, connects with his/her audience and gets messages across with relative ease. Engages spontaneously with his/her audience.	Explains issues and ideas clearly and succinctly. Strikes a good balance between detail and the need for clarity.	Explains even complex issues and ideas clearly and succinctly, simplifies the complex. Convinces sceptics and opponents of his/her points of view.	

	UNSATISFACTORY	IMPROVEMENT NEEDED	MEETS EXPECTATIONS	EXCEEDS EXPECTATIONS	EXCEPTIONAL	
anchor	1 - Extremely Weak 2 - Very Weak	3 - Weak 4 - Fair	5 - Satisfactory 6 - Good	7 - Strong 8 - Very Strong	9 - Excellent 10 - Outstanding	Score
5.	Speaks in an unstructured fashion, jumps from one point to another, does not get to the point, or does not achieve flowing delivery of ideas. Makes contributions that are often unclear or inaccurate. Gives minimalist or no answers to questions.	Gets lost in complexity and does not succeed in making his/her points clearly. Dwells too much on detail and does not get to the point. Is rather vague or evasive when answering questions.	Speaks clearly, persuasively, and concisely. Focuses on the needs of specific individuals and groups. Keeps to a logical order when explaining things. Copes well with questions and provides relevant information.	Uses verbal communication that is consistently clear, persuasive, and adapted to the audience. Illustrates answers to questions with appropriate and relevant examples. Goes straight to the point when answering questions.	Is methodical, precise and structured in speech, is articulate and makes good use of language and gesture. Anticipates information needs and gives full and complete answers to questions.	
6.	Has difficulty tailoring communication to the needs of others; communicates 'too much,' 'too little,' or 'too late.'	Does not always keep the audience in mind.	Tailors information to audience and individual needs.	Effectively adjusts the level of detail and tone to the audience.	Effectively adapts verbal communication to audience; effectively distinguishes between 'need to know' and 'nice to know.'	
7.	Appears distracted or uninterested; frequently interrupts others. Does not listen to what others say.	Interrupts others to express own point of view. Has difficulty getting to the point. Uses facts that are not always accurate or relevant.	Appears knowledgeable and concise. Actively listens to and synthesises perspectives of others.	Appears credible and reliable. Actively listens to and integrates diverse contributions.	Speaks with conviction and authority. Listens to, synthesises, and integrates others' ideas.	
8.	Does not share information in a timely manner, creating problems for colleagues and stakeholders.	Has difficulty distinguishing between critical and noncritical information.	Gives to others the information they need in a timely manner.	Shares accurate, timely information with the right people in the right format.	Displays openness and transparency in sharing information with partners and stakeholders.	

	UNSATISFACTORY	IMPROVEMENT NEEDED	MEETS EXPECTATIONS	EXCEEDS EXPECTATIONS	EXCEPTIONAL	
anchor	1 - Extremely Weak 2 - Very Weak	3 - Weak 4 - Fair	5 - Satisfactory 6 - Good	7 - Strong 8 - Very Strong	9 - Excellent 10 - Outstanding	Score
9.	Avoids contact with co-workers and partners. Is monosyllabic in conversation.	Keeps communication to a minimum. Is reticent to share thoughts and ideas.	Maintains an open and honest dialogue with co-workers and partners.	Encourages others to share ideas and integrates others' thoughts and opinions.	Consistently and effectively seeks and incorporates others' ideas to ensure optimal results.	
10.	Discloses and uses private and confidential information inappropriately, putting the organisation or other individuals at risk.	Does not consistently follow the organisation's confidentiality or privacy practices. Sometimes shares private or confidential information with unauthorised or inappropriate individuals.	Consistently follows confidentiality and privacy policies and practices. Only discloses confidential information to authorised individuals.	Understands and implements confidentiality and privacy policies.	Clearly understands and follows confidentiality and privacy policies and practices. Actively develops practices to protect confidential and private information.	

Total Score

An online version of this questionnaire can be found at:

https://www.johnharperpublishing.co.uk/the-ultimate-eu-career-development-toolkit/

Annex 3.   Self-assessment worksheet for delivering quality and results

Please refer to 'How to use the self-assessment worksheets' on page 21.

Anchors

1. Taking responsibility.

2. Taking initiative.

3. Overcoming obstacles.

4. Delivering quality work on time.

5. Working to a high standard of quality.

6. Manages workload efficiently and effectively.

7. Understands the value of innovation and of quality improvement.

8. Links up the various elements of the work.

9. Demonstrates efficiency and effectiveness in own work.

10. Manages and sustains change initiatives.

Indicators

	UNSATISFACTORY	IMPROVEMENT NEEDED	MEETS EXPECTA-TIONS	EXCEEDS EXPECTA-TIONS	EXCEPTIONAL	
anchor	1 - Extremely Weak 2 - Very Weak	3 - Weak 4 - Fair	5 - Satisfactory 6 - Good	7 - Strong 8 - Very Strong	9 - Excellent 10 - Outstanding	Score
1.	Finds excuses for not dealing promptly with problems and requests. Refers problems to third parties instead of tackling them himself directly. Blames external factors for failure to deliver quality work.	Does not always take responsibility for dealing promptly with problems that arise at work. Is slow to react to developments that affect achievability of results.	Takes his/her work seriously and applies himself to tasks. Is quality-conscious and does the necessary to achieve high standards. Reacts to urgent requests.	Tackles assignments and accepts full responsibility for the outcomes. Reacts to developments that affect achievability of objectives.	Has a highly developed sense of responsibility and accountability. Anticipates problems and has solutions already worked out in advance.	

	UNSATISFACTORY	IMPROVEMENT NEEDED	MEETS EXPECTATIONS	EXCEEDS EXPECTATIONS	EXCEPTIONAL	
anchor	1 - Extremely Weak 2 - Very Weak	3 - Weak 4 - Fair	5 - Satisfactory 6 - Good	7 - Strong 8 - Very Strong	9 - Excellent 10 - Outstanding	**Score**
2.	Does not do more than the minimum required to complete tasks. Sticks strictly to own job description.	Is reluctant to go beyond the call of duty. Never or rarely questions procedures or established ways of working.	Understands procedures and workflow within his/her department. Follows established guidelines where appropriate. Works beyond the confines of job description if necessary.	Keeps up with events and takes initiatives that have a positive impact on quality of work. Acts without waiting to be told: takes initiative.	Goes the extra mile to ensure best possible results. Takes initiatives to make procedures and workflows more efficient or effective.	
3.	Is deflected or stopped by obstacles and does not find ways around them. Goes round in circles instead of narrowing-in on solutions.	Does not deal adequately with complex tasks. Takes the first solution that comes along without standing back to weigh other options.	Achieves satisfactory results when faced with obstacles or complex tasks. Deals appropriately with unexpected developments.	Systematically ensures that desired results are delivered, notwithstanding difficulties. Thinks 'out-of-the-box'.	Demonstrates resourcefulness in finding ways around difficulties. Anticipates problems and has solutions ready.	
4.	Underestimates work, gets his/her planning wrong and runs into time trouble. Spends too long on tasks that add little or no value to the end result.	Does not always take the right decision at the right time. Is perfectionist and loses sight of time constraints.	Deals with matters in appropriate and timely manner. Strikes acceptable balance between quality and deadlines.	Takes remedial actions when quality is in danger or compromised by deadlines. Sees where corners can be cut to meet tight deadlines.	Finds ways of delivering the best possible results under difficult circumstances and tight deadlines.	
5.	Settles for quick and easy solutions.	Does not always meet expectations.	Performs to expected standards and in accordance with procedures in place.	Sets himself demanding standards and does not settle for second best.	Seeks to continuously exceed expectations. Puts a large amount of personal effort and creative thought into work. Thrives in challenging situations.	

	UNSATISFACTORY	IMPROVEMENT NEEDED	MEETS EXPECTATIONS	EXCEEDS EXPECTATIONS	EXCEPTIONAL	
anchor	1 - Extremely Weak 2 - Very Weak	3 - Weak 4 - Fair	5 - Satisfactory 6 - Good	7 - Strong 8 - Very Strong	9 - Excellent 10 - Outstanding	Score
6.	Works inefficiently or becomes overwhelmed with workload. Procrastinates.	Neglects work-life balance. Uses overtime as only strategy to cope with heavy workload or tight deadlines. Is overly perfectionist, indecisive, or impatient with others.	Manages to get all his/her work done in time and to a good quality standard.	Combines good work-life balance with efficient and effective behaviour at work.	Manages own workload as well as the workload of others effectively and efficiently.	
7.	Resists change: prefers to continue to do things as they always have been done.	Has a limited perspective and understanding of the importance of quality improvement.	Understands the value of quality improvement. Identifies weaknesses that impede processes and recommends changes.	Understands and communicates the importance of quality improvement.	Clearly defines the value and imperative for continuous improvement. Consistently offers original, inventive ideas for improving products and services.	
8.	Does not grasp the general picture.	Makes few if any links between separate items of information.	Has a clear understanding of his/her mandate but is less successful in grasping the overall picture and priorities.	Sees how different elements fit together.	Focuses on both the general elements and the details of the situation. Has a clear understanding of the bigger picture. Fits things together and draws conclusions.	

	UNSATISFACTORY	IMPROVEMENT NEEDED	MEETS EXPECTA-TIONS	EXCEEDS EXPECTA-TIONS	EXCEPTIONAL	
anchor	1 - Extremely Weak 2 - Very Weak	3 - Weak 4 - Fair	5 - Satisfactory 6 - Good	7 - Strong 8 - Very Strong	9 - Excellent 10 - Outstanding	Score
9.	Is extremely disorganised and unable to separate 'need to do' from less important tasks. Cannot handle more than one project at a time.	Has difficulty handling more than one task or project at a time. Disorganisation often results in poor quality work.	Successfully manages several projects to achieve desired results.	Manages several projects effectively and efficiently. Results enhance productivity and quality of the department.	Demonstrates efficiency by getting more done in less time while maintaining quality of results. Effectively manages multiple projects to achieve desired outcomes.	
10.	Moves to next project before ensuring successful, sustainable implementation of previous projects.	Rarely monitors change initiatives after implementation.	Sustains change through clear documentation and regular monitoring.	Ensures that operational changes are successfully implemented and sustained over time.	Employs clear post-implementation strategies to ensure sustainability. Encourages continuous improvement.	

Total Score

An online version of this questionnaire can be found at:

https://www.johnharperpublishing.co.uk/the-ultimate-eu-career-development-toolkit/

Annex 4.   Self-assessment worksheet for learning and development

Please refer to 'How to use the self-assessment worksheets' on page 21.

Anchors

1. Explains ideas clearly, simplifies the complex.
2. Actively developing and applying new knowledge, skills, and competencies.
3. Personal development.
4. Asking for advice and assistance.
5. Seeing own role within the organisation.
6. Seeing the 'bigger picture'.
7. Learning other languages.
8. Learning strategy.
9. Active listening.
10. Teaching others.

Indicators

	UNSATISFACTORY	IMPROVEMENT NEEDED	MEETS EXPECTA-TIONS	EXCEEDS EXPECTA-TIONS	EXCEPTIONAL	
anchor	1 - Extremely Weak 2 - Very Weak	3 - Weak 4 - Fair	5 - Satisfactory 6 - Good	7 - Strong 8 - Very Strong	9 - Excellent 10 - Outstanding	Score
1.	Has difficulty in finding the right words to express himself.	Does not always clearly structure ideas; has diffi-culty in articulat-ing thoughts and vision.	Speaks and writes clearly, simplifies the complex.	Explains vision and ideas clearly and succinctly. Strikes a good bal-ance between detail and the need for clarity.	Explains even complex issues and ideas clearly and succinctly, simplifies the com-plex.	

	UNSATISFACTORY	IMPROVEMENT NEEDED	MEETS EXPECTA-TIONS	EXCEEDS EXPECTA-TIONS	EXCEPTIONAL	
anchor	1 - Extremely Weak 2 - Very Weak	3 - Weak 4 - Fair	5 - Satisfactory 6 - Good	7 - Strong 8 - Very Strong	9 - Excellent 10 - Outstanding	Score
2.	Allows knowledge levels to remain constant and/or outdated. Shows little interest in developing new skills or acquiring new knowledge.	Remains fixed in personal ways of working, does not try to develop. Takes a long time to learn new information.	Takes on board new information quickly. Learns from observation. Adapts to new ways of doing things.	Volunteers for new and challenging tasks. Is resourceful when it comes to familiarising with the latest developments in his/her field.	Takes active steps to improve own knowledge and development. Develops new skills on own initiative.	
3.	Stays in comfort zone and settles for routine. Does little to overcome his/her weaknesses.	Sees personal development in exclusively professional terms. Does little to develop his/her strengths.	Knows his/her strengths and weaknesses. Identifies personal failings and tries to overcome them. Sets personal goals.	Sets himself inspiring challenges. Sets and achieves personal goals.	Works actively on developing strengths and overcoming weaknesses. Improves knowledge and skills out of personal interest and natural curiosity.	
4.	Does not take opportunities to ask for personal feedback from others. Fails to learn from mistakes, continues to make them. Does not accept constructive feedback.	Does not learn from experience. Avoids new challenges and learning opportunities. Makes limited use of the experience of colleagues.	Seeks personal feedback on performance from others. Learns from mistakes and avoids repeating them. Responds positively to negative feedback and learns from it.	Rethinks and adjusts approach to take account of feedback received. Learns from input and suggestions from colleagues.	Actively seeks feedback from others to improve own performance. Pools knowledge and expertise.	

	UNSATISFACTORY	IMPROVEMENT NEEDED	MEETS EXPECTATIONS	EXCEEDS EXPECTATIONS	EXCEPTIONAL	
anchor	1 - Extremely Weak 2 - Very Weak	3 - Weak 4 - Fair	5 - Satisfactory 6 - Good	7 - Strong 8 - Very Strong	9 - Excellent 10 - Outstanding	**Score**
5.	Focuses exclusively on own tasks and role. Has limited vision of developments elsewhere. Lacks understanding of how own work contributes to the objectives of the organisation.	Does not always respect the boundaries between his/her responsibilities and those of colleagues.	Knows what his/her department does and where it fits in. Understands the objectives of the organisation and contributes towards their achievement.	Takes initiatives to improve organisation-wide procedures and workflows.	Projects a positive image of his/her organisation to the outside world.	
6.	Makes no efforts to interact with other departments or organisations. Lacks vision of what happens upstream and downstream of own department.	Gives little thought to wider organisational objectives.	Understands how his/her department contributes to the achievement of wider organisational goals. Interacts extensively with other departments and organisations.	Uses the knowledge of wider organisational processes for improving collaboration with other organisations.	Sees the 'bigger picture' and contributes actively. Is aware of the wider political context, and his/her own contribution.	
7.	Besides own mother tongue, is only a basic user (A1, A2) for one of the three working languages.	Besides own mother tongue, is only an independent user (B1, B2) for one of the three working languages.	Is a proficient user (C1) of at least three languages, including mother tongue, one of the working languages, and another official EU language.	Is a proficient user (C1, C2) for the three working languages, or for more than three official EU languages.	Is a proficient user (C1, C2) for at least three official EU languages, and an independent user (B1, B2) for at least one non-EU language.	
8.	Is not aware of own learning style.	Does not apply own preferred learning style systematically.	Knows and applies own preferred learning style.	Has a clear learning strategy, and applies it successfully.	Uses different learning styles in different circumstances.	

	UNSATISFACTORY	IMPROVEMENT NEEDED	MEETS EXPECTATIONS	EXCEEDS EXPECTATIONS	EXCEPTIONAL	
anchor	1 - Extremely Weak 2 - Very Weak	3 - Weak 4 - Fair	5 - Satisfactory 6 - Good	7 - Strong 8 - Very Strong	9 - Excellent 10 - Outstanding	**Score**
9.	Appears distracted or uninterested. Frequently interrupts others. Does not listen to what others say.	Interrupts others to express own point of view.	Listens to and learns from other people's ideas and contributions.	Actively listens to and learns from other people's ideas and contributions.	Listens to, synthesises, and integrates others' ideas into own understanding.	
10.	Keeps own knowledge and understanding to himself. Considers colleagues as competitors.	Teaches others only when explicitly asked to do so.	Considers teaching others as part of his/her job description.	Mentors or coaches others when asked to.	Actively mentors or coaches others. Sees coaching and mentoring as part of his/her job description.	

Total Score

An online version of this questionnaire can be found at:

https://www.johnharperpublishing.co.uk/the-ultimate-eu-career-development-toolkit/

Annex 5.   Self-assessment worksheet for prioritising and organising

Please refer to 'How to use the self-assessment worksheets' on page 21.

Anchors

1. Understands goals and implements plans to achieve them.
2. Mobilises the appropriate resources to achieve goals.
3. Develops and implements metrics to measure results.
4. Anticipates and solves problems.
5. Sets realistic deadlines and milestones.
6. Manages workload efficiently and effectively.
7. Prioritises tasks appropriately.
8. Links up the various elements of the work.
9. Is flexible in taking into account new aspects coming in.
10. Collaborates effectively with others.

Indicators

	UNSATISFACTORY	IMPROVEMENT NEEDED	MEETS EXPECTA-TIONS	EXCEEDS EXPECTA-TIONS	EXCEPTIONAL	
anchor	1 - Extremely Weak 2 - Very Weak	3 - Weak 4 - Fair	5 - Satisfactory 6 - Good	7 - Strong 8 - Very Strong	9 - Excellent 10 - Outstanding	**Score**
1.	Does not follow an orderly method of setting objectives, scoping out difficulties, detailing work, or planning for task completion.	Does not have a clear picture of unit or Institution goals; lacks perspective to pull elements into a strategic view; plans often lack substance and specificity.	Creates effective plans with defined purpose and outcomes. Breaks complex tasks into process steps, prioritises activities, itemises resources and estimates costs.	Plans with unit and Institution goals in mind. Plans clearly identify roles, responsibilities and timeframes.	Creates innovative, ambitious plans, which align with unit and Institution goals and serve as reliable roadmaps to desired outcomes.	

	UNSATISFACTORY	IMPROVEMENT NEEDED	MEETS EXPECTATIONS	EXCEEDS EXPECTATIONS	EXCEPTIONAL	
anchor	1 - Extremely Weak 2 - Very Weak	3 - Weak 4 - Fair	5 - Satisfactory 6 - Good	7 - Strong 8 - Very Strong	9 - Excellent 10 - Outstanding	Score
2.	Is not able to integrate multiple activities and resources into a cohesive, actionable plan.	Has difficulty marshaling and informing resources to work together to achieve desired outcomes.	Organises, informs and supports resources to achieve goals.	Informs and mobilises resources—staff, stakeholders, technical experts—to achieve shared vision, mission, and goals.	Effectively influences, informs, and mobilises resources—staff, stakeholders, technical experts—to achieve shared vision, mission, and goals.	
3.	Is unwilling/unable to create or track metrics. Allows work to continue without monitoring.	Has difficulty defining and implementing appropriate metrics to measure success. Becomes ineffective when plans need to change.	Monitors progress and determine how processes may be changed to improve quality and/or efficiency. Adapts to changes in plans effectively.	Implements metrics that effectively and efficiently measure results. Recommends improvements based on results.	Develops and implements reliable, effective metrics to measure outcomes; identifies and recommends changes to improve efficiency and effectiveness.	
4.	Ignores small problems until they become significant, jeopardising deadlines and effective utilisation of resources.	Identifies problems but does not effectively address them.	Addresses problems in process or resourcing quickly and effectively.	Anticipates and adjusts for problems and roadblocks. Resolves problems in early stages.	Proactively anticipates, analyses and solves problems and motivates others to do the same.	
5.	Sets unrealistic deadlines and milestones.	Sometimes sets unrealistic deadlines and milestones.	Sets realistic deadlines and milestones.	Factors in 'what if' and plans for contingencies.	Consistently sets realistic deadlines and milestones, and always has a 'Plan B'.	

	UNSATISFACTORY	IMPROVEMENT NEEDED	MEETS EXPECTA-TIONS	EXCEEDS EXPECTA-TIONS	EXCEPTIONAL	
anchor	1 - Extremely Weak 2 - Very Weak	3 - Weak 4 - Fair	5 - Satisfactory 6 - Good	7 - Strong 8 - Very Strong	9 - Excellent 10 - Outstanding	Score
6.	Works inefficiently or becomes over-whelmed with workload. Procrastinates.	Neglects work-life balance. Uses over-time as only strat-egy to cope with heavy workload or tight deadlines. Is overly perfec-tionist, indecisive, or impatient with others.	Manages to get all his/her work done in time and to a good quality stan-dard.	Combines good work-life balance with efficient and effective behaviour at work.	Manages own workload as well as the workload of others effectively and efficiently.	
7.	Does not identify main points and gets distracted by side issues.	Leaves the task of establishing priori-ties to others. Does not play an active role in iden-tifying the issues and prioritising accordingly.	Identifies some of the key issues but overlooks others. Identifies issues that are priorities for him/her but not necessarily for their co-workers.	Has a clear picture of the remit of the unit, identifies key issues and pro-poses priorities.	Prioritises tasks appropriately, both for himself/herself and for the unit. Differentiates clearly between matters of primary and secondary importance.	
8.	Does not grasp the general picture.	Makes few if any links between sep-arate items of information.	Has a clear under-standing of his/her mandate but is less successful in grasping the over-all picture and pri-orities.	Sees how different elements fit together.	Focuses on both the general ele-ments and the details of the situa-tion. Has a clear under-standing of the bigger picture. Fits things together and draws conclu-sions.	
9.	Sticks to his/her own views despite consensus.	Puts most of his/her energy into defending own views. Is not inclined to organise and pri-oritise on the basis of points that emerge.	Understands and defends his/her position and links up with new ele-ments. Shows good use of judgement in appraisal of new elements.	Sees how new input affects the state of play and reassesses the situ-ation if necessary.	Builds new ele-ments into the work plan to ensure a well-bal-anced end result.	

	UNSATISFACTORY	IMPROVEMENT NEEDED	MEETS EXPECTATIONS	EXCEEDS EXPECTATIONS	EXCEPTIONAL	
anchor	1 - Extremely Weak 2 - Very Weak	3 - Weak 4 - Fair	5 - Satisfactory 6 - Good	7 - Strong 8 - Very Strong	9 - Excellent 10 - Outstanding	**Score**
10.	Does not collaborate with co-workers and partners. Says 'Yes' to everything. Does everything by himself.	Keeps communication to a minimum and is reticent to share thoughts and ideas.	Maintains an open and honest dialogue with co-workers and partners. Delegates when appropriate.	Encourages others to share ideas and integrates others' thoughts and opinions in own plans and priorities.	Consistently and effectively seeks and incorporates others' ideas to ensure optimal results.	

Total Score

An online version of this questionnaire can be found at:

https://www.johnharperpublishing.co.uk/the-ultimate-eu-career-development-toolkit/

Annex 6.   Self-assessment worksheet for resilience

Please refer to 'How to use the self-assessment worksheets' on page 21.

Anchors

1. Social support.
2. Healthy mind in healthy body.
3. Positive thinking.
4. Communicating and problem solving.
5. Coping with heavy workload and tight deadlines.
6. Adjusting to peaks and troughs in workload.
7. Handling failures and setbacks.
8. Working with management.
9. Facing changes.
10. Self-control.

Indicators

	UNSATISFACTORY	IMPROVEMENT NEEDED	MEETS EXPECTATIONS	EXCEEDS EXPECTATIONS	EXCEPTIONAL	
anchor	1 - Extremely Weak 2 - Very Weak	3 - Weak 4 - Fair	5 - Satisfactory 6 - Good	7 - Strong 8 - Very Strong	9 - Excellent 10 - Outstanding	**Score**
1.	Is socially isolated. Has little or no social contacts with colleagues, friends or family.	Has an operational network, but no personal or strategic network to rely upon. Neglects work-life balance.	Has both an operational and a personal network to rely upon.	Has good operational, personal and strategic networks.	Has very good operational and personal network, combined with an excellent strategic network.	

	UNSATISFACTORY	IMPROVEMENT NEEDED	MEETS EXPECTA-TIONS	EXCEEDS EXPECTA-TIONS	EXCEPTIONAL	
anchor	1 - Extremely Weak 2 - Very Weak	3 - Weak 4 - Fair	5 - Satisfactory 6 - Good	7 - Strong 8 - Very Strong	9 - Excellent 10 - Outstanding	**Score**
2.	Has an unhealthy lifestyle. Uses too much alcohol, caffeine or other drugs. Is a heavy smoker.	Does not do enough physical activity. Is overweight, or has high blood pressure. Has insufficient sleep or rest.	Takes care of physical and mental health. Eats mostly healthy food, sufficient physical activity, gets enough rest and sleep.	Has a good mental and physical condition.	Is mentally and physically in top condition.	
3.	Maintains a negative, pessimistic outlook. Concentrates on negative only.	Has low self-esteem. Lacks trust in colleagues and co-workers.	Is aware of own worth and value, but also of own shortcomings and room for development. Remains in positive mode, despite setbacks.	Maintains an optimistic, positive outlook. Works on self-development.	Always looks on the bright side of life. Continuously works on self-improvement.	
4.	Does not listen to what other people have to say. Is unaware of other people's feelings and emotions.	Is unable to express own feelings and views in a convincing way.	Is assertive, not passive or aggressive.	Listens to, understands, and integrates others' feelings and views in the bigger picture.	Is a 'giver' not a 'taker'.	
5.	Works inefficiently or becomes overwhelmed with workload. Is not capable of adapting to high work pressure. Becomes stressed or panics when under pressure. Displays negative emotions to others inappropriately. Shows complacency.	Uses overtime as only strategy to cope with heavy workload or tight deadlines. Sometimes lacks planning and prioritising skills. Is overly perfectionist, indecisive, or impatient with others.	Generally copes with high levels of work and tight deadlines. Manages to get all his/her work done in time and to a good quality standard. Keeps cool under pressure, works more intensively and longer hours when pressure is on.	Combines good work-life balance with efficient and effective behaviour at work. Has strategies for coping with large volumes of work.	Manages own workload as well as the workload of others effectively and efficiently. Remains calm under pressure. Sees where corners can be cut to meet tight deadlines without sacrificing quality of work.	

	UNSATISFACTORY	IMPROVEMENT NEEDED	MEETS EXPECTATIONS	EXCEEDS EXPECTATIONS	EXCEPTIONAL	
anchor	1 - Extremely Weak 2 - Very Weak	3 - Weak 4 - Fair	5 - Satisfactory 6 - Good	7 - Strong 8 - Very Strong	9 - Excellent 10 - Outstanding	Score
6.	Considers calmer periods as opportunities for complete inactivity, thus wasting time.	Limits himself to catching up on the backlog, deploys no extra activities otherwise.	Takes care of professional and personal development during the calmer periods at work. Expands own operational network.	Anticipates busy periods and prepares for them. Expands own personal and strategic networks.	Makes optimal use of calmer periods to further develop own performance. Prepares mentally and physically for busier periods to come.	
7.	Regards unsuccessful endeavours as personal failures. Loses self-confidence and self-esteem after a failure or setback.	Responds defensively to criticism. Refuses to learn from failures and setbacks. Tends to blame the environment for own failures.	Responds confidently and non-defensively to criticism. Accepts that not everything in life works out fine. Acknowledges own mistakes, and learns from them. Moves on after setbacks and missed opportunities.	Considers failures and setbacks as learning opportunities. Turns setbacks and failures to his/her advantage.	Handles failures and interprets setbacks professionally, not personally. Anticipates failure and has a backup strategy. Has clear strategies for coping with failure.	
8.	Is frustrated by the management, has little tendency to work with it constructively. Intolerant of ambiguity in work content or organisational situation. Externalises frustrations with management.	Does not always alert management to problems. Does not always take steps to establish with management the conditions for smooth working relations. Does not succeed in bringing sceptical superiors to his/her way of thinking.	Tolerates ambiguity in work content or organisational situation. Copes with demands by management and understands their role. Alerts management to problems. Has open and cooperative attitude towards management.	Actively seeks feedback from management and builds on it. Works autonomously but knows when to involve the management. Has gained the confidence of management and is a point of reference.	Understands and works with the management, not against it. Actively manages expectations from management. Endeavours to become involved in decisions related to his/her work.	

anchor	UNSATISFACTORY	IMPROVEMENT NEEDED	MEETS EXPECTATIONS	EXCEEDS EXPECTATIONS	EXCEPTIONAL	
anchor	1 - Extremely Weak 2 - Very Weak	3 - Weak 4 - Fair	5 - Satisfactory 6 - Good	7 - Strong 8 - Very Strong	9 - Excellent 10 - Outstanding	Score
9.	Resists organisational change, and sticks to old habits and traditional ways of working. Reacts negatively to change. Feels threatened by change or reorganisation.	Is suspicious of change and its implications. Has difficulty in adapting to new working environments. Is discouraged by organisational change.	Adapts to new ways of working and broader organisational changes. Sees organisational change as part of life.	Sees change and reorganisation as an opportunity for improvement. Adjusts quickly to unexpected changes.	Embraces change. Proposes more efficient ways of doing things. Sees organisational change as a positive challenge.	
10.	Lacks inner discipline. Shows overindulgence.	Is sometimes caught up by excitement.	Is mindful. Focuses on task and is not distracted by things around. Manages to get rid of bad habits.	Keeps negative emotions under control at all times. Replaces bad habits by good ones.	Is able to control emotions, behaviour and desires in the face of external demands.	

Total Score

An online version of this questionnaire can be found at:

https://www.johnharperpublishing.co.uk/the-ultimate-eu-career-development-toolkit/

Annex 7. Self-assessment worksheet for working with others

Please refer to 'How to use the self-assessment worksheets' on page 21.

Anchors

1. Treats others with respect.
2. Cooperates and collaborates with colleagues.
3. Includes relevant others in decision-making.
4. Working with other cultures.
5. Utilising other backgrounds, skills and motivations.
6. Empathy and sympathy.
7. Assertiveness.
8. Balances individual and team goals.
9. Resolves conflicts among team members.
10. Builds productive working relationships.

Indicators

	UNSATISFACTORY	IMPROVEMENT NEEDED	MEETS EXPECTA-TIONS	EXCEEDS EXPECTA-TIONS	EXCEPTIONAL	
anchor	1 - Extremely Weak 2 - Very Weak	3 - Weak 4 - Fair	5 - Satisfactory 6 - Good	7 - Strong 8 - Very Strong	9 - Excellent 10 - Outstanding	Score
1.	Exhibits behaviour that negatively impacts the morale and accomplishments of the team.	Sometimes displays behaviour inconsistent with workplace courtesy and respect.	Treats others with respect. Encourages and appreciates individual contributions.	Is respectful and welcoming. Reaches out and engages with other people.	Promotes, supports, and influences a culture of respect and courtesy among team members. Inspires collaboration by bridging gaps among diverse individuals and units.	

	UNSATISFACTORY	IMPROVEMENT NEEDED	MEETS EXPECTATIONS	EXCEEDS EXPECTATIONS	EXCEPTIONAL	
anchor	1 - Extremely Weak 2 - Very Weak	3 - Weak 4 - Fair	5 - Satisfactory 6 - Good	7 - Strong 8 - Very Strong	9 - Excellent 10 - Outstanding	Score
2.	Is not a team player. Does not seek consensus and cooperation with others. Often disrupts team process, jeopardizing progress toward common goals. Ignores or belittles the contribution of others.	Has difficulty collaborating with others. Often prefers to work independently. Sees little value in letting everybody have their say.	Works effectively and cooperatively with others. Shares information and knowledge with others. Encourages others to express their views. Takes account of dissenting opinions.	Is highly collaborative. Praises the contributions of others. Seeks new alliances to expand sphere of influence and enhance quality of work.	Demonstrates cooperation and teamwork. Actively involves colleagues in decision-making processes. Creates opportunities for self and others to improve working relationships and work outcomes.	
3.	Makes decisions in isolation without consulting others. Leaves to others the task of liaising with other departments and external stakeholders.	Adopts a silo mentality, does not co-operate across organisational boundaries. Takes little interest in what other parts of the organisation do. Lacks understanding of priorities and key issues for other stakeholders.	Liaises with people outside immediate working environment. Sees when assistance is needed from other departments. Has contacts elsewhere in the organisation to call for support if necessary.	Works co-operatively across organisational boundaries. Is constantly in touch with colleagues from other departments.	Includes relevant others in decision-making. Engages with people outside his/her own team to achieve common objectives.	
4.	Shows lack of cultural sensitivity. Sees cultural differences in terms of national stereotypes. Is prejudiced and biased against people from other cultures; judges them based on personal standards.	Is aware of cultural differences but makes little or no effort to adapt to them. Shows little curiosity for understanding the reasons why people behave as they do.	Is aware of cultural differences and makes an effort to adapt to them. Makes an effort to understand other people in the context of cultural differences	Mixes with people of other nationalities. Understands the importance of non-verbal communication patterns.	Bridges gaps between cultural differences. Is receptive to other cultural approaches. Enjoys working with people from different cultural backgrounds.	

	UNSATISFACTORY	IMPROVEMENT NEEDED	MEETS EXPECTA-TIONS	EXCEEDS EXPECTA-TIONS	EXCEPTIONAL	
anchor	1 - Extremely Weak 2 - Very Weak	3 - Weak 4 - Fair	5 - Satisfactory 6 - Good	7 - Strong 8 - Very Strong	9 - Excellent 10 - Outstanding	**Score**
5.	Fails to consider individual differences in background, skills, or motivations. Sees things in terms of black or white.	Is dismissive of ideas that are not his/her own. Holds strong views and is reluctant to see things from other angles.	Holds strong views but is willing to consider other opinions. Listens to reason. Sees the shades of grey between black and white.	Encourages people to voice their opinions and express their views.	Effectively utilises the diverse range of backgrounds, skills and motivations of others. Actively seeks input from others.	
6.	Shows no concern for the emotional state of others. Does not take steps to deal with underlying tensions at work.	Misreads other people's feelings or states of mind. Steps on other people's toes. Is dismissive of ideas that are not his/her own.	Is sensitive to the feelings of other people. Assists colleagues when asked to do so.	Is diplomatic when drawing attention to errors in other people's work or understanding of a situation.	Shows a genuine concern for the emotional state of others. Speaks up for colleagues in distress.	
7.	Has low self-esteem. Lets himself/herself be dictated to by other people. Is 'invisible' in group discussions. Plays games, is sarcastic, or remains silent.	Bottles up feelings that eventually explode, leaving no room for communication. Is not sufficiently assertive when defending his/her views.	Is clear about what he feels, what he needs and how it can be achieved. Is able to communicate calmly without attacking other people.	Is happy to defend own position, even if it provokes conflict. Is able to say 'no', rather than agreeing to do something just to please someone else.	Understands how to negotiate if two people want different outcomes. Is able to talk openly about self and able to listen to others.	
8.	Is unwilling to work outside comfort zone to support team goals.	Resistant to new challenges. Seems uninterested in building skills and knowledge.	Demonstrates flexibility and willingness to step out of comfort zone to support team and goals.	Is always willing to try something new. Balances individual and team goals.	Consistently goes beyond direct responsibilities to achieve team and department goals. Welcomes new challenges.	

	UNSATISFACTORY	IMPROVEMENT NEEDED	MEETS EXPECTA-TIONS	EXCEEDS EXPECTA-TIONS	EXCEPTIONAL	
anchor	1 - Extremely Weak 2 - Very Weak	3 - Weak 4 - Fair	5 - Satisfactory 6 - Good	7 - Strong 8 - Very Strong	9 - Excellent 10 - Outstanding	**Score**
9.	Often avoids conflict. Is not prepared or willing to resolve conflict.	Is unable to resolve or constructively manage conflicts.	Works effectively with others to resolve conflict.	Manages conflict competently and efficiently. When possible, looks for and proposes middle ground solutions.	Skillfully and proactively addresses conflict. Seeks and achieves 'win-win' resolutions.	
10.	Shows lack of interest in and respect for peers and partners.	Has difficulty building strong, mutually beneficial working relationships.	Builds and maintains effective working relationships with peers and partners.	Successfully builds productive, mutually beneficial relationships to solve problems and achieve common goals.	Leads colleagues to inspired cooperation and teamwork in support of department and organisational goals.	

Total Score [ ]

An online version of this questionnaire can be found at:

https://www.johnharperpublishing.co.uk/the-ultimate-eu-career-development-toolkit/

Annex 8. Self-assessment worksheet for leadership

Please refer to 'How to use the self-assessment worksheets' on page 21.

Anchors

1. Explains ideas clearly, simplifies the complex.
2. Adapts communication to the level of the audience.
3. Communicates clearly and knowledgeably.
4. Shares information with others.
5. Seeks input from others.
6. Understands and supports organisational goals.
7. Helps others perform at their best.
8. Self-aware and open to feedback.
9. Leads by example.
10. Delegates effectively.

Indicators

	UNSATISFACTORY	IMPROVEMENT NEEDED	MEETS EXPECTA-TIONS	EXCEEDS EXPECTA-TIONS	EXCEPTIONAL	
anchor	1 - Extremely Weak 2 - Very Weak	3 - Weak 4 - Fair	5 - Satisfactory 6 - Good	7 - Strong 8 - Very Strong	9 - Excellent 10 - Outstanding	**Score**
1.	Has difficulty in finding the right words to express himself.	Does not always clearly structure his/her ideas; has difficulty in articulating his/her thoughts and vision. Is hesitant and transmits uncertainty with body language or tone of voice.	Speaks and writes clearly, connects with his/her audience and gets messages across with relative ease. Engages spontaneously with his/her audience.	Explains vision and ideas clearly and succinctly. Strikes a good balance between detail and the need for clarity.	Explains even complex issues and ideas clearly and succinctly; simplifies the complex. Convinces sceptics and opponents of his/her points of view.	

	UNSATISFACTORY	IMPROVEMENT NEEDED	MEETS EXPECTA-TIONS	EXCEEDS EXPECTA-TIONS	EXCEPTIONAL	
anchor	1 - Extremely Weak 2 - Very Weak	3 - Weak 4 - Fair	5 - Satisfactory 6 - Good	7 - Strong 8 - Very Strong	9 - Excellent 10 - Outstanding	**Score**
2.	Has difficulty tailoring communication to the needs of others; communicates 'too much,' 'too little,' or 'too late.'	Does not always keep the audience in mind.	Tailors information to audience and individual needs.	Effectively adjusts the level of detail and tone to the audience	Effectively adapts communication to audience; effectively distinguishes between 'need to know' and 'nice to know.'	
3.	Appears distracted or uninterested. Does not listen to what others say.	Interrupts others to express own point of view. Has difficulty getting to the point. Uses facts that are not always accurate or relevant.	Appears knowledgeable and enthusiastic. Actively listens to and synthesises perspectives of others.	Appears credible and reliable. Actively listens to and integrates diverse contributions.	Speaks with conviction and authority. Listens to, synthesises, and integrates others' ideas.	
4.	Does not share information in a timely manner, creating problems for colleagues and customers. Shies away from delivering tough messages.	Tends to 'hold on' to information; has difficulty distinguishing between critical and non-critical information.	Gives others the information they need in a timely manner.	Shares accurate, timely information with the right people in the right format.	Displays openness and transparency in sharing information with others. Is prepared to deliver tough messages when necessary.	
5.	Avoids contact with co-workers and partners.	Keeps communication to a minimum; is reticent to share thoughts and ideas.	Maintains an open and honest dialogue with co-workers and partners.	Encourages others to share ideas and integrates others' thoughts and opinions.	Consistently and effectively seeks and incorporates others' ideas to ensure optimal results.	

	UNSATISFACTORY	IMPROVEMENT NEEDED	MEETS EXPECTA-TIONS	EXCEEDS EXPECTA-TIONS	EXCEPTIONAL	
anchor	1 - Extremely Weak 2 - Very Weak	3 - Weak 4 - Fair	5 - Satisfactory 6 - Good	7 - Strong 8 - Very Strong	9 - Excellent 10 - Outstanding	**Score**
6.	Resists change. Maintains focus on immediate, routine tasks. Work efforts do not align with unit and department goals.	Contributions and work efforts often do not reflect an understanding of unit and department goals.	Effectively aligns work efforts with organisational and department goals.	Understands and supports the need to align work with organisational initiatives and goals.	Encourages and leads changes that enhance organisational and workforce effectiveness.	
7.	Hinders sharing of knowledge and/or expertise, focused largely on own development. Fails to spot or nurture future talent. Fails to create development opportunities for others.	Does not openly share expertise or information with others. Spots future talent but fails to nurture it.	Assists others in developing skills and knowledge. Helps people to resolve problems and overcome obstacles.	Consistently and actively assists others in expanding and developing skills and knowledge. Coaches and/or mentors others. Creates targeted development opportunities for others.	Inspires and helps others develop skills and competencies to perform at their best. Spots and nurtures potential future talent.	
8.	Is not motivated to learn and grow, believes that others are responsible for his/her development.	Often resists feedback on performance. Rarely asks for help or feedback.	Is self-aware and open to feedback from others. Displays integrity.	Very self-aware; asks others for feedback in an effort to improve skills and knowledge.	Demonstrates a high degree of self-awareness; asks others for feedback on performance; is a continuous learner. Is authentic in everything he/she does or says.	

	UNSATISFACTORY	IMPROVEMENT NEEDED	MEETS EXPECTATIONS	EXCEEDS EXPECTATIONS	EXCEPTIONAL	
anchor	1 - Extremely Weak 2 - Very Weak	3 - Weak 4 - Fair	5 - Satisfactory 6 - Good	7 - Strong 8 - Very Strong	9 - Excellent 10 - Outstanding	**Score**
9.	Demotivates others. Betrays lack of conviction in chances of success.	Keeps too low a profile to make a leadership impact. Does not react when developments require assertive action. Is inconsistent in supporting staff to achieve defined goals.	Is enthusiastic about his/her work and transmits enthusiasm to others. Encourages and supports employees to achieve performance and development goals.	Sets a good example in terms of enthusiasm and commitment. Encourages and engages staff to make optimal use of skills and knowledge. Makes himself visible and accessible to colleagues.	Leads and motivates by example. Inspires staff to perform at their best. Shows drive and determination to succeed.	
10.	Does not delegate; does most of the work by himself/herself. Assigns work inappropriately. Does not keep development and performance goals in mind. Has unrealistic expectations and perception of staff skills and knowledge.	Doesn't effectively match work assignments to staff talent and proficiencies. Does little to monitor team progress or provide follow-up.	Plans ahead and organises work. Thoughtfully delegates work to develop staff and achieve goals. Monitors team progress and provides follow-up.	Effectively links work assignments to achieve individual and unit performance goals.	Effectively delegates work to develop skills and knowledge. Ensures optimal outcomes, aligns work with individual, unit, and organisational goals.	

Total Score

An online version of this questionnaire can be found at:

https://www.johnharperpublishing.co.uk/the-ultimate-eu-career-development-toolkit/

Annex 9. Your competency passport

Plot your total scores for the general competencies in Annexes 1 to 8 on this spider's web (there is an example in Figure 1.3 on page 7). Then go to Annex 10.

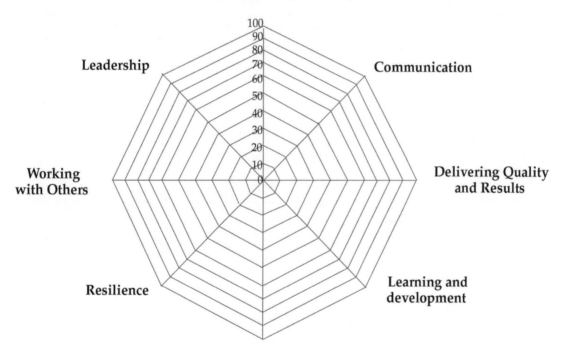

Annex 10. Your development plan

Your highest priority competencies are the three with the lowest scores on the spider's web in Annex 9.

Competency	Goal	Reality	Options	Will
Only the 3 with the highest priority for the moment	Set SMART, operational goals	List of anchors and scores in ascending order	Possible solutions	Choose one solution and set yourself a realistic deadline

Annex 11. Glossary

360-degree feedback

The term 360-degree feedback refers to an appraisal and feedback system in which an employee (typically someone in a managerial or supervisory position) is evaluated by one or more supervisors, peers, and subordinates.

70-20-10 model

The 70-20-10 model is a learning and development model, usually credited to Morgan McCall and his colleagues, Lombardo and Eichinger, working at the Centre for Creative Leadership (CCL).

80/20 principle

This principle can be applied to prioritising your tasks, based on the idea that most of the results (output) will be generated by a small amount of your effort (input).

ABC method

The ABC method is a powerful priority setting technique. Behind every item you put a letter A, B or C depending on the following criteria: A - Very important. This is something that you must do. This is a task for which there can be serious consequences if you fail to do it; B - A task that you should do, but only has mild consequences if you don't. This means that someone may be unhappy or inconvenienced if you don't do it, but that's about it; C – A task that would be nice to do, but for which there are no consequences at all.

Accountability

What are you going to do? By when will you do this? How will I know? It does NOT include blame or judgement!

Active listening

A technique used in counselling, training and conflict resolution, which requires the listener to feed back what they hear to the speaker, by way of re-stating or paraphrasing what they have heard in their own words, to confirm what they have heard and moreover, to confirm the understanding of both parties. (Wikipedia)

Analysing and problem solving

General competency: Identify the critical facts in complex issues and develop creative and practical solutions.

Anchor

See behavioural anchors.

Appraisal

See performance appraisal.

Assertiveness

Assertiveness is an attitude and a way of relating to the outside world, backed up by a set of abilities.

Assessment

A way to understand a person's goals and where they are at physically, mentally and spiritually. Assessments may measure strengths and skills, or may identify areas for improvement.

Authentic leadership

Authentic leadership is an approach to leadership that emphasises building the leader's legitimacy through honest relationships with followers that value their input and are built on an ethical foundation. (Wikipedia)

Behavioural anchors

Behavioural anchors are specific, easy-to-apply examples of behaviours that demonstrate a given competency. In practical application, behavioural anchors can be used to define the level someone has reached on a particular competency, for example from level 1 to 10.

Body language

Body language is non-verbal communication, where thoughts, intentions, or feelings are expressed by physical behaviours, such as facial expressions, body posture, gestures, eye movement, touch and the use of space. (Wikipedia)

Boreout

Boreout consists of three elements: boredom, lack of challenge, and lack of interest.

Brainstorming

Brainstorming is a group creativity technique by which efforts are made to find a solution for a specific problem by gathering a list of ideas spontaneously contributed by its members.

Burnout

Burnout is a state of physical, emotional or mental exhaustion combined with doubts about your competence and the value of your work.

Career development

The management of careers by individuals and organisations (e.g. through skills development, job moves and promotions).

Career guidance

Career guidance aims to help staff manage their careers (e.g. by providing advice on how to make best use of their skills, and develop new skills, in line with their aspirations).

Certification

In the EU administration a procedure allowing officials from the Assistant (AST) function group to become members of the Administrator (AD) function group following successful completion of training and examinations.

CLEAR

Challenging, Legal, Environmentally sound, Agreed, Recorded.

Coach

A person who offers support, advice, skills and 'tough love'. A coach plays a vital role in the spiritual, mental and physical development of the coachee.

Coaching

Coaching is unlocking a person's potential to maximise their performance. Coaching is helping people to learn rather than teaching them. Coaches need not have first-hand experience of the coachee's line of work. Coaching is focusing on the 'vertical' development of the coachee.

Comfort zone

Your comfort zone is any type of behaviour that keeps you at a low anxiety level.

Communicating

General competency: Communicate clearly and precisely both orally and in writing.

Competency

A competency is a set of defined behaviours that provide a structured guide enabling the identification, evaluation and development of the behaviours in individual employees.

Competency framework

The competency framework used by the European Personnel Selection Office is the result of a comprehensive job analysis undertaken in 2009 for all entry grades of EU officials across the institutions.

Competency passport

A competency passport gives an overview of a person's general competencies, usually in a graphical format.

Continuous improvement

Continuous (also called continual) improvement is a permanent commitment and effort by a business or organisation to improve its products, services, or processes.

Core competencies

Core competencies are general competencies common to all European institutions and therefore suitable for use in open competitions and appraisal procedures.

Creative thinking

Creative thinking involves a relaxed, open, and playful approach. 'Thinking outside the box' is a metaphor that means to think differently, unconventionally, or from a new perspective; it refers to creative thinking.

Critical thinking

Critical thinking is the process we use to reflect on, assess, and judge the assumptions underlying our own and others' ideas and efforts.

Delegation

Delegation is giving others the authority to act on your behalf, accompanied with a degree of accountability for results.

Deliberate practice

Deliberate practice involves awareness, attention, rehearsal and repetition, and leads to new knowledge or skills that can later be developed into more complex knowledge and skills.

Delivering quality and results

General competency: Take personal responsibility and initiative for delivering work to a high standard of quality within set procedures.

Eisenhower matrix

A way of dividing and prioritising tasks into one of four categories: important and urgent, important but not urgent, not important but urgent, and neither important nor urgent.

Emotional intelligence

The ability to identify, use, understand, and manage emotions in positive ways to relieve stress, communicate effectively, empathise with others, overcome challenges, and defuse conflict.

ENFJ

One of the 16 Myers-Briggs Personality Type Indicators (MBTI). Warm, empathetic, responsive, and responsible. Highly attuned to the emotions, needs, and motivations of others. Find potential in everyone, want to help others fulfil their potential. May act as catalysts for individual and group growth. Loyal, responsive to praise and criticism. Sociable, facilitate others in a group, and provide inspiring leadership. ('Introduction to Type' by Isabel Briggs Myers published by CPP. Inc.)

ENFP

One of the 16 Myers-Briggs Personality Type Indicators (MBTI). Warmly enthusiastic and imaginative. See life as full of possibilities. Make connections between events and information very quickly, and confidently proceed based on the patterns they see. Want a lot of affirmation from others, and readily give appreciation and support. Spontaneous and flexible, often rely on their ability to improvise and their verbal fluency. ('Introduction to Type' by Isabel Briggs Myers published by CPP. Inc.)

ENTJ

One of the 16 Myers-Briggs Personality Type Indicators (MBTI). Frank, decisive, assume leadership readily. Quickly see illogical and inefficient procedures and policies, develop and implement comprehensive systems to solve organizational problems. Enjoy long-term planning and goal setting. Usually well informed, well read, enjoy expanding their knowledge and passing it on to others. Forceful in presenting their ideas. ('Introduction to Type' by Isabel Briggs Myers published by CPP. Inc.)

ENTP

One of the 16 Myers-Briggs Personality Type Indicators (MBTI). Quick, ingenious, stimulating, alert, and outspoken. Resourceful in solving new and challenging problems. Adept at generating conceptual possibilities and then analysing them strategically. Good at reading other people. Bored by routine, will seldom do the same thing the same way, apt to turn to one new interest after another. ('Introduction to Type' by Isabel Briggs Myers published by CPP. Inc.)

EPSO

European Personnel Selection Office: EPSO organises and conducts selection procedures on behalf of the European Union institutions. The decisions to recruit successful candidates are taken by each institution.

ESFJ

One of the 16 Myers-Briggs Personality Type Indicators (MBTI). Warm-hearted, conscientious, and cooperative. Want harmony in their environment, work with determination to establish it. Like to work with others to complete tasks accurately and on time. Loyal, follow through even in small matters. Notice what others need in their day-by-day lives and try to provide it. Want to be appreciated for who they are and for what they contribute. ('Introduction to Type' by Isabel Briggs Myers published by CPP. Inc.)

ESFP

One of the 16 Myers-Briggs Personality Type Indicators (MBTI). Outgoing, friendly, and accepting. Exuberant lovers of life, people, and material comforts. Enjoy working with others to make things happen. Bring common sense and a realistic approach to their work, and make work fun. Flexible and spontaneous, adapt readily to new people and environments. Learn best by trying a new skill with other people. ('Introduction to Type' by Isabel Briggs Myers published by CPP. Inc.)

ESTJ

One of the 16 Myers-Briggs Personality Type Indicators (MBTI). Practical, realistic, matter-of-fact. Decisive, quickly move to implement decisions. Organise projects and people to get things done, focus on getting results in the most efficient way possible. Take care of routine details. Have a clear set of logical standards, systematically follow them and want others to also. Forceful in implementing their plans. ('Introduction to Type' by Isabel Briggs Myers published by CPP. Inc.)

ESTP

One of the 16 Myers-Briggs Personality Type Indicators (MBTI). Flexible and tolerant, they take a pragmatic approach focused on immediate results. Theories and conceptual explanations bore them – they want to act energetically to solve the problem. Focus on the here-and-now, spontaneous, enjoy each moment that they can be active with others. Enjoy material comforts and style. Learn best through doing. ('Introduction to Type' by Isabel Briggs Myers published by CPP. Inc.)

Ethics and Integrity

In the European Commission, Ethics and Integrity is now a compulsory one-day course, classified under the heading 'internal procedures' and not under any of the general competencies. The focus is on six key principles: independence, impartiality, objectivity, loyalty, responsibility and circumspection.

Expectancy theory

Vroom's expectancy theory suggests that behaviour results from conscious choices among alternatives whose purpose is to maximise pleasure and minimise pain.

Fight-or-flight

The fight-or-flight response, also called the acute stress response, is a physiological reaction that occurs in response to a perceived harmful event, attack, or threat to survival.

Fishbone diagram

A fishbone, or Ishikawa, diagram identifies the possible causes for an effect or problem.

Flow

Flow is a state of complete immersion in an activity, being completely involved in an activity for its own sake.

Formal learning

Intentional learning organised in terms of objectives within a structured setting. Examples are enrolling in a programme of study, attending lectures, preparing coursework, engaging in seminar/tutorial discussions.

See also informal learning.

Four stages of competence

Individuals are initially unaware of how little they know, or unconscious of their incompetence. As they recognise their incompetence, they consciously acquire a skill, and then consciously use it. Eventually, the skill can be operated without it being consciously thought through: the individual is said to have acquired unconscious competence.

Gantt chart

Gantt charts plot the activities necessary to complete a project on a timeline using a bar or a line, which begins and ends at a definite time. The Gantt chart also provides milestones, or markers, for assuring that a project is on track.

General adaptation syndrome (GAS)

A term used to describe the body's short-term and long-term reactions to stress; it was originally described by Hans Selye.

General competencies

General competencies are competencies – or behaviour – that are expected from all employees regardless of their position or function in the organisation.

Generational thinking

Labelling people according to their birth years. According to this, Baby Boomers, born between 1946 and 1964, are competitive and loyal to their employer. Gen Xers, born between 1965 and 1977, are more likely to be sceptical and independent-minded. Gen Ys, also known as Millennials, were born in 1978 or later, and like teamwork, feedback and technology. Finally, there is Gen Z. Born after 1995, they grew up in a highly sophisticated media and computer environment and will be more internet savvy and expert than their Gen Y ancestors. This theory is highly controversial and at best a generalisation.

Goal setting

Goals keep you focused and on track towards what you aim to become. Goals are not the same as action; they are the desired result of action.

Groupthink

The term groupthink was first described in 1972 by social psychologist Irving Janis. It is a phenomenon that occurs when a group makes incorrect decisions because group pressures lead to a deterioration of 'mental efficiency, reality testing, and moral judgement'.

GROW

The GROW model is a simple but powerful method for goal setting and problem solving. It was developed in the United Kingdom, mainly by Sir John Whitmore and is used extensively in corporate coaching. The acronym stands for: Goals – Reality – Options (or Obstacles) – and Will (or Way Forward).

GRPI

Goals, Roles, Processes and Interpersonal Relationships are four critical and interrelated aspects of teamwork. The GRPI is a four-step project-planning tool to help team leaders ensure productivity, efficiency and quality.

Hard skills

Hard skills are teachable abilities or skills that are easy to quantify. Examples of hard skills include: proficiency in a foreign language, a degree or certificate, typing speed, machine operation, computer programming, etc.
See also soft skills.

Herzberg's hygiene and motivational factors

According to Herzberg, 'hygiene factors' must be present (without them there is dissatisfaction) before motivators stimulate an employee. He used the term job enrichment to describe the process of redesigning work to build motivators.

IDEAL

Identify the problem; Define the problem; Examine the options; Act on a plan; Look at the consequences.

Indicators

Indicators – or behaviours – can be associated with multiple behavioural anchors. A behavioural anchor is something that is used to define the level someone has reached on a particular competency, say from 1 to 10. In this sense it is very similar to an indicator, but indicators tend to be simple 'positive' and 'negative' poles, whereas the anchors define all points in between.

INFJ

One of the 16 Myers-Briggs Personality Type Indicators (MBTI). Seek meaning and connection in ideas, relationships, and material possessions. Want to understand what motivates people and are insightful about others. Conscientious and committed to their firm values. Develop a clear vision about how best to serve the common good. Organised and decisive in implementing their vision. ('Introduction to Type' by Isabel Briggs Myers published by CPP. Inc.)

Informal learning

Informal learning is learning that originates from activities external to a structured learning context, or unstructured learning within a structured learning environment (e.g. coaching, on-the-job learning, sharing experiences with colleagues).
See also formal learning.

Information overload

Information overload (also known as 'infobesity' or 'infoxication') refers to the difficulty a person can have understanding an issue and making decisions that can be caused by the presence of too much information.

INFP

One of the 16 Myers-Briggs Personality Type Indicators (MBTI). Idealistic, loyal to their values and to people who are important to them. Want an external life that is congruent with their values. Curious, quick to see possibilities, can be catalysts for implementing ideas. Seek to understand people and to help them fulfil their potential. Adaptable, flexible, and accepting unless a value is threatened. ('Introduction to Type' by Isabel Briggs Myers published by CPP. Inc.)

Interpersonal skills

See soft skills.

INTJ

One of the 16 Myers-Briggs Personality Type Indicators (MBTI). Have original minds and great drive for implementing their ideas and achieving their goals. Quickly see patterns in external events and develop long-range explanatory perspectives. When committed, organise a job and carry it through. Sceptical and independent, have high standards of competence and performance, for themselves and others. ('Introduction to Type' by Isabel Briggs Myers published by CPP. Inc.)

INTP

One of the 16 Myers-Briggs Personality Type Indicators (MBTI). Seek to develop logical explanations for everything that interests them. Theoretical and abstract, interested more in ideas than in social interaction. Quiet, contained, flexible, and adaptable. Have unusual ability to focus in depth to solve problems in their area of interest. Sceptical, sometimes critical, always analytical. ('Introduction to Type' by Isabel Briggs Myers published by CPP. Inc.)

IQ

Intelligence Quotient. The definition of Intelligence is somewhat controversial amongst psychologists, but by far the most widely used in practical settings is the psychometric approach, trying to capture the complex concept into a single score known as the Intelligence Quotient, or IQ.

ISFJ

One of the 16 Myers-Briggs Personality Type Indicators (MBTI). Quiet, friendly, responsible, and conscientious. Committed and steady in meeting their obligations. Thorough, painstaking, and accurate. Loyal, considerate; notice and remember specifics about people who are important to them, concerned with how others feel. Strive to create an orderly and harmonious environment at work and at home. ('Introduction to Type' by Isabel Briggs Myers published by CPP. Inc.)

ISFP

One of the 16 Myers-Briggs Personality Type Indicators (MBTI). Quiet, friendly, sensitive, and kind. Enjoy the present moment, what's going on around them. Like to have their own space and to work within their own time frame. Loyal and committed to their values and to people who are important to them. Dislike disagreements and conflicts, do not force their opinions or values on others. ('Introduction to Type' by Isabel Briggs Myers published by CPP. Inc.)

ISTJ

One of the 16 Myers-Briggs Personality Type Indicators (MBTI). Quiet, serious, earn success by thoroughness and dependability. Practical, matter-of-fact, realistic, and responsible. Decide logically what should be done and work towards it steadily, regardless of distractions. Take pleasure in making everything orderly and organized – their work, their home, their life. Value traditions and loyalty. ('Introduction to Type' by Isabel Briggs Myers published by CPP. Inc.)

ISTP

One of the 16 Myers-Briggs Personality Type Indicators (MBTI). Tolerant and flexible, quiet observers until a problem appears, then act quickly to find workable solutions. Analyse what makes things work and readily get through large amounts of data to isolate the core of practical problems. Interested in cause and effect, organise facts using logical principles, value efficiency. ('Introduction to Type' by Isabel Briggs Myers published by CPP. Inc.)

Johari Window

The Johari Window was invented by Joseph Luft and Harrington Ingham in the 1950s as a model for mapping personality awareness.

Kaizen

Kaizen is a Japanese word used in English to mean 'continuous improvement'.

KISS

KISS is an acronym for 'Keep it simple, stupid', a design principle adopted by the US Navy in the early 1960s.

Lateral thinking

Lateral thinking deliberately distances itself from standard perceptions of creativity as either 'vertical' logic (the classic method for problem solving: working out the solution step-by-step from the given data) or 'horizontal' imagination (having many ideas but being unconcerned with the detailed implementation of them). The term was coined by Dr Edward de Bono.

Leadership

General competency: Manage, develop and motivate people to achieve results.

Learning and development

General competency: Develop and improve personal skills and knowledge of the organisation and its environment. The process of acquiring or improving knowledge and skills.

Lifelong learning

The process of constantly striving to learn and understand new information and practices. Offers a way for individuals to grow continuously and stay in touch with their selves and their world.

Maslow's hierarchy of needs

Ethics, ideas and behaviour differ from country to country and from culture to culture, but all humans have similar needs. Abraham Maslow used the terms 'physiological', 'safety', 'belongingness' and 'love', 'esteem', 'self-actualisation', and 'self-transcendence' to describe the pattern that human motivations generally move through. Maslow's theory suggests that the most basic level of needs must be met before the individual will strongly desire the secondary or higher level needs.

MBTI

Myer-Briggs Type Indicator: MBTI is based on the idea that each personality type is composed of four pairs of preferences – or dichotomies – thus resulting in 16 different personality types.

Mentoring

Mentoring is a pairing of a more skilled or experienced person, usually in the same field of knowledge, with a less experienced person. Ideally mentors have no line management relationship to the mentee. Mentors will often provide direction and advice and should open organisational doors for mentees. Mentors can provide a neutral sounding board, assure total confidentiality, and have no agenda other than assisting their mentees in their development and to reach their goals. Mentoring involves helping people to develop their career, skills and expertise, often drawing upon the experiences of the mentor. Mentoring focuses on the 'horizontal' development (learning) of the mentee.

Mind mapping

A mind map is a powerful graphic method that provides a universal key to unlock the potential of your brain.

Motivation

Motivation is what drives us to achieve our goals. Daniel Pink defines Motivation 1.0, 2.0, and 3.0 as steps in the development over time of human motivational 'operating systems', sets of assumptions and protocols about how the world works and how humans behave, that run beneath our laws, economic arrangements, and business practices.

Multitasking

Multitasking is doing multiple things – performing multiple tasks – 'at the same time'.

Networking

Networking is about making connections and building enduring, mutually beneficial relationships.

Nice guy syndrome

The 'nice guy syndrome' refers to a behavioural pattern of being overly nice to others.

People skills

See soft skills.

Performance appraisal

A performance appraisal is a systematic and periodic process that assesses an employee's job performance and productivity in relation to pre-established criteria and organisational objectives, as well as the identification of potential for future improvement.

Performance development

Performance development is a broad term that includes performance management and employee development. It describes both assessing and managing the work that needs to be done and providing opportunities for professional growth and development.

Personality

There are many theories on personality, and most are in some way based on or related to the work of Carl Jung. There are both type and trait theories: trait personality questionnaires are useful in selection and recruitment as they can be more readily mapped to job requirements, whilst the type models are useful in personal and team development, as the type categories are helpful in understanding oneself and others.

PERT/CPM

PERT/CPM graphs provide a general overview of a project. They consist of activities and events. Activities are operations in the project that consume resources and take time. Events occur at a point in time and represent the beginning, the end (or both) of an activity.

Pervasive learning

Learning at the 'speed of need' through formal, informal and social learning modalities. (Dan Pontrefact)

Prioritising and organising

General competency: Prioritise the most important tasks, work flexibly and organise own workload efficiently.

Problem analysis

Gaining more information about a problem and increasing understanding. This phase is all about fact finding and analysis, building a more comprehensive picture of both the goal(s) and the barrier(s).

Problem identification

Problem identification involves detecting and recognising that there is a problem, identifying the nature of the problem or, in other words, defining the problem. Identifying a very clearly defined and specific problem is the first critical step to successful problem solving.

Process

A specific ordering of work activities across time and place, with a beginning and an end, clearly defined inputs and outputs, a structure for action. (Thomas Davenport)

Procrastination

Procrastination is carrying out less urgent tasks in preference to more urgent ones, or doing more pleasurable things in place of less pleasurable ones, and thus putting off tasks to a later time, sometimes to the 'last minute' before the deadline.

Productivity

Productivity is an average measure of efficiency. It can be expressed as the ratio of output to inputs used, i.e. output per unit of input.

Professional competencies

Professional competencies are skills, knowledge and attributes that are valued by the other professionals that are connected to your profession; professional competencies may also be referred to as 'technical competencies'.

PMBOK

'A Guide to the Project Management Body of Knowledge' (PMBOK Guide) is a book that presents a set of standard terminology and guidelines (a body of knowledge) for project management.

PRINCE2

Acronym for 'PRojects IN Controlled Environments, version 2'. It is a project management methodology.

PURE

Positive, Understood, Relevant, Ethical.

QA

Quality Assurance.

Resilience

General competency: Remain effective under a heavy workload, handle organisational frustrations positively and adapt to a changing work environment.

Root cause analysis

A root cause analysis is a systematic way of uncovering the 'roots' – or underlying causes – of an identified problem, or the symptom of a problem.

Six Thinking Hats

'Six Thinking Hats' is a self-help book by Edward de Bono that describes a tool for group discussion and individual thinking involving six coloured hats. Six Thinking Hats and the associated idea of parallel thinking – a process where focus is split in specific directions – provide a means for groups to plan thinking processes in a detailed and cohesive way, and in doing so to think together more effectively.

Skills

Ability to carry out tasks proficiently.

SMART

SMART is a goal-setting tool. The acronym stands for Specific – Measurable – Attainable (or Achievable) – Relevant (or alternatively, Realistic) – and Time-framed.

Soft skills

Also known as 'people skills' or 'interpersonal skills,' soft skills relate to the way you relate to and interact with other people: to the way you behave.

Solution focused coaching (SFC)

A coaching model; an alternative to the GROW model.

STAR

STAR is the acronym for Situation, Task, Actions, Results. It is a very efficient way of telling a story, particularly useful in behavioural interviews.

STOP

STOP is an acronym for Stop – Think – Organise – and Proceed.

Strategic thinking

Strategic thinking is a mental process that is applied by an individual in the context of achieving success in a game or other endeavour.

Team

A team is a small group of people who regularly meet, in person or online, to discuss shared agendas, causes, or interests. Each team is unique and draws on the backgrounds and abilities of its members. Depending on the situation, teams can have a different name: task force, work group, study group, commission, committee, or such like.

Technical competencies

See professional competencies.

Theory X and theory Y

Douglas McGregor developed a view of humanity with his theory X and theory Y. These are two opposing perceptions about human behaviour at work.

Timeboxing

Timeboxing is a time management technique whereby the schedule is divided into a number of separate time periods – or timeboxes. Each timebox has its own deliverables, deadline and budget. It is also used for individual use to address personal tasks in a shorter time frame in order to improve the productivity of the user.

Time management

Taking conscious control (awareness and responsibility) over the amount of time you spend on specific activities.

TQM

Total quality management (TQM) consists of organisation-wide efforts to install and make permanent a climate in which an organisation continuously improves its ability to deliver high-quality products and services to customers. (Wikipedia)

Type I behaviour

Type I behaviour is a way of thinking and an approach to life built around intrinsic, rather than extrinsic, motivators. It is powered by our innate need to direct our own lives, to learn and create new things, and to do better by ourselves and our world. (Daniel Pink)

Type X behaviour

Type X behaviour is fuelled more by extrinsic desires than intrinsic ones and concerns itself less with the inherent satisfaction of an activity and more with the external rewards to which the activity leads. (Daniel Pink)

Working with others

General competency: Work co-operatively with others in teams and across organisational boundaries and respect differences between people.

Work-life balance

The equilibrium between how much time a person spends in their job and how much time they spend at home, with family and friends. A good equilibrium supports long-term health and happiness.

Annex 12. Bibliography

'Applied Imagination: Principles and Procedures Creative Problem Solving' (1953) by Alex F. Osborn (ISBN: 9780930222734)

'A Sense of Urgency' (2008) by John P. Kotter (ISBN: 9781423369356)

'A theory of goal setting and task performance' (1990) by Edwin Locke et al. (ISBN 9780139131387)

'Authentic Leadership – Rediscovering the Secrets of Creating Lasting Value' (2003) by Bill George (ISBN: 9780787969134)

'A Whole New Mind: Why Right-Brainers will rule the Future' (2006) by Daniel Pink (ISBN: 9781594481710)

'Boreout – Overcoming workplace demotivation' (2008) by Peter Werder and Philippe Rothlin (ISBN: 9780749453398)

'Brief: Make a Bigger Impact by Saying Less' (2014) by Joseph McCormack (ISBN: 9781118704967)

'Ces gestes qui vous trahissent' (2011) by Joseph Messinger (ISBN: 9782290035016)

'Coaching for Performance – GROWing human potential and Purpose' (2009) by Sir John Whitmore (ISBN: 9781857885354)

'Cultures and Organisations – Software of the Mind' (2010) by Geert Hofstede, Gert Jan Hofstede and Michael Minkov (ISBN: 9780071664189)

'Der Europäische Landbote: die Wut der Bürger und der Friede Europas' by Robert Menasse (ISBN: 9783552056169)

'Drive: The Surprising Truth about What Motivates Us' (2011) by Daniel H. Pink (ISBN: 9781594484803)

'Effective Business Communications' (1997) by Herta A. Murphy et al. (ISBN: 9780070443983)

'Emotional Intelligence: Why It Can Matter More Than IQ' (1995) by Daniel Goleman (ISBN: 9780553383713)

'Find Your Focus Zone' (2011) by Lucy Jo Palladino (ISBN: 9781416532019)

'Finding Flow' (1998) by Mihaly Csíkszentmihályi (ISBN 9780465024117)

'First Things First' (1996) by Stephen Covey (ISBN 9780684802039)

'Flat Army: Creating a Connected and Engaged Organisation' (2016) by Dan Pontrefact (ISBN: 9781943425419)

'Fried – Why you Burn Out and how to Revive' (2012) by Joan Borysenko (ISBN: 9781401925512)

'Gamestorming: A Playbook for Innovators, Rulebreakers, and Changemakers' (2010) by Dave Gray, Sunny Brown and James Macanufo (ISBN: 9780596804176)

'Give and Take – Why Helping others Drives our Success' (2014) by Adam Grant (ISBN: 9780143124986)

'Growing Pains' (2007) by Flamholtz and Randle (ISBN 9780787986162)

'HBR Guide to Persuasive Presentations' (2012) by Nancy Duarte (ISBN: 9781422187104)

'Hot, Flat, and Crowded' (2009) by Thomas L. Friedman (ISBN: 9780141036663)

'How the EU Institutions Work and How to Work with the EU Institutions' by Alan Hardacre and Erik Akse (ISBN: 9780992974886)

'How to be a Productivity Ninja' (2015) by Graham Allcott (ISBN: 9781848316836)

'How to win Friends and Influence People' (1998) by Dale Carnegie (ISBN: 9780671027032)

'Kaizen: The Key to Japan's Competitive Success' (1986) by Masaaki Imai (ISBN: 9780075543329)

'Leaders eat last: Why some teams pull together and others don't' (2014) by Simon Sinek (ISBN: 9781591845324)

'Leadership Development: Maturity and Power.' (1994) by Barr, L., & Barr, N. (ISBN: 9780890159453)

'Leadership in a Diverse and Multicultural Environment' (2005) by Mary Connerly and Paul Pedersen (ISBN: 9780761988601)

'Management of Organizational Behaviour' (2012) by Kenneth Hersey et al. (ISBN 9780132556408)

'Metaphors we live by' (1980) by George Lakoff and Mark Johnson (ISBN: 9780226468013)

'No More Mr Nice Guy' (2003) by Robert Glover (ISBN: 9780762415335)

'Our Iceberg is Melting' (2006) by John Kotter (ISBN: 9780230014206)

'Parkinson's Law: or the Pursuit of Progress' (2002) by C. Northcote Parkinson (ISBN: 9780141186856)

'Prendre la parole en public' (2009) by Bernard Blein (ISBN: 9782035843562)

'Primal Leadership' (2013) by Daniel Goleman et al. (ISBN 9781422168035)

'Quiet: The Power of Introverts in a World that can't stop Talking' (2013) by Susan Cain (ISBN: 9780141029191)

'Real Leaders Don't Do Powerpoint – How to Speak so People Listen' (2009) by Christopher Witt (ISBN: 9780749942601)

'Six Thinking Hats' (1999) by Edward de Bono (ISBN: 9780316178310)

'Solution Focused Coaching in Practice: Essential Coaching Skills and Knowledge' (2012) by O'Connell, B., Palmer, S., & Williams, H. (ISBN: 9780415447072)

'Start with Why – How Great Leaders Inspire Everyone to take Action' (2009) by Simon Sinek (ISBN: 781591846444)

'Targeting Success' (2011) by Lorii Myers (ISBN 9780986790003)

'The Art of Conversation' (1936) by Milton Wright (ASIN: B000H1DGTE)

'The Art of Conversation – A guided Tour of a Neglected Pleasure' (2009) by Catherine Blyth (ISBN: 9781592404971)

'The Attention Economy: Understanding the New Currency of Business' (2002) by Thomas H. Davenport and John C. Beck (ISBN: 9781578518715)

'The Career Architect Development Planner' (2000) by Michael Lombardo and Robert Eichinger (ISBN: 9780965571241)

'The European Commission – A Practical Guide' by Manuel Szapiro (ISBN: 9780957150133)

'The European Parliament' by Richard Corbett et al. (ISBN: 9780965450852)

'The Gen Z Effect – The Six Forces Shaping the Future of Business' (2014) By Tom Koulopoulos and Dan Keldsen (ISBN: 9781629560311)

'The Gifts of Imperfection' (2010) by Brené Brown (ISBN: 9781592858491)

'The Human Condition' (1998) by Hannah Arendt (ISBN: 9780226025988)

'The Human Side of Enterprise' (1960) by Douglas McGregor (ISBN: 9780070450929)

'The Inner Game of Work: Overcoming Mental Obstacles for Maximum Performance' (2000) by Timothy Gallwey (ISBN: 9781842030158)

'The Managerial Grid III: The Key to Leadership Excellence' (1985) by Blake, R., Mouton, J. (ISBN: 9780872014701)

'The Passage to Europe' (2013) by Luuk van Middelaar (ISBN: 9780300195408)

'The Peter Principle: Why Things Always go Wrong' (2011) by Laurence J. Peter and Raymond Hull (ISBN: 9780062092069)

'The Shallows: What the Internet is doing to our Brains' (2011) by Nicholas Carr (ISBN: 9780393339758)

'The Thinker's Guide to the Art of Socratic Questioning' (2007) by Richard Paul and Linda Elder (ISBN: 9780944583319)

'The Truth About Burnout – How Organisations Cause Personal Stress and What to Do About it' (2000) by Christina Maslach and Michael P. Leiter (ISBN: 9781118692134)

'The Ultimate EU Test Book: Assessment Centre Edition' (2015) by András Baneth and Jan De Sutter (ISBN: 9780992974879)

'The Upside of Stress – Why Stress is good for You, and how to get Good at It' (2015) by Kelly McGonigal (ISBN: 9781583335611)

'The Use of Lateral Thinking' (1967) by Edward de Bono (ISBN: 9780140137880)

'The World is Flat' (2011) by Thomas L. Friedman (ISBN: 9783125737990)

'Thinkertoys – A Handbook of Creative Thinking Techniques' (2006) by Michael Michalko (ISBN: 9781580087735)

'Thinking, fast and slow' (2012) by Daniel Kahneman (ISBN: 9780141033570)

'Thinking for a Living' (2005) by Thomas H. Davenport (ISBN: 9781591394235)

'Too Many Bosses, Too Few Leaders' (2012) by Rajeev Peshawaria (ISBN: 9781451646672)

'Victims of Groupthink: A psychological Study of foreign-policy decisions and fiascoes' (1972) by Irving Janis (ISBN: 9780395140444)

'Visual meetings: How Graphics, Sticky Notes & idea mapping can transform group productivity' (2010) by David Sibbet (ISBN: 9780470601785)

'Who moved my Cheese?' (1999) by Spencer Johnson (ISBN: 9780091816971)

'Wikinomics: How Mass Collaboration Changes Everything' (2010) by Don Tapscott and Anthony D. Williams (ISBN: 9781591843672)

'Working with Emotional Intelligence' (1998) by Daniel Goleman (ISBN: 9780553378580)

Index

Note: the letter g following a page number denotes an entry from the glossary.